Auftakt 1

Get ahead in German

Zwei deutsche Städte

Christiane Hermann and Corinna Schicker

Menschenbilder

Mirjam Hauck and Evelyn Reisinger

Hodder & Stoughton
A MEMBER OF THE HODDER HEADLINE GROUP

Writers

Christiane Hermann is Senior Lecturer in the Business School at Buckinghamshire College, a college of Brunel University

Corinna Schicker is a freelance educational author

Mirjam Hauck is Lecturer in Modern Languages at The Open University

Evelyn Reisinger is Tutor and Research Assistant at City University

Language and German Studies Consultant

Ragnhild Gladwell, Goethe Institut, London

Open University

Book Co-ordinator, Duncan Sidwell

Academic Editor, Monica Shelley

Programme Chair, Lore Arthur

Acknowledgements

The course team would like to thank Eva Kolinsky, Professor of Modern German Studies, Keele University for her support in the development of the course. Our thanks also to Margaret Winck of Tübingen and Christoph Sorger of Leipzig for help and support in the preparation of the audio-visual material and for all the information and contacts which they provided. Thanks, too, to all the people of Tübingen and Leipzig who took part in the filming and recording in this course.

A catalogue record for this title is available from the British Library

ISBN 0 340 67329 X

First published 1996

Impression number 10 9 8 7 6 5 4 3 2 1

Year 2001 2000 1999 1998 1997 1996

Typeset and designed by David La Grange.

Printed in Great Britain for Hodder & Stoughton Educational, a division of Hodder Headline Plc, 338 Euston Road, London NW1 3BH and for the Open University by Butler and Tanner, Frome, Somerset.

Contents

Introduction

What is *Auftakt*?

Auftakt is a German course for individual adult learners studying on their own without the support of a classroom teacher, but is also suitable for use in adult education classes. It aims to help you, the learner, develop confidence in speaking, listening, reading and writing German, so that you will be able to communicate effectively and accurately in German. When you have worked through all four books you should have achieved a language level equivalent to just below A level standard.

How much German am I expected to know?

At the beginning of the course it is assumed that you will have an elementary knowledge of German. This means that you should be able to get by when visiting a German-speaking country and understand simple German speech in everyday contexts. You should have achieved the approximate level of GCSE or the equivalent of a rusty O level, either through formal classroom teaching or through regular contact with native speakers of German.

What does *Auftakt* consist of?

Course books

Auftakt consists of four graded books, *Auftakt 1*, *2*, *3* and *4*. The books are carefully structured to assist the learning process and can either be used separately or studied in sequence. They are divided into two sections, each with a distinct theme (*Thema*), and each *Thema* consists of four parts (*Teile*). The *Themen* are numbered sequentially through the course. The first three *Teile* introduce and practise new topics, language structures and grammar items, while the fourth provides revision and consolidation. Each *Teil* is further divided into three units, with one unit (*Lerneinheit*) representing roughly two hours of study.

Clear introductions, study charts and precise instructions will guide you through each part and activity of the course. In *Auftakt 1* and *2* these instructions are in English, but in *Auftakt 3* and *4* most of them are in German. In addition, there are study tips (*Lerntips*) to help you learn the language more effectively, and cultural background notes (*Wissen Sie das?*).

You will find a *Checkliste* at the end of *Teile 1–3*, which summarises the key learning points. Answers for each activity are provided at the end of the book in the *Lösungen* section. Both the *Lösungen* and *Checkliste* are designed to help you assess your progress through the book or throughout the course.

Audio-visual material

A 30-minute **video** accompanies each book. Filmed in two German towns – Leipzig, an industrial city in the east, and Tübingen, a smaller university town in the south – the video features a wide variety of German people talking about their ways of life, their work, their interests, their hopes for the future. Occasionally, where the language may be slightly difficult, German subtitles have been added. All video sections are clearly numbered for ease of use.

Two **audio cassettes** accompany each book. Cassette One opens with an episode of the drama (*Hörspiel*), which runs throughout the course. This is followed by a documentary feature (*Hörbericht*) linked to the main theme of each *Thema*. Both the drama and feature sections are followed by simple fluency and pronunciation activities and can be used independently of the course book. Cassette Two (*Übungskassette*) consists of numerous speaking and listening exercises, which are closely integrated into the main course-book activities.

Transcript booklets

There is a separate transcript booklet, containing transcripts of both the video and audio cassettes which accompany each book. The language is transcribed as it is actually spoken, that is with hesitations, incomplete utterances, repetitions and, occasionally, incorrect German.

Additional resources

To study *Auftakt* you will need a grammar book and dictionary. The writers of this course have referred to *The Oxford German Grammar* by William Rowlinson (available in paperback and mini-reference form) and the new *Langenscheidt Standard German Dictionary.* Furthermore, you will find the Open University's *The Language Learner's Good Study Guide* full of useful advice on all aspects of language learning.

German spelling

The German federal states have agreed to introduce changes in the spelling of some German words from 1 August 1998. The reform, which aims to simplify German spelling, is based on recommendations of a commission set up in 1988 by the Austrian government. The commission consisted of experts from Germany, Belgium, Denmark, Italy, Liechtenstein, Luxembourg, Austria, Romania, Switzerland and Hungary. New rules for spelling will be taught in German schools and introduced in all official documents, in the media, commerce and other institutions. It is expected that the process of change will be completed by 1 August 2005. These rules have not been applied in this book.

Viel Spaß und Erfolg beim Deutschlernen!

DÄNEMARK
OSTSEE
Nordfriesische Inseln
Husum
NORDSEE
Kiel
Schleswig-
Holstein
Rostock
Ostfriesische Inseln
Lübeck
Mecklenburg-
Vorpommern
Norden
Bremerhaven
Hamburg
Bremen
POLEN
Ems
Niedersachsen
Amsterdam
Berlin
Hannover
NIEDERLANDE
Brandenburg
Salzgitter
Magdeburg
Nordrhein-
Westfalen
Elbe
Sachsen-
Anhalt
Duisburg
Dortmund
Essen
BUNDESREPUBLIK
DEUTSCHLAND
Düsseldorf
Wuppertal
Leipzig
Sachsen
Köln
Erfurt
Rhein
Maastricht
Bonn
Dresden
Thüringen
BELGIEN
Hessen
Koblenz
Frankfurt
Rheinland-
Pfalz
Prag
Mainz
LUXEMBURG
Main
TSCHECHISCHE
REPUBLIK
Luxemburg
Saarland
Nürnberg
Mannheim
Mosel
Saarbrücken
Bayern
Regensburg
Stuttgart
Ingolstadt
Nancy
Donau
Straßburg
Tübingen
Ulm
Baden-
Württemberg
Linz
FRANKREICH
München
ÖSTERREICH
Freiburg
Mülhausen
Schaffhausen
Salzburg
Basel
Zürich
km
SCHWEIZ
LIECHTENSTEIN
Innsbruck
0
150
Vaduz
Bern

Thema 1

Zwei deutsche Städte

The first *Thema* of *Auftakt* is called *Zwei deutsche Städte*. The two German cities are Tübingen in Baden-Württemberg and Leipzig in Sachsen (Saxony). *Thema 1* introduces you to these towns and to some local inhabitants, including students, people who have lived there all their lives, newcomers and families, who will describe where and how they live.

In the first part of the book, *Teil 1*, *Ein erster Eindruck*, you will take a tour round the two towns with the help of the video. In *Teil 2*, *Meine vier Wände*, you will listen to the first episode of the audio drama (*Hörspiel*), *Begegnung in Leipzig*, and work on describing places where you and other people live. *Teil 2* also includes an audio feature (*Hörbericht*), *Kein Platz für Autos*. *Teil 3*, *Hier wohne ich*, develops the theme of describing homes and helps you to express positive and negative opinions about homes and places.

Teil 4, *Wiederholung*, is a revision section, which will help you revise and consolidate the most important aspects of the work done in *Teile 1–3*. By the end of *Thema 1*, you should be familiar with aspects of Leipzig and Tübingen. You will have revised the basic grammar which you will need to help you progress through the course and you will have practised useful skills such as finding your way and describing and expressing opinions about where you live.

Teil 1

Ein erster Eindruck

Teil 1 will give you an initial impression of Tübingen and Leipzig and what they look like. You will hear about some of the successes and problems of each town.

Lerneinheit 1, Tübingen, takes you round this old Swabian university town on the rivers Ammer and Neckar. *Lerneinheit 2, Leipzig*, moves northeastwards to Sachsen to introduce you to one of east Germany's largest industrial cities. *Lerneinheit 3, Wo treffen wir uns?*, is about making arrangements.

By the end of *Teil 1*, you should be able to ask for directions around a town and follow the instructions given in reply and know how to make comparisons, for example, between two towns.

Lerneinheit 1 Tübingen

Lerneinheit 1 introduces Tübingen through photographs, video and text about the town. You will hear about the importance of its university in past and present-day Tübingen.

The first topic is *Getting to know Tübingen*, which should give you an idea of what the town looks like. The second topic, *Finding out more about Tübingen*, provides information about the history of the town and the importance of tourism today. The third topic, *Asking your way*, helps you to practise directions. The final topic, *Writing about Tübingen*, suggests how to write a summary of what you have learned in *Lerneinheit 1*.

STUDY CHART

Topic	Activity and resource	Key points
Getting to know Tübingen	**1 Text**	studying photographs and information about Tübingen
	2–3 Video	checking you've understood information from the video
Finding out more about Tübingen	**4 Text**	reading about Tübingen past and present
	5 Text	checking you've understood information about Tübingen
	6 Text	recognising the accusative case
Asking your way	**7 Text**	practising asking for directions
Writing about Tübingen	**8 Text**	writing a description of the town

Here are some photographs of important places in Tübingen. Study the captions to each photograph, which give you some general information about the town. Then use the information to do the exercise which follows.

Bild links: Das Rathaus steht am Marktplatz. Es wurde im Jahre 1435 gebaut.

Bild rechts: Die Universität dominiert die wirtschaftliche Struktur der Stadt. Sie ist der größte Arbeitgeber.

Bild links: Das Schloß ist in der Altstadt.

Bild rechts: Es gibt in Tübingen viele schöne, alte Fachwerkhäuser. Hier wohnten früher die reichen Bürger.

Bild links: In der Fußgängerzone gibt es montags, mittwochs und freitags einen Markt.

Bild rechts: Die Neckarbrücke. Die Stadt liegt an zwei Flüssen. Die Ammer, die sehr klein ist, fließt im Norden der Stadt, und der Neckar fließt im Süden.

wirtschaftlich *economic*

der Arbeitgeber (-) *employer*

der Bürger (-) *citizen*

Now rewrite these statements correcting the errors in each of them. The first has been done for you.

1. Der größte Arbeitgeber ist das Rathaus. → *Der größte Arbeitgeber ist die Universität.*
2. Die Universität steht am Marktplatz.
3. Die Ammer fließt an der Südseite der Stadt.
4. Das Schloß liegt am Stadtrand.
5. Donnerstags gibt es einen Markt.
6. Die Arbeiter wohnten früher in den Fachwerkhäusern.

00.00–04.31

Now that you have seen some of the main buildings in Tübingen, the video will tell you more about the town and introduce you to Dr. Setzler who has lived there for many years. Watch the video, then write down the answers to the questions overleaf in English.

1. How many people live in Tübingen?
2. How old is the town?
3. Where is the old university situated?
4. Where did the manual workers use to live?
5. Why did Dr. Setzler originally come to Tübingen?

WISSEN SIE DAS?

There is an important difference between the way you fill in questionnaires and forms in German and in English. Germans always use a ✗ to identify the appropriate option. The ✓ is never used.

00.00–04.31

Are the statements below *richtig* (true) or *falsch* (false)? Put a cross in the appropriate box to indicate the correct answer. Then rewrite the false statements correctly in German.

		RICHTIG	FALSCH
1	Dr. Setzler ist in Tübingen geboren.	❑	❑
2	Im Jahr 1845 wurde die Altstadt zu klein für die Universität.	❑	❑
3	Das neue Universitätszentrum liegt in der Stadtmitte.	❑	❑
4	Etwa 16 000 Studenten leben in der Stadt.	❑	❑
5	12 000 Studenten pendeln jeden Tag.	❑	❑
6	In Tübingen gibt es auch Hochhäuser und moderne Wohngebiete.	❑	❑
7	In Tübingen findet man immer noch idyllische Viertel.	❑	❑

USING a *Notizbuch*

It is a good idea to have a *Notizbuch* (notebook) where you write down words as you learn them. There are many ways you can organise this – perhaps by grouping words by subject as you come across them in *Auftakt*, or by grouping all the words of a similar type together. You will find it helpful if you note down the gender and the plural of the more common nouns, then memorise them by saying both singular and plural forms out loud, e.g. *die Mutter, die Mütter, der Sohn, die Söhne*, and so on. You can record new words in your *Notizbuch* like this, writing the plural in brackets:

die Mutter (¨) *mother* **der Sohn (¨e)** *son*

On page 5 there is an extract from a tourist brochure about Tübingen. First read through the extract, making sure that you understand it, then answer the questions below in English.

Unsere Geschichte

Die alte Universitätsstadt Tübingen liegt an den Flüssen Ammer und Neckar im Vorland der Schwäbischen Alb. Tübingen ist 1 500 Jahre alt – die Siedlung Tvvigia wurde im 6. Jahrhundert von den Alemannen gegründet. Schon im 11. Jahrhundert war Tübingen eine bedeutende Stadt mit Marktplatz und Stadtmauer. Im Jahre 1477, als die Stadt 3 000 Einwohner hatte, gründete dort Graf Eberhart im Bart die Universität, die sich in der Stadtmitte befindet. Heute ist Tübingen das kulturelle Zentrum der Schwäbischen Alb. Das Landestheater Tübingen und die Tübinger Kunsthalle sind in ganz Deutschland berühmt. Es gibt zahlreiche Museen, Galerien, Konzerthallen und Kinos.

Wirtschaft und Industrie

Tübingen ist eine Stadt mit wenig Industrie und Landwirtschaft aber auch wenig Arbeitslosigkeit. Die Universität dominiert die wirtschaftliche Struktur der Stadt. Die meisten Einwohner Tübingens arbeiten für die Universität. Auch der Tourismus ist schon seit langem sehr wichtig für die Stadt. Jedes Jahr kommen Besucher aus aller Welt in die berühmte Universitätsstadt.

die Geschichte (-n) *history, story*
das Vorland *foothills*
die Schwäbische Alb *a range of hills south of Tübingen*
die Siedlung (-en) *settlement, estate*
die Alemannen *Alemanni, a German tribe*
gegründet (*from* gründen) *founded*
bedeutend *significant*
die Stadtmauer (-n) *town wall*
der Graf (-en) *earl, count*
sich ... befindet (*from* befinden) *is situated*
berühmt *famous*
zahlreich *numerous*
die Landwirtschaft *agriculture*
die Arbeitslosigkeit *unemployment*

1 What features did Tübingen have by the 11th century?
2 Give examples of cultural activities to be found in Tübingen.
3 Who is the main employer in Tübingen?
4 Name one important industry.

This text contains information about Tübingen that you have read or heard on the video. Fill in the gaps using words from the selection overleaf.

Tübingen liegt in Südwestdeutschland ____________ Neckar. Die Stadt ist 1 500 Jahre alt und wurde von den Alemannen gegründet. Tübingen ist eine schöne ____________ Stadt ____________ einer Universität. Sie hat viele kleine, ____________ Gassen und schöne Fachwerkhäuser . ____________ Jahr 1477, als die Stadt 3 000 Einwohner hatte, wurde die Universität gegründet. Das alte Universitätsgebäude befindet sich in der ____________ . Schon im ____________ war die Altstadt zu klein für die Universität und man hat ein ____________ Universitätszentrum am ____________ gebaut. Tübingen ist ein kulturelles Zentrum ____________ Theatern, Museen und Galerien.

Die Stadt hat wenig Industrie, aber auch wenig ____________ : Die meisten Einwohner arbeiten für die Universität und ein ____________ aller Einwohner sind ____________ . Tourismus ist auch eine wichtige Industrie.

Die Stadt hat aber auch einige ____________ . Die Verkehrsprobleme sind besonders schlimm: Es gibt zu viele ____________ und zu wenig ____________ .

mit Probleme am 19. Jahrhundert Stadtrand Studenten mit alte Parkplätze neues im Stadtmitte enge Arbeitslosigkeit Autos Drittel

USING subjects and objects

A simple sentence would normally have **subject**, **verb** and **object**. Here is an example in English: **Tübingen** (*subject*) **has** (*verb*) **a castle** (*object*).

In a German sentence of this sort the subject is in the nominative case and the object is in the accusative. To sort out which is which, the easiest thing to do is first to look for the verb, then look for who performs the action of the verb (the subject), finally, look for the thing or person who is on the receiving end (the object).

These German sentences have been set out to show which words are in the nominative and which in the accusative cases.

Subject: nominative	**Verb**	**Object: accusative**
Tübingen	hat	einen Bahnhof.
Die Universität	dominiert	die Stadt.
Ich	suche	ein Museum.

This is how the accusative is formed:

	Masculine	**Feminine**	**Neuter**	**Plural**
Nominative	der	die	das	die
Accusative	**den**	**die**	**das**	**die**
Nominative	ein	eine	ein	—
Accusative	**einen** **meinen** **keinen**	**eine** **meine** **keine**	**ein** **mein** **kein**	**—** **meine** **keine**

CONTINUED

As you can see, the main thing to look out for when using the accusative is the *-en* ending of the masculine article.

It is important to understand that the object of a verb is in the accusative and to be able to recognise the case ending, because this helps you to understand the meaning of the sentence. Germans often alter the word order of a sentence, and it need not start with the subject as it often does in English. Word order is changed for purposes of emphasis in ways that are not possible in English; this is done frequently, particularly in writing. So you need to be able to identify the subject and object of the verb, either from the context or from the case ending. Look at this example:
Ich suche die Froschgasse.

Here the subject is *Ich* and the object is *Froschgasse*. Suppose you wanted to change the emphasis, you could say:
Nein. Die Froschgasse suche ich und nicht die Bachstraße.

In the following sentence, the case endings show which is the subject and which the object.
Diesen Mann sucht die Polizei. *The police are looking for this man.*
'The police' is the subject (in the nominative) and 'this man' is the object (in the accusative).

You will probably remember that the verb 'to be' (*sein*) does not have an object. In the sentence *„Die Froschgasse ist eine kleine Straße."*, both *Froschgasse* and *Straße* are in the nominative case, and *Straße* is described as the **complement** of the verb.

Here is a short activity to help you to practise recognising subject and object. Work through these sentences and mark which word is in the nominative (the subject) and which in the accusative (the object).

1 Er sucht das Schloß.
2 Das Hotel Hospiz sucht er.
3 Am Rande der Stadt gibt es viele Hochhäuser.
4 Ich möchte etwas essen.
5 Den Bahnhof suchen Sie?
6 Oben auf dem Berg gibt es ein Schloß.

ASKING how to find places

Here are a few simple phrases to help you find places in town. Note that these sentences use the accusative of *der, die, das* or *ein, eine, ein*, because the place you are looking for is the object of the verb:
Gibt es hier in der Nähe einen/eine/ein ...? *Is there a ... near here?*
Ich suche den/die/das ... *I'm looking for the ...*

CONTINUED

Gibt es hier einen/eine/ein ...? *Is there a … here?*
Wo gibt es hier einen/eine/ein ...? *Where is there a … around here?*

If you are visiting somewhere new in Germany, these phrases might come in useful:
Entschuldigung. Ich bin hier fremd. *Excuse me, I'm a stranger here.*
Entschuldigen Sie, können Sie mir bitte helfen? *Excuse me, can you help me, please?*

Now you can practise using these expressions.

Here are some reasons why you might be looking for a particular place in Tübingen. Read through and check that you understand them.

1 Ich möchte etwas essen.
2 Ich habe Kopfweh und hätte gern ein Aspirin.
3 Ich möchte einige Bücher kaufen.
4 Ich muß Briefmarken kaufen.
5 Ich möchte Geld umtauschen.
6 Ich möchte parken.
7 Ich interessiere mich für moderne Kunst.
8 Ich fahre mit dem Zug nach Mannheim.

Ich habe Kopfweh *I've got a headache*
umtauschen *to change (money)*
die Kunst (¨e) *art*

Now make up an appropriate enquiry or question to go with each reason, choosing words and expressions from the table below and using the correct accusative form either of *ein* or of *der*, *die*, *das*, whichever you feel is appropriate. Here is an example:

Entschuldigung. Ich bin hier fremd. Ich suche die Post.

<table>
<tr><td>Ich suche …</td><td rowspan="3">Parkhaus (n)
Bahnhof (m)
Apotheke (f)
Bank (f)
Kirche (f)
Restaurant (n)
Café (n)
Post (f)
Gaststätte (f)
Buchhandlung (f)
Galerie (f)</td></tr>
<tr><td>Gibt es hier (in der Nähe) …?</td></tr>
<tr><td>Wo gibt es hier (in der Nähe) …?</td></tr>
</table>

8

To round off this *Lerneinheit* on Tübingen, write a short text of up to 50 words describing the town. Before doing so, reread the information on Tübingen. Here are some phrases and suggestions to help you.

- liegt in ...
- Größe ...
- Einwohnerzahl ...
- Alter ...
- Universität (wie alt?) ...
- Prozentsatz von Studenten ...
- neues Universitätszentrum (wo?) ...
- Industrie ...
- was es noch in der Stadt gibt ...

Lerneinheit 2 Leipzig

Lerneinheit 2 introduces you to Leipzig. This is one of the great industrial cities of Germany, where much new building has been undertaken since the unification of Germany. You will explore Leipzig, sometimes on your own, sometimes in the company of Johanna Schmidt, a tourist guide who has lived there all her life.

The first topic, *Getting to know Leipzig*, will help you to find out more about the city's major buildings and institutions. The second topic, *Making comparisons*, provides yet more information and structures to help you to compare Leipzig and Tübingen. The third topic, *Writing about Leipzig and Tübingen*, helps you to describe Leipzig and make further comparisons with Tübingen.

STUDY CHART

Topic	Activity and resource	Key points
Getting to know Leipzig	**1 Text**	studying photographs and information about Leipzig
	2 *Übungskassette*	hearing more about Leipzig
	3 *Übungskassette*	practising dates
	4 Text	reading about the history of Leipzig
	5 Text	checking you've understood the text about Leipzig
	6 Video	checking you've understood information from the video
Making comparisons	**7 Text**	practising comparative adjectives
	8 *Übungskassette*	talking about facts and figures
Writing about Leipzig and Tübingen	**9 *Übungskassette***	answering questions about the history of Leipzig
	10 Text	writing a description of Leipzig and comparing it with Tübingen

Here are some photographs of important buildings in Leipzig. Study the captions and answer the questions below in English.

Dieses große Renaissancegebäude steht am Marktplatz. Heute dient das Alte Rathaus als Museum der Geschichte der Stadt.

Das Neue Gewandhaus. Hier spielt das weltberühmte Gewandhaus-Orchester.

das Gebäude (-) *building*

weltberühmt *world famous*

das Friedensgebet (-e) *prayer for peace*

die Festung (-en) *fortress*

errichtet *built*

der Turm (¨-e) *tower*

Die Nikolaikirche hat eine bedeutende Rolle in der modernen Geschichte Deutschlands gespielt. Hier fanden die Friedensgebete und, im Jahre 1989, die Friedensdemonstrationen statt.

Das Neue Rathaus sieht fast wie eine Festung aus. Es wurde 1905 errichtet und hat den höchsten Rathausturm Deutschlands.

1. Where is the old town hall?
2. What is the old town hall used for nowadays?
3. The Neue Gewandhaus is the headquarters of what?
4. What is the significance of the Nikolaikirche?
5. What feature of the town hall is mentioned?

SAYING that something was done

In the next activity you will hear the guide use *wurde*, which in this context means 'was' in English. You are likely to hear it being used on occasions such as guided tours, so it is useful to be familiar with it. Here is an example from what the guide says:

Die Nikolaikirche wurde im zwölften Jahrhundert gebaut.

The Nikolaikirche was built in the twelfth century.

This structure is known as the passive, and it is used here in the past tense.

2

In this activity you will hear extracts from a guided tour of Leipzig in German. Before listening to the cassette, study the vocabulary given below. Then listen to *Hörabschnitt 1* on the *Übungskassette*. Finally, read the questions below and write out the answers in English, listening once more to *Hörabschnitt 1*, if you need to.

1. How is the Nikolaikirche described?
2. Why is the church significant?
3. On what day of the week did the demonstrations take place?
4. At what time of the year did they take place?
5. What was the Gewandhaus famous for in the 19th century?
6. Why was Luther's visit to Leipzig significant?
7. Where did Bach die?
8. What was Bach's job?
9. Where was the old town hall built?

der Ausgangspunkt (-e) *point of departure*
berühmt *famous*
errichten *to build, erect*
gestorben (*from* sterben) *died*
der Leiter (-) *director*
der Knabenchor (¨-e) *boys' choir*
aus ... stammt (*from* stammen) *originates in*

USING dates

When you want to give the year in German, for example 'in 1992', there are two ways of saying it – either *im Jahre 1992,* (also, *im Jahr 1992*) or by simply giving the year, *1992.*

When you specify the century you always use a preposition, such as *in dem (im), aus dem* or *vor dem.* Here are some examples:
aus dem neunten Jahrhundert
vor dem sechzehnten Jahrhundert
im zwanzigsten Jahrhundert

The number ends in *-ten* (after *zwanzig, dreißig* etc.) or in *-sten* when you say or write it in full. To abbreviate it, write *im 20. Jahrhundert.*

3

Listen once more to what the guide says in *Hörabschnitt 1* and complete the sentences which follow. In each case you will need a date or century to complete the sentence.

1. Die Nikolaikirche wurde ____________ gebaut.
2. Die Revolution war im Jahre ____________ .

3 Das Neue Gewandhaus wurde ______________ eröffnet.

4 Das Gewandhaus-Orchester war schon ______________ berühmt.

5 Luther hat ______________ in der Thomaskirche gepredigt.

6 Der Thomanerchor stammt aus ______________ .

7 Das Alte Rathaus wurde ______________ errichtet.

4 The text which follows is about Leipzig. As well as giving you information about the history of the town, it contains some language and grammar you will need in later activities. Read the text, on which some later activities are based.

Leipzig – eine Stadt mit Geschichte und Zukunft

Leipzig hat 1165 die Stadtrechte bekommen und blickt auf eine lange Geschichte als Handels- und Messestadt zurück. Die Stadt entstand am Kreuzungspunkt von zwei großen Handelsstraßen, der Reichsstraße und der Königsstraße, und durch diese günstige Lage wurde Leipzig zunehmend bedeutender und reicher. Der Buchdruck ist seit dem 16. Jahrhundert von großer Bedeutung für die Stadt. Später, im 19. Jahrhundert, entwickelte sich die Metall- und die Elektroindustrie. Leipzig ist noch heute eine wichtige Drehscheibe für den Ost-West-Handel.

die Stadtrechte bekommen *to receive a charter*

blickt ... zurück (*from* zurückblicken) *looks back*

der Handel *trade*

die Messe (-n) *trade fair*

entstand (*from* entstehen) *grew up*

günstig *favourable*

bedeutender *more important*

der Buchdruck *printing*

die Bedeutung (-en) *importance*

später *later*

entwickelte sich (*from* sich entwickeln) *developed*

die Drehscheibe (-n) *literally turntable, here: axis*

5

Read the following statements about Leipzig, which refer back to the information given in Activity 4. Decide whether you think they are *richtig* or *falsch*, indicating this by putting a cross in the appropriate box. Then rewrite the false statements correctly in German.

		RICHTIG	FALSCH
1	Leipzig ist seit dem 13. Jahrhundert eine Stadt.	❑	❑
2	Die Stadt entstand an zwei Handelsstraßen.	❑	❑
3	Man hat schon im 15. Jahrhundert Bücher in Leipzig gedruckt.	❑	❑
4	Im 19. Jahrhundert war die Schwerindustrie wichtig.	❑	❑
5	Leipzig liegt nicht sehr günstig zwischen Ost und West.	❑	❑

On the video, you will hear Frau Schmidt mention the revolutionary events of 1989. The *DDR – die Deutsche Demokratische Republik* (German Democratic Republic – GDR) – collapsed in 1989. *Die Wende* (literally the change or turning point) is the name given to describe the events which brought about the end of the communist regime and eventually the end of the 40 year division of Germany. Leipzig played a key part in that revolution, as you will hear. The video commentary also refers to the Karl-Marx-Platz. Since the 1989 revolution, this has reverted to its original name, the Augustus-Platz. Renaming of this sort has taken place throughout the towns in Germany's new *Bundesländer* (federal states). A number of towns have reverted to their earlier names: Karl-Marx-Stadt, for instance, is now Chemnitz again.

04:33–09:05

Now comes your opportunity to see Leipzig on video. The city is introduced by Frau Johanna Schmidt, a tourist guide.

Read the statements overleaf, then watch the second part of the video at least twice. Look up any words you do not understand. Then fill in the gaps in the statements from the choices given.

Johanna Schmidt ist gebürtige Leipzigerin und hat ihr ganzes Leben in Leipzig verbracht. Sie arbeitet als Gästebetreuerin für die Stadt. Sie fährt gern Rad und geht einmal in der Woche schwimmen.

gebürtig *native to, born in*
die Gästebetreuerin (-nen) *tourist guide*
ich freue mich *I am glad*
zeigen *to show*
der Kreuzungspunkt (-e) *junction point*
diese Straßen kreuzten sich *these roads crossed*
war … geworden (*from* werden) *became*
die Oper (-n) *opera*
in den zahlreichen Gasthäusern *in the many pubs*
die Heldenstadt genannt (*from* nennen) *named the 'Town of Heroes'*
ohne Gewalt *without violence*
eine große Unzufriedenheit *great discontent*
… versammelten sich (*from* sich versammeln) *to assemble*
friedlich *peaceful*
ohne Blutvergießen *without bloodshed*

1 Johanna Schmidt wohnt ______ ______ ______ in Leipzig.

seit 59 Jahren   seit 38 Jahren   seit 69 Jahren

2 Sie ist ______ von Beruf.

Gastgeberin   Gästebetreuerin   Gastwirtin

3 Leipzig ist ungefähr ______ ______ alt.

450 Jahre   850 Jahre   950 Jahre

4 Wo Leipzig sich befindet, kreuzten sich zwei alte Handelsstraßen. Sie waren ______ ______ und ______ ______.

die Königsstraße   die Rechtsstraße   die Reichsstraße

5 Eine der Handelsstraßen führte von ______ bis nach ______.

Italien   Holland   Rußland   Frankreich   Spanien

6 Die andere Handelsstraße führte von ______ nach ______.

Rußland   Dänemark   Skandinavien   Spanien   Italien

7 Leipzig ist eine bedeutende Musikstadt. Die Oper ist ______ Jahre alt und das Gewandhaus ist ______ alt.

300   200   350   400   250

8 Felix Mendelssohn-Bartholdy gründete ______ die Musikhochschule.

1834   1883   1843

9 Johann Sebastian Bach, der Komponist, lebte ______ Jahre in Leipzig.

23   33   27

10 Johann Wolfgang von Goethe, der Dichter, ______ in Leipzig.

studierte   arbeitete   schrieb Bücher

11 In der Zeit der Wende bekam Leipzig den Namen ______.

Hafenstadt   Heldenstadt   Helferstadt

12 Während der Revolution von 1989 fanden die Friedensgebete ______________ ______________ ______________ statt.

vor dem Gewandhaus   in der Nikolaikirche   in der Thomaskirche

13 Die Bürger versammelten sich auf dem ______________ .

Gewandhausplatz   Bahnhofplatz   Karl-Marx-Platz

Johann Wolfgang von Goethe (1749–1832) was one of Germany's greatest poets. He greatly influenced the German romantic movement, later moving to more classical forms. As well as writing poems, plays and novels he pursued scientific interests. His principal works, in addition to his considerable poetic writings, are the early romantic novel *Die Leiden des jungen Werthers* and the drama *Faust*.

MAKING comparisons

In the passage about Leipzig which you read in Activity 4, a number of comparatives are used such as *reicher*, meaning richer. Here are two other examples from the passage:
Leipzig wurde zunehmend *bedeutender*.
***Später*, im 19. Jahrhundert, entwickelte sich die Metall- und die Elektroindustrie.**

Note how the comparative is used:
more modern than **moderner als**
not as modern as **nicht so modern wie**
as modern as **so modern wie**
almost as modern as **fast so modern wie**

The comparative is formed in German by adding *-er* to the adjective and, in some cases, changing the vowel sound by using an umlaut:
klar → klarer   schön → schöner   alt → älter   groß → größer

A few comparatives are irregular:
viel → mehr   gut → besser   hoch → höher

7

Here is an activity to give you practice in using the comparative. Complete the statements by choosing appropriate adjectives from the selection below, changing them into their comparative forms. Add *als*, *wie* and *so* as necessary.

1. Seit der Wende ist es hier viel ______________ .
2. Die vielen Bäume machen die Stadt viel ______________ .
3. Das Neue Rathaus ist viel ______________ das Alte.
4. Im 14. Jahrhundert war die Stadt nicht ______________ im 16. Jahrhundert.
5. Die Universität von Leipzig ist ______________ die Universität von Tübingen.
6. Die Messestadt Frankfurt ist eines der Finanzzentren Europas, aber als Industriemessestadt ist Leipzig vielleicht ______________ .

alt reich bedeutend gut groß schön

8

Here are some statistics (from 1995) about population figures in Germany, Tübingen and Leipzig and the *Länder* where they are situated. Read through the statistics – you will use them to answer questions in this activity. Use a map of Germany to look up all the *Länder* and, in particular, Sachsen and Baden-Württemberg, to get an idea of their relative positions.

This is an opportunity to talk about the facts and figures you have been given in *Lerneinheit 2*. The facts you will need about population are set out below. One or more of your answers will require you to use numbers which include decimals. When you write a decimal figure in German, a comma is used, instead of the decimal point used in English. You say it as it is written, e.g. *2,5 Millionen = zwei Komma fünf Millionen.*

- Die Bundesrepublik Deutschland – 80 Millionen Einwohner in 16 Ländern (1996)
- Sachsen – 4,9 Millionen Einwohner
- Dresden (Hauptstadt von Sachsen) – 488 000
- Leipzig – 500 234
- Baden-Württemberg – 10,0 Millionen
- Stuttgart (Hauptstadt von Baden-Württemberg) – 584 000
- Tübingen – 85 000

Now listen to the questions in *Hörabschnitt 2* on the *Übungskassette* and reply in the pauses which follow.

ab *from*

In this dialogue activity in *Hörabschnitt 3* imagine that you are helping a tourist to check up on some dates. Read through these dates relating to Leipzig's history in preparation for your answers.

Leipzig – einige Daten

Nikolaikirche	12. Jahrhundert
Thomaskirche	13. Jahrhundert
Altes Rathaus	1556
Neues Gewandhaus	1981
Bach	18. Jahrhundert
Schumann	ab 1831 Student in Leipzig
Mendelssohn-Bartholdy	gründete 1843 die Musikhochschule

Now listen to the questions in *Hörabschnitt 3* on the *Übungskassette* and reply in the pauses which follow.

10

In the course of *Lerneinheit 2* you have been learning about Leipzig. In this final activity you are asked to write a short description of the town (up to 70 words) covering the points made below. Then write a paragraph (of about 50 words) comparing it to Tübingen. To help you to make this comparison a number of facts have been listed below. Use as many examples of comparatives as you can as you write about Leipzig and Tübingen. Before doing this part of the activity, look back at *Lerneinheit 1*.

Leipzig

- die Anfänge
- die Lage
- die Messe
- die Industrie
- die Größe
- die Kulturgeschichte

Einige Tatsachen

	Tübingen	**Leipzig**
Stadtrecht	1231	1165
Universität	1477	1409
Einwohner	85 000	500 234
Lage	südlich	nordöstlich
Wirtschaft	wenig Industrie	viel Industrie

Lerneinheit 3 Wo treffen wir uns?

When you visit new places you often meet new people and have to make arrangements for meeting them. The final *Lerneinheit* of *Teil 1* concentrates on the language and structures which will help you to do this effectively.

The first topic, *Planning to meet*, includes useful vocabulary and phrases. The second topic, *Fixing the time*, will help you to specify the time you want to meet. The third topic, *Making arrangements*, will help you practise this useful skill. The fourth topic, *Describing what you've been doing*, helps you to describe recent activities.

STUDY CHART

Topic	Activity and resource	Key points
Planning to meet	1 ***Übungskassette***	checking you've understood three telephone conversations
Fixing the time	**2 Text**	listing expressions of time
	3 Text	matching German and English phrases
Making arrangements	4 ***Übungskassette*** **5 Text**	practising making arrangements
Describing what you've been doing	**6 Text**	analysing what people have written about their activities
	7 Text	writing about what you've been doing

1

Study the vocabulary below, then listen to each of the three dialogues in *Hörabschnitt 4* on the *Übungskassette*. You will hear three phone conversations. The first two (Herr Eltges and Frau Schneider, Frau Schaan and Herr Finkler) are between visitors to Tübingen and local people who are inviting them out. After each dialogue answer the questions given on page 19.

Hätten Sie Lust … zu …? *Would you like to …?*

Wo treffen wir uns? (*from* sich treffen) *Where shall we meet?*

ich freue mich darauf *I'm looking forward to it*

verabredet *booked, engaged*

ich bedanke mich für die Einladung *thank you for the invitation*

ich muß mich ausruhen *I must have a rest*

todmüde *dead tired*

tschüs *cheerio, 'bye*

Dialog 1 Herr Eltges and Frau Schneider

1 What activity is suggested?
2 At what time?
3 Where will they meet?
4 Where exactly is that?

Dialog 2 Frau Schaan and Herr Finkler

5 What activity is suggested?
6 What is the response?
7 What are the alternatives? (two things are suggested)
8 At what time?

Dialog 3 Klaus and Karin

9 What is the second speaker doing this evening? (three things)
10 What is suggested to him/her?
11 Why does he/she refuse? (two things)
12 What is suggested instead?
13 When will they meet?
14 Where?

USING *du* and *Sie*

The use of *du* or *Sie* is quite subtle. In general, German practice is more formal than in English, where first names are used more readily. German adults generally ask each other if they can use *du* to another person (*Duzen wir uns?*) once they get to know each other well. Young people tend to use *du* immediately. When you hear in the audio drama the meeting between two people in their twenties who were students together, you will notice that they immediately use *du*. When in doubt, the safest thing to do is to follow the lead of your German friend or acquaintance.

2 In Activity 1, you will also have noticed some expressions of time which relate either to the day, or to the time when people are arranging to meet. Listen to *Hörabschnitt 4* on the *Übungskassette* once more and make a list of the expressions of time. You will need to use them later on when you are making up dialogues for yourself. Your list should include expressions such as *Guten Abend* and *um 12*.

LERNTIP

Für's Notizbuch

These expressions will help you to translate 'would', and 'could' from English. Make a note of them in your *Notizbuch,* as they will be particularly useful for making arrangements.

Wie wäre es mit (3 Uhr)? *How would (3 o'clock) do?*

Hätten Sie Lust (ins Kino zu gehen)? *Would you like (to go to the cinema)?*

Dann könnten wir vielleicht (spazieren gehen). *Perhaps we could (go for a walk).*

3 Another set of expressions that you probably noticed in the dialogues were those that people used to make requests, to decline an invitation and so on. Below is a list of such expressions (A), plus a list of their English equivalents. Link each German expression to the equivalent English one by writing the letter of the English expression against the German one. Then read list B and write the German translation against each English expression.

A

1 leider
2 ich bin schon verabredet
3 Wie wäre es mit ...?
4 Was würden Sie am liebsten machen?
5 bei Ihnen
6 Wo treffen wir uns?
7 Geht das?
8 ich weiß, wo ...
9 Hätten Sie Lust?
10 Wissen Sie, wo ...?
11 bis 8 Uhr
12 ja, gerne

a Would you like to?
b Where shall we meet?
c I know where ...
d How about ...?
e Is this OK?
f see you at eight
g Do you know where ...?
h yes, I'd like to
i I'm already booked up
j at your place
k unfortunately
l What would you most like to do?

B

1 I'm sorry
2 at 8
3 Are you acquainted with ...?/Do you know ...?
4 that's not possible
5 at your place
6 I'm resting
7 I don't feel like it
8 perhaps

4

Now it's your turn to practise making arrangements. You might like to listen to the recorded conversations in *Hörabschnitt 4* again first, as some of the expressions in those conversations reappear in this activity. The responses to this activity involve using times. Remember that in German there are two ways of expressing half past the hour. 'Three thirty' can be *drei Uhr dreißig* or *halb vier*. Now take part in the two recorded conversations in *Hörabschnitt 5* on the *Übungskassette*, following the prompts given.

USING expressions of time

In Activity 2 you made a note of expressions of time that the speakers used. These can be grouped according to how they're used.

guten Tag *hello*
guten Abend *good evening*
guten Morgen *good morning, hello*

jeden Tag *every day*
nächsten Sonntag *next Sunday*
vorigen Samstag/letzten Sonnabend *last Saturday*

(Note that German has two words for 'Saturday', *Samstag* and *Sonnabend*, but *Sonnabend* is not usually used in the South.)

jeden Monat *every month*
jedes Jahr *every year*
jede Woche *every week*
am Samstag *on Saturday*

am Dienstagabend *on Tuesday evening*
am Nachmittag *in the afternoon*
am Morgen *in the morning*

No preposition is used in expressions such as 'today', 'tomorrow' and 'yesterday':

Heute abend gehe ich ins Kino.
Gestern habe ich Italienisch gegessen.
Morgen treffen wir uns bei dir.
Morgen nachmittag gehen wir spazieren.

With time, *um* is used:

Wir sehen uns um 5 Uhr. *We'll meet/see each other at 5.*

Note also the use of the expression *Wie wäre es mit ...?*

Wie wäre es mit 8 Uhr? *How about 8 o'clock?*

5

Now practise making up dialogues on your own, using the details given in the table overleaf. An example is given to start you off. You should write your dialogues out first, then record them for yourself. Use the *Sie* form (since you don't know the other person that well), as shown in the example overleaf. Begin your dialogues with the invitation *Hätten Sie Lust ... zu ...?*, like the example. You might find it helpful to read the transcripts of the dialogues you worked on in Activity 1.

Note that if you are giving a time as well as a place to meet in the same sentence, the rule for German word order is to put the time **before** the place.

– Hätten Sie Lust, schwimmen zu gehen?
– *Ja. Wann gehen wir?*
– Wie wäre es mit heute nachmittag?
– *Ja. Sagen wir um drei Uhr?*
– Ja. Wir treffen uns also um Viertel vor drei bei mir?
– *Ja. Bei Ihnen. Bis später.*

	was?	wann?	ja/nein?	Uhr?	wo?
1	ins Kino gehen	heute	ja	20.00	bei mir
2	einkaufen	am (Dienstag)	ja	14.00	bei Ihnen
3	essen gehen	um (acht)	verabredet? morgen abend	19.30	im Restaurant Griechisch essen?

In the last two activities of *Lerneinheit 3* you are going to read and use the past tense in order to say what you did, for example, at the weekend or last Friday. Before starting these activities, read the following explanation of some basic aspects of the perfect tense.

TALKING about the past

When talking or writing about the past in German you would normally use either the **perfect** or the **imperfect** tense. The perfect tense is most common because you will hear it being used in speech and also in informal letters.

To form the perfect tense you use two verbs, just as you do in English:
Ich habe es gemacht. *I have done it.*

The two verbs used here are *haben* (to have) and *machen* (to do). *Haben,* the auxiliary verb, is used in the present tense *(ich habe)*, and *machen* in its past participle form, *gemacht.*

The general principle in forming past participles is that for regular verbs you take the prefix *ge-* and add the stem of the verb (the infinitive minus the *-en* ending) and a *-t* ending e.g. *machen – gemacht.* Irregular verbs take *ge-*, the (usually) changed stem of the verb and an *-en* ending e.g. *singen – gesungen.* (Past participles will be dealt with further in *Thema 2, Teil 1, Lerneinheit 1.*) Most perfect tenses are formed with the auxiliary verb *haben,* but a few take *sein* (to be). Many of the verbs which take *sein* in the perfect tense are to do with movement or transition. Common verbs that take *sein* are *fahren* (to travel), *gehen* (to go) and *sterben* (to die), though *sein* (to be) and *bleiben* (to stay) also take *sein.*

Although the formation of the perfect tense in German is similar to that in English, there is one important difference in that *Ich habe das schon gemacht* means both 'I **have done** it' and 'I **did** it' in

CONTINUED

English. Here are examples with *haben* and *sein*:
Sie hat mit Herrn Eltges gegessen. *She has had a meal with Herr Eltges./She had a meal with Herr Eltges.*
Ich bin zu Hause geblieben. *I have stayed at home./I stayed at home.*

In the perfect tense, separable verbs such as *fernsehen* or *einladen* behave as shown below. You will see that the past participle is split and -ge- goes between the parts of the separable verb. For example:
Ich habe den ganzen Abend ferngesehen. *I (have) spent all evening watching television.*
The perfect tense will be covered in greater detail in *Thema 2.*

Here are some short extracts from letters that Hans Drösser, Christine Launer and Oliver Förster have written about what they have been doing. Read the extracts and answer the questions below. Then go through the extracts again and write out the infinitives of the verbs used in the perfect tense, putting a star against those that take *sein*. For example, if a letter contained the phrase *Wir sind nach Tübingen gefahren*, you would write down *fahren**.

Hans Drössers Brief

... und dann sind wir alle spazierengegangen. Wir hatten einen sehr schönen Tag. Wir sind ein ganzes Stück die Ammer entlanggelaufen. Am Abend war ich sehr müde und bin zu Hause geblieben. Ich habe nur ferngesehen – dann bin ich früh ins Bett gegangen.

grüßen lassen
to send best wishes

1 What did they do during the day?
2 What did Hans Drösser do in the evening?

Christine Launers Brief

... und am Samstag habe ich Tennis gespielt. Ja, Tennis! Ich habe mit Claudia und ihrem Freund gespielt. Am Abend sind wir in eine Kneipe gegangen. Claudia läßt Dich grüßen. Am nächsten Tag sind beide zu mir gekommen und wir haben gut gegessen und sonst nichts gemacht.

3 Who did Christine Launer play tennis with?
4 What did they do in the evening?
5 What is the message from Claudia?
6 What did they do next day apart from eating?

Oliver Försters Brief

> *... Ich habe den neuen Film von Wenders gesehen. Fantastisch. Du mußt ihn sehen. Ich bin am Wochende mit Sabine gegangen. Das war nach dem Einkaufen. Wir sind am Nachmittag für die neue Wohnung einkaufen gegangen, und haben unheimlich viel gekauft.*

7 When did Oliver Förster go to the cinema?
8 What had he been doing beforehand?
9 Why did they shop?

7

In this activity you are asked to answer questions about what you did yesterday or at the weekend. The questions are below, with suggestions as to how you might answer. Write three short paragraphs of up to 30 words each. Draft your answers, then read the answers in the *Lösungen* to find out whether you are on the right track, correcting your version where necessary. It will help to reinforce this learning if you redo the activity in a day or so for more practice.

1 Was haben Sie am Wochenende gemacht?

Friday: evening to cinema with Karla. Saw a Spielberg film.
Saturday: shopping
Sunday: nothing

2 Hast du gestern etwas Interessantes gemacht?

No. Stayed at home, watched TV and went to bed early.

3 Wie war das Wochenende?

OK
Saturday: played tennis. In the evening ate Italian food.
Sunday: had an outing and went for a walk in the Sachsenwald.

Checkliste

By the end of *Teil I* you should be able to

- ○ recognise and use simple expressions required for finding your way around and have revised the use of the definite and indefinite article (*Lerneinheit 1*, Activity 7)
- ○ write a short descriptive passage, about a town (*Lerneinheit 1*, Activity 8)
- ○ express numbers and dates (*Lerneinheit 2*, Activities 3 and 8)
- ○ recognise and use comparatives (*Lerneinheit 2,* Activity 7)
- ○ use 'would' and 'could' in simple phrases (*Lerneinheit* 3, Activities 3–4)
- ○ use a range of expressions of time (*Lerneinheit* 3, Activity 5)
- ○ make an arrangement to meet and respond to an invitation (*Lerneinheit 3*, Activity 5)

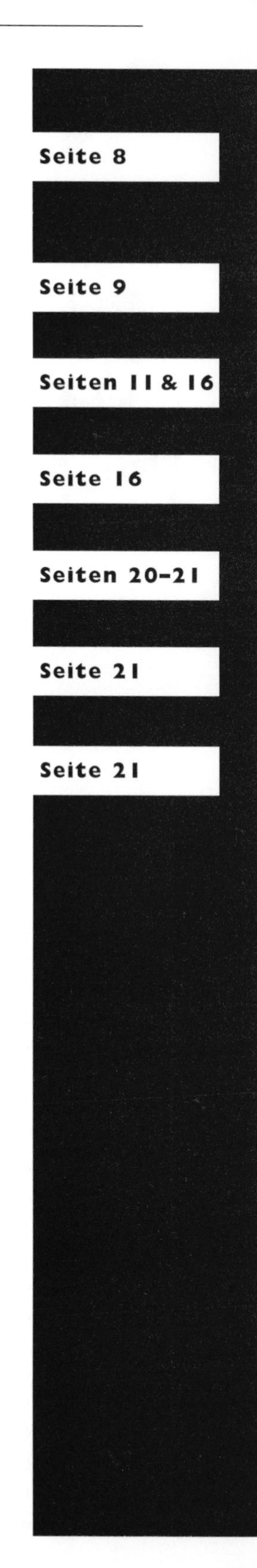

Teil 2

Meine vier Wände

The theme of *Teil 2* is housing – your own and other people's. It will help you to describe your home and its contents and to consider its advantages and disadvantages. You will hear a wide variety of people talking about their homes, and what they think about them. The first episode of the *Hörspiel* (audio drama), *Begegnung in Leipzig*, and the first *Hörbericht* (audio feature), *Kein Platz für Autos* (set in Tübingen), provides opportunities to discuss practical issues concerning housing.

Lerneinheit 4, Ich suche Unterkunft, starts with the first episode of *Begegnung in Leipzig*: you will meet the main characters, Bettina, Sonja and Thomas. Bettina is flat hunting in Leipzig, so you will be find out how to deal with flat and house advertisements and the process of moving into a new home. *Lerneinheit 5, Wohnen Sie schon immer dort?*, concentrates on listening to people in Leipzig and Tübingen describing their homes, particularly in comparison with where they have lived before. In *Lerneinheit 6, Zu viel Verkehr*, you will work on the *Hörbericht*, which uses the example of an innovative housing estate in Tübingen called *Schafbrühl* to discuss ways of dealing with traffic problems.

By the end of *Teil 2*, you should be able to understand housing advertisements and make comparisons between different houses and flats, and you will have practised writing short letters.

Lerneinheit 4 Ich suche Unterkunft

Lerneinheit 4 is about describing your home and its contents. The first topic is *Listening to the drama*. This is followed by *Working on advertisements*, which will enable you to begin to describe flats and houses. *Moving in* introduces the language of furniture and *Telling your friends* concentrates on letter-writing.

STUDY CHART

Topic	Activity and resource	Key points
Listening to the drama	1 *Hörspiel*	working on the drama
	2 *Hörspiel*	checking you've understood the drama
	3 *Hörspiel*	summarising the drama
Working on advertisements	4 Text	analysing housing advertisements
Moving in	5 Text	practising the accusative and using words for furniture
	6 Text	comparing flat details
Telling your friends	7 Text	writing about your new home

Hörspiel, Folge 1

Turn to the *Hörspiel, Begegnung in Leipzig*. First, listen to *Folge 1* right through, then listen once more and indicate whether you think the statements below are *richtig* or *falsch* by putting a cross in the appropriate box. Finally, rewrite the false statements correctly in German.

		RICHTIG	FALSCH
1	Die Szene spielt in Tübingen auf der Straße.	❑	❑
2	Bettina und Sonja wohnen zusammen.	❑	❑
3	Es ist Dienstag.	❑	❑
4	Bettina ist Lehrerin.	❑	❑
5	Sonja wohnt schon länger in der Stadt als Bettina.	❑	❑
6	Sonja ist todmüde und möchte einen Kaffee trinken.	❑	❑
7	Bettina mag Straßenmusikanten.	❑	❑
8	Sonja geht alleine nach Hause.	❑	❑

Hörspiel, Folge 1

Now read the following statements, correcting those that are incorrect. Listen to the *Hörspiel* again if you are uncertain.

1 Sie treffen sich um sieben Uhr vor der Arbeit.
2 Sonja würde gern am Wochenende spazieren gehen.
3 Bettina möchte ins Kino gehen. Sie ist todmüde.
4 Sie müssen einkaufen gehen. Sie brauchen etwas zu essen.
5 Vor dem Einkaufen möchte Sonja einen Tee trinken.
6 Sonja kennt ein Café gegenüber der Universität.
7 Bettina interessiert sich für die Heroldstraße.
8 Sonja geht nach Hause.
9 Bettina und der Straßenmusikant waren Studenten in Ulm.
10 Bettina und der Straßenmusikant gehen essen.

Hörspiel, Folge 1

Now write a summary in German of this episode of the drama, using the present tense. Listen to the *Hörspiel* as many times as you need to, to do this activity. You should aim to write about 100 words.

In Germany, houses are described in terms of how many families live in them, and flats in terms of how many rooms they have. So a house can be an *Einfamilienhaus* or a *Zweifamilienhaus,* and a flat with a living room and one bedroom might be described as a *Zweizimmerwohnung.* The other families who live in the house are often referred to as *die (zwei) anderen Parteien.* In houses divided into several homes, people frequently share facilities such as cellars.

In Activity 4 you will work on four typical advertisements for accommodation, which include a number of advertising conventions. The size of a flat or a house is expressed by giving its floor area in square metres. The number of usable rooms is shown by an abbreviation such as *2ZKB*, which means two rooms plus kitchen and bathroom. Houses in Germany nearly always have a cellar, and flats often have a shared one (see advertisement **a**). Cellars are used as storerooms and utility rooms, so often contain a washing machine. Ownership of a house or a flat is rarer in Germany than in any other west european country.

As you heard in *Begegnung in Leipzig*, Bettina has got a teaching job in Leipzig and will be looking for accommodation. But she won't see a 'For Sale' notice outside a house or flat. In Germany, accommodation is advertised through agents and privately in newspapers, so she will see examples such as those given on page 29.

Read through the advertisements, checking that you understand them, and then read the statements given below. Imagine that the statements have been made by people describing the flats or houses in response to an enquiry. Link the statements to the advertisements by putting the letter of the advertisement against the appropriate statement.

die Lage *position*

die Kaution (-en) *deposit*

MM (Monatsmiete) *monthly rent*

NK (Nebenkosten) *additional costs*

die Benutzung *use*

die Kaltmiete (-n) *rent excluding heating bills*

die Verkehrsverbindung (-en) *public transport connections*

das Angebot (-e) *offer*

Ztrlhzg. (Zentralheizung) *central heating*

a Altbauwohnung, 3ZKB, im 1. Stock. Günstige Lage in der Stadtmitte, 114 m², mit Zentralheizung, Balkon und Fahrradkeller. Nähe Uni. 2MM Kaution, MM DM 1500 + NK – Tel. 0341 9804183

b Suche Mitbewohner(in) für Dachgeschoßwohnung in Leipzig Nord. Nähe Bahnhof und Bushaltestelle. Eigenes Zimmer (32 m²), gemeinsame Küche und Bad, mit Gartenbenutzung, Kaltmiete DM 550, - Tel. 0341 4010574 ab 18 Uhr

c Einfamilienhaus (186 m²) mit Garten, ruhige Lage, gute Verkehrsverbindungen, MM DM 2000, Auskunft: Immobilien Alt, Tel. 0341 2612427

d Zu verkaufen: Haus am Waldrand, großer Garten, Ztrlhzg., Doppelgarage. Angebote ab DM 350 000 an M. Müller, Tel 0341 6842154

1. Das Haus liegt sehr ruhig direkt am Wald.
2. Wir teilen uns die Küche.
3. Man kann am Abend noch sehr schön auf dem Balkon sitzen.
4. Es gibt keinen Balkon, aber man kann im Garten sitzen.
5. Die Wohnung ist im ersten Stock in einem schönen, alten Haus.
6. Die Wohnung ist sehr schön – unterm Dach.
7. Mit dem Auto ist man in zehn Minuten in der Stadt. Öffentliche Verkehrsmittel gibt es nicht.
8. Man kommt sehr leicht in die Stadt. Die Bushaltestelle ist vor der Tür.
9. Die Lage ist sehr günstig für Studenten.
10. Es gibt sehr wenig Verkehr.

USING the accusative or dative case after *in*, *an*, *auf* and *vor*

Certain German prepositions can be followed by either the accusative or dative case. The commonest are *in*, *an*, *auf*, and *vor*. The decision whether to use the accusative or the dative after them depends upon whether movement is involved or not.

In Activity 4, statement 8 begins as follows:
Man kommt sehr leicht in die Stadt. *You can get into town very easily.*

Here the preposition *in* is followed by the accusative case; this indicates that the phrase means 'into the town' rather than 'in the town' – that is, movement is involved. This contrasts with the use of *in* in Activity 4 statements 4 and 7 where it is followed by the dative case, as no movement is involved. In these examples 'in' does not mean 'into':
Man kann im Garten sitzen. *You can sit in the garden.*
Mit dem Auto ist man in zehn Minuten in der Stadt. *By car you are in town in ten minutes.*

CONTINUED

The nominative, accusative and dative forms of the definite article are as follows:

	masculine	feminine	neuter	plural
nominative	*der*	*die*	*das*	*die*
accusative	*den*	*die*	*das*	*die*
dative	*dem*	*der*	*dem*	*den*

In Activity 4 you can find examples of the use of *an, auf, vor* and other examples of *in* where the dative is used, because no movement is involved.

In the next activity you will be practising the use of *in* with the accusative, indicating movement. Here are some more examples where movement is involved. These statements are all responses to the question *Wohin?*.

der Keller Die Waschmaschine kommt in den Keller.
die Küche Karla geht in die Küche.
das Schlafzimmer Max geht in das (ins) Schlafzimmer.

In German there are two words for the English 'where'. These are *wohin*, meaning 'where to' (indicating movement), and *wo* meaning 'where (is)' (indicating rest).

Wohin fährt Julia? Sie fährt in die Stadt.
Wohin gehst du? Ich gehe in den Garten.
Wo ist Sonja? Sie ist in der Stadt.
Wo ist Max? Er ist im Garten.

You will get a chance to practise the use of the dative after prepositions on page 35.

5 Now you need to imagine that you are moving into the house shown on the next page and are telling the removal people where things should go. A plan of the house has been provided. Complete the questions below by writing down the name of the piece of furniture in German, then write where the furniture should go (also in German). This activity aims to help you practise the use of the accusative of movement – so you need to use the accusative in all your answers. Here is an example of what you should do:

Frage: Wohin kommt  ?

Wohin kommt der Teppich?

Antwort: Ins Wohnzimmer.

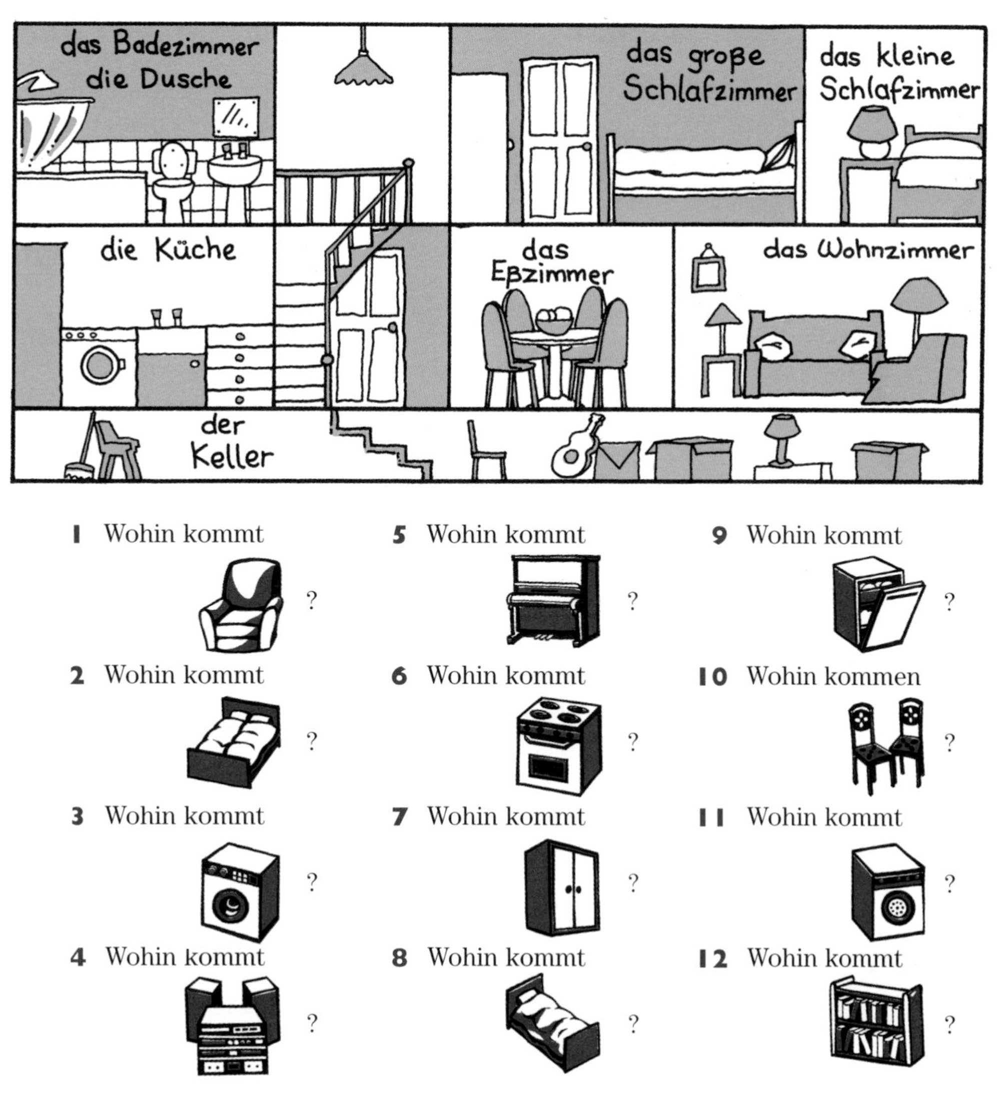

6

This activity should help you to learn how to describe your own place. Two estate agents' descriptions of flats are given overleaf. In Activity 7 you will be asked to describe them. First of all, check that you understand the advertisements. Then look at the statements below, which have been made by the two owners, Herr Wagner and Frau Mühlen. Label each statement with the name of the owner you think made it.

unmittelbar *immediate*
erhalten *maintained*
der Parkettboden *parquet flooring*
die Küchenzeile (-n) *kitchenette*
m.d. Zug *mit dem Zug*
die Einheit (-en) *unit*
die Tiefgarage (-n) *underground garage*
die Fußbodenheizung (-en) *underfloor central heating*
der Kamin (-e) *fire place*
der Zugang (¨-e) *access, entrance*
eingerichtet *furnished*
die Landschaft (-en) *countryside*

Herr Wagners Wohnung

Miete: DM 945,–

Wohnfläche: 79 m²

Lage: Citylage – Zentrum Leipzig (Altstadt 5 Min.); Einkaufsmöglichkeiten und Bushaltestelle in unmittelbarer Nähe

Zimmer: 3

Gut erhaltene Garten-Altbauwohnung (Erdgeschoß). Ruhige und sonnige Lage. Zentralheizung. Parkettboden. Wohnzimmer mit Küchenzeile und Tür zum Garten. Badezimmer mit neu installierter Dusche, Toilette, Waschbecken.

Frau Mühlens Wohnung

Miete: DM 1 200,–

Wohnfläche: 104 m²

Lage: Lindental (nördlich von Leipzig)

Gute Verkehrsverbindungen; 5 Automin. bis zu Bahnhof Lindental, 20 Min. m.d. Zug zum Hbf Leipzig

Zimmer: 5

Komfortable Neubauwohnung. Neue Siedlung mit Wohneinheiten. Landschaftlich schöne Lage. Intensi Begrünung. Tiefgarage. Grüne Innenhöfe n Spielplätzen. Fußbodenheizung. Wohnzimmer n Kamin und Zugang zum Balkon mit Blick auf Innenh Komplett eingerichtete Küche. Eßzimmer mit Durchga zur Küche. Luxus-Badezimmer. 3 weitere Zimmer.

1 You look out on to woods from my flat.
2 Let's walk. We'll be right in the middle of town in a matter of minutes.
3 I had the bathroom done up just a month ago.
4 I much prefer these older buildings.
5 It's very safe for children. There is a play area at the back.
6 Lots of sunshine here, you know – it comes right in.
7 You can get up and walk straight into the garden.
8 Leipzig lies to the south – over there.

7

Imagine that you have just moved into either Herr Wagner's or Frau Mühlen's fla choose the one you prefer. Read through the estate agent's description again of flat you have chosen and make brief notes of the essential features. Use the not to write a letter in German to a friend, describing your new home. There are so suggestions below for points you could cover. Also included are the beginning a end of a letter, and a sentence you could use to start off, which tells your friend how long ago you moved in. Add whatever details you wish – the colours of the rooms, for example. Make your letter about 100 words long.

- type of flat
- rent
- size
- rooms
- fittings
- location

Liebe/Lieber ____________ ,

ich bin/wir sind vor ____________ umgezogen. Die neue Wohnung ist …

Viele Grüße,

____

Lerneinheit 5 Wohnen Sie schon immer dort?

Lerneinheit 5 develops the theme of housing from *Lerneinheit 4*. It features recordings of people from Tübingen and Leipzig talking about where they live. You will learn how to describe where you live more fully and you will also practise spelling.

The first topic is *Talking about your home* – some of the people you will hear live in flats, others in houses. The second topic, *Other people describe their homes*, could be useful when you are talking to people from a German twin town. The final topic is *Comparing homes*.

STUDY CHART

Topic	Activity and resource	Key points
Talking about your home	1 ***Übungskassette***	listening to people talking about their homes
	2 ***Übungskassette***	practising the accusative and dative cases
	3 **Text**	practising the dative of rest and accusative of movement
	4 ***Übungskassette***	practising German spelling
Other people describe their homes	5 ***Übungskassette***	identifying useful words in the description of someone's home
	6 ***Übungskassette***	checking you've understood the description of someone's home
Comparing homes	7 ***Übungskassette***	noting advantages and disadvantages of a home
	8 ***Übungskassette***	practising talking about where you live
	9 **Text**	comparing where you live now and lived before

Before listening to *Hörabschnitt 6*, which comprises five short descriptions of where different people live, study the vocabulary overleaf. You will notice that in German there are several words for the floors of a building.

Listen to the five descriptions, and then answer the following questions in English about each of the speakers, playing *Hörabschnitt 6* again, if you need to.

teuer *expensive*

die Eigentumswohnung (-en) *private flat, owner occupied; flat of one's own*

die Wohnverhältnisse (*pl*) *living conditions*

die Wohnfläche (-n) *living space*

das Doppelhaus (¨-er) *semi-detached house*

das Stockwerk (-e) *floor, storey*

das Dachgeschoß *floor under or in the roof*

eingezogen (*from* einziehen) *moved in*

Herr Winter

1 What is special about the area he lives in?
2 Do they own or rent their flat?
3 How big is it?
4 How many families live in the building?
5 What do they share?
6 What do some families also have?

Herr Hartmann

7 Does he live in or outside Tübingen?
8 What is the population of the place he lives in?
9 What sort of house is it?
10 How big is it?
11 What do you know about his garden?

Professor Möhle

12 What is the area of the plot of land?
13 What was done to his house?
14 When was the house built?

Frau Storr

15 What sort of house is it?
16 How many rooms does it have?
17 How many floors does it have?
18 List the rooms on each floor.

Frau Patzwahl

19 How does she describe the three flats or houses that she has lived in?
20 When did they move to the two bedroomed flat?
21 When did they move into their present home?

REVISING *der, die, das* and *ein, eine, ein*

In *Lerneinheit 4* you learned to use the accusative after certain prepositions (*an, auf, in* and *vor*) when movement is involved. You also learned that the dative is used after the same prepositions when there is no movement.

Accusative of movement: **Wohin geht sie? Sie geht in die Küche.**
Dative of rest: **Wo ist sie jetzt? Sie ist in der Küche.**

Remember that definite and indefinite articles which follow a preposition need to change their endings. For quick revision, refer to the tables on pages 6 and 30.

2

In the following sentences the articles have been omitted. Put them back in, using either the accusative or the dative, as appropriate. You might find it helpful to listen to *Hörabschnitt 6* again before doing this activity.

Herr Winter wohnt in ____________ Eigentumswohnung. Die Wohnung hat vier Zimmer und ____________ Keller. Die vier Parteien haben ____________ Waschküche und ____________ Fahrradkeller zusammen. Seine Wohnung hat ____________ Dachboden.

Herr Hartmann wohnt in ____________ Einfamilienhaus mit ____________ Wohnfläche von 140 m^2 und mit ____________ großen Garten.

Die Möhles wohnen in ____________ Zweifamilienhaus.

Frau Storr wohnt in ____________ Doppelhaus. Ihr Büro ist in ____________ Dachgeschoß.

Frau Patzwahl hat jetzt ____________ Vierzimmerwohnung. Früher wohnte sie in ____________ Dreizimmerwohnung.

3

In this activity you will practise using the accusative and the dative in contrasting ways, depending on whether movement or rest is involved. Answer the questions using the clues you are given. The arrow (➔) indicates movement, the circle with the dot (◉) indicates that there is none. For example:

Wo ist Heinz? ➔ Garten.
Er ist in den Garten gegangen. (*He's gone into the garden.*)
Ist Tanja da? ◉ Wohnzimmer.
Nein, sie ist im Wohnzimmer. (*She's in the living room.*)

1. Ist Karl da? ➔ Stadt
2. Wo ist Heti? ◉ Schlafzimmer
3. Wohin ist Lutz gefahren? ➔ Dorf
4. Ich suche Herrn Hartmann. ◉ Haus
5. Wissen Sie, wo Margret ist? ➔ Keller
6. Haben Sie Axel hier gesehen? ➔ Garten
7. Wo ist Benno? ➔ Küche
8. Ist Christine da? ◉ Balkon

4

This activity concentrates on spellings. Listen to the short extracts of conversation in *Hörabschnitt 7* in which people spell names of places and people. Note down the words that they spell and then go over the dialogues again, listening to the spellings and repeating them several times.

When you have completed the activity, practise words you are likely to need to spell in Germany, such as your own name, the name of the place where you live and the names of members of your family.

buchstabieren
to spell

5

Frau Hilde Rösner lives in Lustnau near Tübingen. In *Hörabschnitt 8* you can he her describing her flat. Before listening to her, look at the words below. You will hear one word from each pair in *Hörabschnitt 8* – though it will, of course, be in German. Tick each one as you hear it and write it down in German.

1 **a** two-family house **b** flat
2 **a** second floor **b** first floor
3 **a** third floor **b** ground floor
4 **a** surface area **b** shared accommodation
5 **a** purchase price **b** rent

6

In *Hörabschnitt 8* you will hear Frau Rösner say how long she has lived in Lustnau. Remember that in German the structure is *seit* plus the present tense. F example, *„Ich wohne seit 5 Jahren in Mannheim."* means 'I have lived in Mannheim for 5 years.'

Now listen to *Hörabschnitt 8* again and answer these questions in English.

1 How long has Frau Rösner lived in Lustnau with her family?
2 Who else lives in the house?
3 How big is their flat?
4 How much rent do they pay?

7

In *Hörabschnitt 9* you can hear Frau Rösner listing the good and bad points abo where she used to live, in the centre of town. In doing this, she sometimes uses t imperfect tense. The words she uses are given in the vocabulary. Write down in English the advantages and disadvantages she mentions. She mentions two good points and five or six bad points, depending on how you interpret what she says.

bezahlt (from *bezahlen*) *paid*
es gab *there was*
der Lärm *noise*
die Verschmutzung *dirt, pollution*
sie konnten *they could*
deshalb *for that reason*
wir wollten *we wanted to*
wir haben ... gefunden (*from* finden) *we found*
wir sind ... umgezogen (*from* umziehen) *we moved house*

8

To help you to practise talking about where you live, imagine that you live in Leipzig. Listen to the questions in *Hörabschnitt 10* on the *Übungskassette* and answer them in German. You will get some prompts in English, as you see below You can prepare your answers beforehand if you wish.

Interviewer	Wo wohnen Sie?
You	*(I live in a suburb in the south of Leipzig.)*
Interviewer	Wohnen Sie in einem Einfamilienhaus?
You	*(No, I have a flat in a house for three families.)*
Interviewer	Wohnen Sie gerne dort?
You	*(Yes. The flat is quite big – I have 95 m^2 and five rooms.)*

Interviewer	Wo haben Sie früher gewohnt?
You	*(I used to live in a flat in an old building in the centre of Leipzig.)*
Interviewer	Warum sind Sie dort weggezogen?
You	*(There was too much traffic there.)*
Interviewer	Gab es noch weitere Gründe?
You	*(Yes, the rent was too high and the flat was too small.)*

9

Now it's time to talk about your own home and compare it with where you used to live. Read the following questions out loud and answer them in German, as if you were having a conversation with yourself. Record yourself as well. Then write out the answers and look at the feedback in the *Lösungen*.

- Wo wohnen Sie?
- Wohnen Sie in einem Hochhaus?
- Wie viele Zimmer haben Sie?
- Was für Zimmer gibt es in Ihrer Wohnung oder in Ihrem Haus?
- Wohnen Sie gerne dort? Warum oder warum nicht?
- Wo haben Sie früher gewohnt?
- Warum sind Sie umgezogen?

Lerneinheit 6 Zu viel Verkehr

Lerneinheit 6 is based almost entirely around the *Hörbericht, Kein Platz für Autos*, which describes Tübingen's traffic problems and how the town is trying to solve them. One particular solution which they are trying in their attempts to minimise the impact of the car is a housing development called Schafbrühl.

The three topics *Lerneinheit 6* covers are *Working on the feature*, which outlines the situation and what the people of Tübingen think about it; *Discussing the problem and a solution*, where you will practise interviewing and being interviewed; and *Summing up the situation*.

STUDY CHART

Topic	Activity and resource	Key points
Working on the feature	1 **Text**	checking relevant vocabulary
	2 ***Hörbericht***	listening to *Kein Platz für Autos*
	3 ***Hörbericht***	transcribing extracts from the feature
	4 ***Hörbericht***	checking you've understood the feature
Discussing the problem and a solution	5 ***Übungskassette***	being interviewed about Tübingen's traffic problems
	6 ***Übungskassette***	answering questions about Schafbrühl
	7 **Text**	writing questions for an interview
Summing up the situation	8 ***Hörbericht***	writing a summary of the feature

Before listening to the *Hörbericht* about Tübingen's traffic problems, study the list on page 39 of words which are used in it. Read the list through twice, then cover the English side and see how many meanings you can remember. Repeat the process if you feel you need to. At this stage you don't need to be able to use the German words, just understand them.

In Tübingen gibt es zu viele Autos, so wie in vielen anderen Städten Deutschlands auch. Nur sind die Verkehrsprobleme in Tübingen besonders schlimm. Warum?

erwerbstätig *employed*

in der Lage sein, etwas zu machen *to be able, or in a position to do something*

der Grundstückspreis (-e) *cost of land*

der Pendler (-) *commuter*

der Durchschnitt (-) *average*

der Stau (-s) *traffic jam*

der Lärm *noise*

am Rande *on the edge, outskirts*

der Innenhof (¨-e) *courtyard*

der Teich (-e) *pond*

der Bach (¨-e) *stream*

das Gemeinschaftsgefühl (-e) *community feeling*

der Nachbar (-n) *neighbour*

sich begegnen *to meet one another*

toll *great, fantastic; literally: mad*

Hörbericht 1

Now listen to *Hörbericht 1* right through. Don't worry if you don't understand all of it, just pick up what you can. Then listen to it again and write down the answers to the following questions.

1. What percentage of people who work in Tübingen commute to work?
2. Why do they commute rather than live in the town?
3. What is the average number of people travelling in each car?
4. Where are cars allowed in Schafbrühl?
5. What three things do you know about Frau Patzwahl and her family?
6. Where was the recording of Frau Patzwahl made?
7. What is there in the courtyard by her house?
8. List the advantages of Schafbrühl that are mentioned, seen from Frau Patzwahl's point of view.

Hörbericht 1

To fill in the gaps in these sentences you will need words and short phrases from *Hörbericht 1*. Some have already been given in the vocabulary list in Activity 1, others you will find on the tape. Write out the sentences in full and check your answers.

1. Die ______ in der Stadt sind besonders schlimm.
2. Die meisten Pendler sind ______ ______ ______ ______ die Miet- und Grundstückspreise zu bezahlen.
3. Die Autos ______ ______ ______ mit 1,1 Personen besetzt.
4. ______ ______ ist Tübingen praktisch eine Großstadt durch die Einpendler.
5. Schafbrühl ist eine neue ______. Die Autos ______ ______ ______ der Siedlung bleiben.

6 Zwischen ______________ ______________ gibt es Innenhöfe, wo die Kinder ______________ können.

Hörbericht I

This text contains a number of factual inaccuracies. Read it through and write out the correct version, using information from the *Hörbericht.*

Dreißig Prozent der Leute, die in Tübingen arbeiten, sind Pendler. Sie pendeln, weil sie gern außerhalb der Stadt wohnen. Sie fahren meistens mit dem Bus. Nur wenige Autos kommen in die Stadt. Die Pendler fahren in die Stadt, um Einkäufe zu machen.

Seit den 70er Jahren gibt es eine neue Art Siedlung. Sie heißt Schafbrühl und liegt in der Innenstadt. Die Häuser sind um Parkplätze gruppiert. Schafbrühl hat kein starkes Gemeinschaftsgefühl und die sozialen Kontakte sind schlecht.

5

Now imagine that someone from the local radio station has stopped you in the street to interview you about the traffic problems of Tübingen and about the solutions that are being tried. The interviewer's questions are given below, together with prompts in English. Listen again to the *Hörbericht* if you wish and then prepare your replies in German. Read the completed dialogue a couple of times out loud to yourself. Then turn to *Hörabschnitt 11* on the *Übungskassette* and answer the interviewer's questions as they are put to you.

Die Siedlung Schafbrühl

Interviewer Haben Sie Verkehrsprobleme in Tübingen?
You *(Yes. The traffic problems are especially bad.)*
Interviewer Warum?
You *(Because too many people commute.)*
Interviewer Warum pendeln so viele Leute?
You *(They are not in a position to pay the rents.)*
Interviewer Ich habe hier viele parkende Autos gesehen.
You *(Yes. There are too many cars in the town centre.)*
Interviewer Man hat hier aber Versuche mit einer neuen Art Siedlung gemacht.
You *(Yes. The new estate is called Schafbrühl. It's on the edge of town.)*
Interviewer Was macht man dort mit den Autos?
You *(They have to stay outside the estate.)*

6

The radio interviewer has found out that you live in Schafbrühl and wants to ask you about the estate and what you think about it. You will be given English prompts, as in Activity 5. Listen to *Hörabschnitt 12* on the *Übungskassette* and answer the interviewer's questions as they are put to you.

This time, the answers have been provided and you have to write the questions. Frau Hüber from the *Stadtsanierungsamt* (the town planning office) is being interviewed about Tübingen's traffic problem and about housing. Write down the questions that the interviewer would need to ask. Here are some suggestions you could adapt to use in the activity.

How?	**Wie macht man das? Wie kommt es, daß so viele Leute pendeln?**
How many?	**Wie viele Autos kommen in die Stadt?**
Since when?	**Seit wann gibt es diese Probleme?**
What is there ...?	**Was gibt es ...?**
What does the town planning office want to do?	**Was will das Stadtsanierungsamt machen?**
What is/are ... like?	**Wie ist/sind ...?**
Where?	**Wo haben Sie neue Parkplätze gebaut?**
Why?	**Warum sind die Probleme so schlimm?**

Interviewer	...
Frau Hüber	*Die meisten Leute fahren mit dem Auto in die Stadt. Einige fahren mit dem Bus und einige wenige fahren mit dem Rad.*
Interviewer	...
Frau Hüber	*Sie wohnen nicht in der Stadt, weil es zu teuer ist. Die Mietpreise sind zu hoch.*
Interviewer	...
Frau Hüber	*Im Durchschnitt sitzen nur 1,1 Personen in jedem Auto. Es gibt viel zu viele Autos in der Stadt. Wir haben aber eine neue Siedlung, wo man praktisch ohne Auto leben kann.*
Interviewer	...
Frau Hüber	*Die Siedlung gibt es seit 1980.*
Interviewer	...
Frau Hüber	*Sie liegt am Stadtrand.*
Interviewer	...
Frau Hüber	*Parkplätze? Ja, es gibt Parkplätze, aber sie sind am Rand der Siedlung.*
Interviewer	...
Frau Hüber	*Es gibt Innenhöfe dazwischen.*
Interviewer	...
Frau Hüber	*Die Innenhöfe sind sehr schön. Es gibt Teiche und Bäche.*

8

Hörbericht 1

To sum up, write a short passage of about 100–120 words about Tübingen's traffic problems and about Schafbrühl. Try to write your first draft without referring to the activities you have just done, just listen to *Hörbericht 1* again. When you have completed your draft, go through the activities in this *Lerneinheit* and see whether you can improve your summary. Cover the following points:

- Verkehrsprobleme
- pendeln
- Mietpreise
- Lebensqualität
- Schafbrühl
- Autoparken
- Innenhöfe – spielen

Checkliste

By the end of *Teil 2* you should be able to

- ○ compose a short summary in the present tense (*Lerneinheit* 4, Activity 3)
- ○ understand advertisements for flats and houses (*Lerneinheit* 4, Activity 4)
- ○ describe a flat or house briefly and use the words for furniture (*Lerneinheit* 4, Activities 5 & 7)
- ○ use the conventions for writing informal letters (*Lerneinheit* 4, Activity 7)
- ○ use the accusative case after prepositions where there is movement and the dative case where there is none (*Lerneinheit* 5, Activity 3)
- ○ spell in German (*Lerneinheit* 5, Activity 4)
- ○ understand percentages in German (*Lerneinheit* 6, Activities 2 & 4)
- ○ formulate questions using *w-* words (*wie, was, wo, warum* (*Lerneinheit* 6, Activity 7)

Teil 3

Hier wohne ich

So far in this book you have seen what Tübingen and Leipzig look like and heard local people talk about their homes. *Teil 3* centres on how people feel about where they live. How does their house or flat suit them? Do they like their neighbourhood? *Lerneinheit 7, In Tübingen and Leipzig*, gives you a chance to find out more about the kinds of places where people live in these two towns. *Lerneinheit 8, Mir gefällt es hier*, concentrates on people's opinions about their homes, and *Lerneinheit 9, Aus den Zeitungen*, introduces some wider housing issues through two newspaper articles.

By the end of *Teil 3*, you should have developed skills in describing your home and its neighbourhood and have practised expressing opinions about them. You will have gained some insights into how some people live in Tübingen and Leipzig.

Lerneinheit 7 In Tübingen und Leipzig

In *Lerneinheit 7* you will see and hear people from Tübingen and Leipzig talking about their homes. They describe the size and the location of their house or flat and talk about their reasons for living there.

The first topic is *Living in Tübingen and Leipzig*; the second topic is *Describing where people live*. You will be able to use these activities to improve the way you describe things and express your opinions about them.

STUDY CHART

Topic	Activity and resource	Key points
Living in Tübingen and Leipzig	**1 Video**	checking you've understood a video about where people live
	2 Video	picking out who said what
	3 Video	working on prepositions
	4 Text	working on prepositions and articles in the dative and accusative
Describing where people live	**5 *Übungskassette***	answering questions about flats
	6 Text	making up short texts about where people live

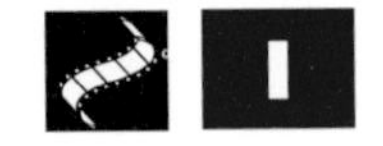

09:07–13:57

Ar *unit of measurement of 100 square metres*

die Wohngemeinschaft (-en) *shared accommodation*

lustig *cheerful, jolly*

die Eltern (*pl*) *parents*

eine alleinerziehende Mutter *single mother*

aus Kostengründen *for reasons of cost*

zirka *approximately*

der Landkreis (-e) *district*

es ist natürlich Plattenbau *it is, of course, prefabricated*

bis vor kurzem *until a short while ago*

billig *cheap*

Toilette auf der Treppe *toilet off the staircase*

ursprünglich *originally*

In this activity you will be working from the third part of the video. Watch the accounts of where people live, then answer the following questions in English.

Dr. Wilfred Setzler ist Leiter des Kulturamts der Stadt Tübingen. Die Setzlers wohnen in einem Einfamilienhaus in der Stadtmitte. Sie haben drei Kinder.

Tanja Lindl stammt aus Heilbronn. Seit drei Jahren studiert sie Skandinavistik und Anglistik in Tübingen, wo sie mit sechs Frauen in einer Wohngemeinschaft wohnt. Sie geht gern ins Kino, reist gern und sie treibt manchmal Sport.

Sibylle Metzger studiert Englisch und Deutsch. Sie wohnt in Reutlingen und fährt jeden Tag mit dem Zug nach Tübingen. Sie schwimmt gerne, joggt und fährt im Winter Ski.

Günter Leypoldt ist Germanistik- und Anglistikstudent an der Tübinger Universität, wo er auch einen Teilzeit-Job hat. Er wohnt in der Stadtmitte von Tübingen.

Daniela Krafak kommt aus Berlin und hat in Leipzig studiert. Nach der Wende war sie ein Jahr in London. Sie arbeitet in einem Reisebüro.

Frau Frenzel und ihr Mann haben drei Kinder: Christine, Antje und Lukas. Sie arbeitet als Teilzeitbeschäftigte bei einem Optiker.

1. What sort of house does Dr. Wilfried Setzler live in?
2. How many rooms does it have?
3. What does he say about the garden?
4. What part of town does Tanja Lindl live in?
5. She mentions two possible problems about living with six other women. What are they?
6. Describe Sibylle Metzger's flat.
7. Where does Günter Leypoldt live?
8. For how long has Gesine Jüttner shared a house with her parents?
9. How much space does she have in the house?
10. Describe the building Ruth Stabenow lives in.
11. What does she say about the size of her flat?
12. What did Daniela Krafak and her boyfriend decide to do about accommodation?

13 When did they move?
14 How big is Angelika Frenzel's flat?
15 Is it an old or a new building?
16 What sort of house does Renate Baumeister live in?
17 Who lives in the middle flat?

Plattenbau in Leipzig

In this part of the video, Frau Stabenow refers to the block of flats where she lives as *Plattenbau*. Under the DDR much housing was provided in large prefabricated tenement blocks built of concrete slabs and known as *Plattenbauten* (prefabricated buildings). *Plattenbauten* were built to satisfy demand for housing using relatively limited resources. Though they have now come to symbolise drabness and uniformity of living, they did provide a reasonable standard of housing for a great number of people.

2
09:07–13:57

This activity highlights how people describe where they live. Read the statements below, then watch the video again and write the name or initials of the person to whom it refers against each statement.

1 Es gibt im Haus zwei Arbeitszimmer.
2 Dort zu wohnen ist sehr praktisch.
3 Die Wohnung ist ohne Komfort und Luxus.
4 Ein großer Balkon gehört zur Wohnung.
5 In der alten Wohnung war die Toilette auf der Treppe.
6 Ein Paar ohne Kinder wohnt unter dem Dach.
7 Sie wohnt in einer Wohngemeinschaft in der Stadtmitte.
8 Er wohnt 20 Minuten von der Stadtmitte entfernt.
9 Der Hausbesitzer wohnt im selben Haus.
10 Sie wohnt mit den Eltern und mit dem Sohn zusammen.

USING prepositions

In *Lerneinheiten 4* and *5* you worked on prepositions that take the accusative or the dative depending upon whether movement is involved or not. There are other German prepositions that are followed only by the accusative or only by the dative.

These prepositions are followed only by the accusative case:

durch *through*
für *for*
gegen *against*
ohne *without*
um *around*

CONTINUED

The following prepositions are followed only by the dative case:

aus *out of, from*
bei *near, by, at, for, with*
gegenüber *opposite*
mit with
nach *after, to*
seit *since*
von *from, of*
zu *to*

Note these shortened forms:

zum **= zu dem** ***zur*** **= zu der** ***beim*** **= bei dem** ***vom*** **= von dem**

The prepositions that you studied earlier, which are followed by either the accusative or the dative, were *an, auf, in* and *vor.* There are more – here is a complete list:

an *up to, over to, on*
auf *on, onto*
hinter *behind, beyond*
in *in, into*
neben *beside, next to*
über *over, across*
unter *under*
vor *before, in front of*
zwischen *between*

Note these shortened forms:

am **= an dem** ***ans*** **= an das** ***im*** **= in dem** ***ins*** **= in das**

10:42–11:18

Read the passage below, which is a transcript of the video sequence you have just watched, and insert the appropriate prepositions in the gaps provided. Then watch the video sequence again and check your answers.

das Gebiet (-e)
district

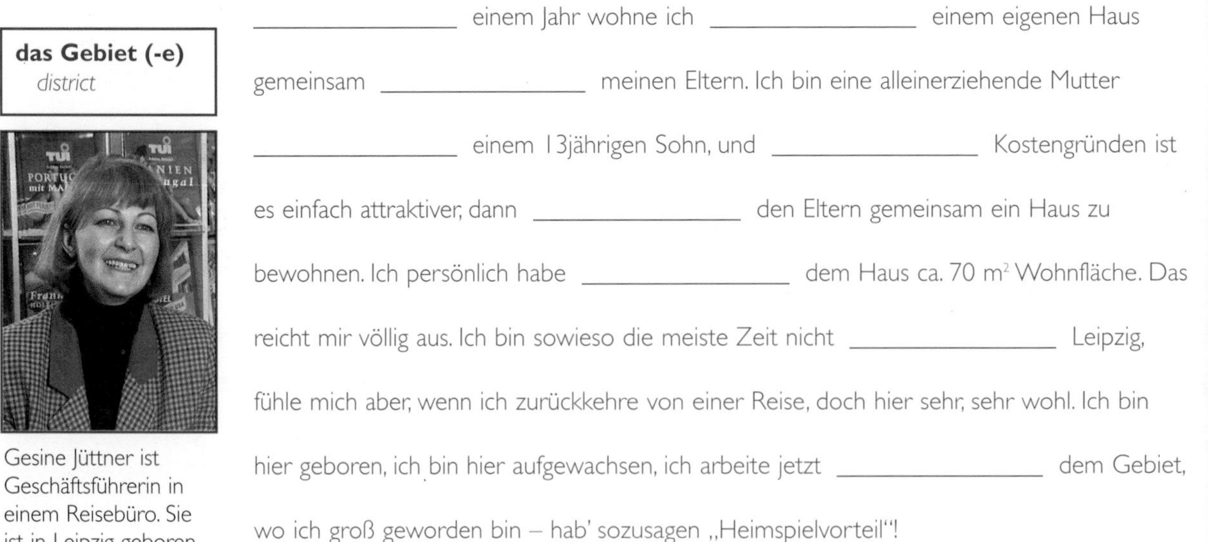

Gesine Jüttner ist Geschäftsführerin in einem Reisebüro. Sie ist in Leipzig geboren und erzieht ihren Sohn allein.

__________ einem Jahr wohne ich __________ einem eigenen Haus gemeinsam __________ meinen Eltern. Ich bin eine alleinerziehende Mutter __________ einem 13jährigen Sohn, und __________ Kostengründen ist es einfach attraktiver, dann __________ den Eltern gemeinsam ein Haus zu bewohnen. Ich persönlich habe __________ dem Haus ca. 70 m^2 Wohnfläche. Das reicht mir völlig aus. Ich bin sowieso die meiste Zeit nicht __________ Leipzig, fühle mich aber, wenn ich zurückkehre von einer Reise, doch hier sehr, sehr wohl. Ich bin hier geboren, ich bin hier aufgewachsen, ich arbeite jetzt __________ dem Gebiet, wo ich groß geworden bin – hab' sozusagen „Heimspielvorteil"!

4

Here are brief descriptions of where some other people live. There are gaps in the descriptions where the German word for 'a' (the indefinite article) and 'the' (the definite article) have been omitted. Fill in the gaps, checking whether the word you insert should be in the dative or accusative. This will depend on the preposition and in some cases on whether movement or rest involved.

1 Ich wohne in ____________ kleinen Wohnung in ____________ Hochhaus. Meine Wohnung ist in ____________ Stadtmitte und ich wohne dort seit ____________ Jahr.

2 Ich wohne mit ____________ Freund zusammen. Unsere Wohnung ist sehr schön und besteht aus ____________ Wohnzimmer, ____________ Küche und drei weiteren Zimmern. Im Sommer essen wir auf ____________ Balkon.

3 Ich wohne in ____________ Haus mit ____________ Garten. Man kann direkt von ____________ Wohnzimmer in ____________ Garten gehen. Das Haus liegt an ____________ Stadtrand und ist zwei Kilometer von ____________ Stadtmitte entfernt. Ich kann also zu Fuß in ____________ Stadt gehen, was sehr praktisch ist.

5

The last two activities in *Lerneinheit 7* will give you some practice in writing a description of your home.

Now it's your turn to describe a flat as if it were your own. To do this, you should use phrases from the statements and transcripts in Activities 1–4. Listen to the questions in *Hörabschnitt 13* on the *Übungskassette*, then answer in German in complete sentences, following the prompts in English.

6

Here is some information you can use as a basis for making up descriptions of where people live and how long they've lived there. Use it to make up two complete descriptions, adding adjectives such as *schön*, *groß*, *attraktiv* and so on, where appropriate. Here is an example to show how such information can be expanded.

Name	**seit + *dative***	**Haus/Wohnung**	**Lage**
Reus	seit 3 Jahren	Altbauwohnung Balkon 2ZKB	im Norden 5 km von der Autobahn Wald in der Nähe Geschäfte um die Ecke

Frau Reus wohnt seit drei Jahren in einer kleinen Altbauwohnung. Sie hat einen Balkon und zwei Zimmer mit Küche und Bad. Die Wohnung liegt im Norden der Stadt, 5 Kilometer von der Autobahn entfernt. Der Wald liegt in der Nähe und die Geschäfte sind um die Ecke.

Here are two sets of information for you to work from.

Name	seit + *dative*	Haus/Wohnung	Lage
Schelling	ein Monat	Einfamilienhaus 130 m² Garten	im Osten am Stadtrand ... km von ... in der Nähe von Sportzentrum Bahnhof Bushaltestelle vor der Tü
Braun und Klausewitz	zwei Jahre	Wohnung 3ZKB Balkon 120 m²	Stadtmitte 500 m – Bahnhof Geschäfte in der Nähe

Lerneinheit 8 Mir gefällt es hier

In *Lerneinheit 8* you will meet people from all over Germany who give their opinions about where they live. You will work on describing why people like or dislike living where they do.

The first topic, *Discussing people's homes*, will provide you with the necessary vocabulary and linguistic structures to do that. In the second topic, *Talking about where you live*, you will hear opinions from people living in cities all over Germany. The third topic, *Considering where you live*, will help you to sum up your own situation. *Lerneinheit 8* ends with the poem *„Die Stadt"*, by the north German writer Theodor Storm.

STUDY CHART

Topic	Activity and resource	Key points
Discussing people's homes	**1 Text**	reading what people say about where they live
	2 *Übungskassette*	listening to descriptions of the same people
	3 Text	practising using possessives and pronouns
	4 Text	writing about the people whose opinions you've heard
Talking about where you live	**5 Text**	reading about people who live in other German cities
	6 Text	practising using *weil*
	7 Text	explaining why people like or dislike places
Considering where you live	**8 Text**	summing up the advantages and disadvantages of where you live
Die Stadt	**9 *Übungskassette***	listening to and reading a poem

This is the first of a sequence of four activities. First, read the personal accounts of four people who live in Tübingen and Leipzig, then answer the questions below in English.

Frau Stabenow stammt aus Glauchau in der Nähe von Chemnitz, aber hat mehr als 50 Jahre in Leipzig gelebt. Sie ist Witwe, und bevor sie Rentnerin wurde, hat sie in einer großen chemischen Firma in Leipzig gearbeitet.

Frau Stabenow

„Ich bin seit 53 Jahren Leipzigerin. Ich wohne in einer kleinen Wohnung am Stadtrand in der Nähe des Wildparks. Ich finde es sehr schön hier, weil die Lage ruhig ist und die Nachbarn freundlich sind. Wenn ich das Haus verlasse, treffe ich immer Freunde. Ich gehe gern spazieren und mache oft Stadtbummel in Leipzig, was mir sehr gefällt."

Renate Baumeister ist Hausfrau und arbeitet auch als Erzieherin in einem Kindergarten. Frau Baumeister hat drei Kinder: Lucy, Max und Till.

Frau Baumeister

„Ich wohne seit 20 Jahren in Tübingen. Mein Haus steht am Stadtrand im Dorf Hirschau, ungefähr vier Kilometer von der Stadtmitte entfernt. Die Lebensweise in Süddeutschland gefällt mir sehr, und ich würde mich in Norddeutschland nicht so wohl fühlen. Mit meiner Familie mache ich oft Wanderungen in den Wäldern hier in der Nähe, weil wir sehr gern in der Natur sind."

Dr. Setzler

„Ich wohne seit vielen Jahren in Tübingen. Mit meiner Frau und drei Kindern wohne ich in der Stadtmitte. Ich fühle mich sehr wohl in Tübingen. Ich habe hier viele soziale Kontakte und Freunde. Mein Haus steht in der Stadtmitte, was ich sehr praktisch finde. Ich gehe zu Fuß in mein Büro und meine Kinder gehen auch zu Fuß einkaufen. Gaststätten und Geschäfte liegen ganz in der Nähe."

Herr Rübling ist in Königsberg in Ostpreußen (heute Kaliningrad in Rußland) geboren. Er hat den größten Teil seines Lebens in Leipzig verbracht. Nach der Wende ist er Besitzer einer Taxifirma geworden.

Herr Rübling

„Ich wohne seit vielen Jahren in Leipzig und fühle mich ganz zu Hause in dieser Stadt. Ich wohne mit meiner Frau in einem neuen Haus am Stadtrand, eine Gegend, die ich sehr schön finde. Wir haben das Grundstück vor einigen Jahren gekauft. Leipzig gefällt uns gut. Ich habe hier viele Verwandte und Freunde. Weil ich Taxifahrer bin und einen ziemlich langen Arbeitstag habe, habe ich wenig Zeit für mich."

1. Where is Frau Stabenow's flat?
2. What three reasons does she give for liking living there?
3. What does Frau Baumeister like about living where she does? (two points)
4. Why does Dr. Setzler like living where he does? (two reasons)
5. Why does Herr Rübling like living in Leipzig?

TALKING about others

In Activity 1, people talked about themselves. They used what is called 'the first person' (I, me, my, mine; we, us, our, ours). When, however, you are talking about someone else, you use the third person. In Activities 2–4 you will hear personal pronouns and possessive adjectives being used in the third person – he, his, she, her, hers, it, its; they, their, theirs. Here are some examples:

Third person personal pronouns in the nominative and the dative

Er *hat eine Wohnung gekauft. Sie gefällt* ***ihm*** *gut.*
Leipzig gefällt ***ihr*** *gut. Sie wohnt dort mit Max zusammen.*
Sie *haben ein Haus am Stadtrand. Es gefällt* ***ihnen*** *gut, dort zu wohnen.*

Third person possessive adjectives in the nominative and the dative

Meine *Wohnung ist in der Bismarckstraße.*
Seine *Kinder gehen zu Fuß in die Schule.*
Anna? ***Ihr*** *Haus steht in der Lerchengasse.*
Sabina wohnt mit ***ihrem*** *Freund zusammen.*
Sie hat eine große Familie und ***ihre*** *Kinder wohnen alle in der Nähe.*

2 In this activity you will listen to *Hörabschnitt 14*, on the *Übungskassette*, where you will hear some of the same information as in Activity 1. However, instead of the four people describing themselves and using the first person (I and we), the *Hörabschnitt* describes them, using the third person (he, she, they). It uses the personal pronouns and possessive adjectives you have just read about. Listen to the *Hörabschnitt* twice. The first time, concentrate on the personal pronouns an write them down; the second time listen for the possessive adjectives and list them. You will need both for Activity 3.

3 Now, using the information you have read and heard in Activities 1 and 2, fill in t gaps in these statements, using the correct pronoun or possessive adjective.

1 **Frau Stabenow** Leipzig gefällt ______________ . Sie trifft ______________ Freunde. ______________ Kinder wohnen in einer anderen Stadt.

2 **Frau Baumeister** ______________ Haus steht in einem Dorf. Süddeutschland gefällt ______________ sehr. Sie geht mit ______________ Mann oft spazieren.

3 **Dr. Setzler** wohnt mit ______________ Familie in der Stadtmitte. Er kann zu Fuß ______________ Büro gehen. ______________ Kinder können auch zu Fuß einkau gehen.

4 **Herr Rübling** Mit ______________ Frau wohnt er in einem neuen Haus. Leipzig gefällt ______________ gut.

4 This activity gives you the chance to write more fully about the four people abov Complete the descriptions of where they live, using information from their personal accounts and *Hörabschnitt 14*. You will notice that these descriptions all in the third person singular. This means that in some sentences you will need use the personal pronouns and possessive adjectives given in Activity 3.

1 **Frau Stabenow** Die Lage ______________ ______________ . Die Nachbarn ______________ ______________ . Wenn sie das Haus verläßt, ______________ ______________ ______________ . Spazieren gehen gefällt ______________ ______________ .

2 **Frau Baumeister** Die Lebensweise in Süddeutschland ______________ ______________ ______________ . Sie macht gern ______________ ______________ ______________ . Sie ist ______________ ______________ ______________ ______________ .

3 Dr. Setzler Er fühlt ____________ ____________ ____________

____________ ____________ . Wohnen in der Stadtmitte ist ____________

____________ . Er geht zu Fuß ____________ ____________

____________ .

4 Herr Rübling Er fühlt ____________ ____________ ____________

____________ ____________ ____________ ____________ . Er wohnt mit

____________ ____________ ____________ ____________

____________ ____________ .

5

In this activity four people introduce themselves and tell you what they think about where they live. Read through the extracts and write down answers to the questions below in German.

…ßerdem *besides*

…er Nachteil (-e) *disadvantage*

…er Grund (¨-e) *reason*

…nstrengend *strenuous, stressful*

Andrea Schreiner „Ich mag Magdeburg, denn ich bin hier großgeworden. Meine Familie und Freunde leben hier, und ich kenne mich hier aus. Außerdem ist Magdeburg eine ziemlich große Stadt, und es gibt viele Unterhaltungsmöglichkeiten und Kultur. Ich liebe klassische Musik und gehe gern ins Konzert. Der einzige Nachteil für mich ist, daß es ein bißchen weit von Berlin und Leipzig entfernt liegt, wo gute Gruppen spielen."

Thomas Neuner „Bremen gefällt mir, und zwar aus verschiedenen Gründen. Es ist eine historische Stadt mit vielen alten und interessanten Häusern und das ist mir sehr sympathisch. Meine Wohnung liegt direkt in der Innenstadt. Das ist sehr praktisch zum Einkaufen und zum Ausgehen. Mein Supermarkt liegt gleich um die Ecke, und am Abend kann ich zu Fuß in die Kneipe gehen. Ins Büro fahre ich mit dem Fahrrad."

Marion Schelling „Frankfurt ist mir persönlich unsympathisch. Ich finde, es gibt zu viel Verkehr und Hektik. Das Wohnen im Zentrum ist so teuer – die Mieten kann man nicht bezahlen. Ich wohne 20 km außerhalb von Frankfurt und fahre mit dem Bus und der S-Bahn zur Arbeit. Das heißt, ich bin jeden Tag zwei Stunden unterwegs und das finde ich anstrengend."

Dieter Pleines „In Rostock fühle ich mich zu Hause. Hier ist mein Arbeitsplatz, und hier habe ich vor einigen Jahren mit meiner Frau ein Haus gebaut. Wir wohnen am Stadtrand von Rostock. Da ist genug Platz für einen Garten. Das ist wichtig für mich und meine Frau, weil wir gern in der Natur sind. Unsere Kinder und Enkelkinder wohnen in der Nähe und besuchen uns oft."

1. Wohin geht Frau Schreiner gerne?
2. Wann geht Herr Neuner in die Kneipe?
3. Ist der Supermarkt weit von seiner Wohnung entfernt?
4. Wie fährt er zur Arbeit?
5. Wie fährt Frau Schelling zur Arbeit?

6 Wie lange dauert ihre Fahrt zur Arbeit hin und zurück?
7 Warum ist ein Garten wichtig für Herr Pleines und seine Frau?
8 Was hat er vor einigen Jahren gemacht?

GIVING reasons

In the texts on page 53 there is an example of the use of *weil*:

Das ist wichtig für uns, *weil* wir gern in der Natur sind.

That is important to us, because we like being out in the country.

When *weil* is used, the verb in the same phrase goes to the end. As you can see in the example above, *weil* is always preceded by a comma when it occurs in the middle of a sentence. You will practise using this construction in the next activity.

In this activity you should write sentences using *weil* that give reasons for people's attitudes to where they live. Information from Activity 5 to help you is given below. Some advice is given at first, to help you.

1 Frau Schreiner

Sie mag Magdeburg, …

a ist dort groß geworden (*You would write*, Sie mag Magdeburg, weil sie dort groß geworden ist.)
b ihre Familie und Freunde
c es gibt viel Unterhaltung und Kultur

2 Herr Neuner

Bremen gefällt ihm, …

a Wohnung in der Innenstadt (*You would write*, ... weil seine Wohnung …)
b Supermarkt gleich um die Ecke
c zu Fuß in die Kneipe

3 Frau Schelling

a Sie mag Frankfurt nicht, …
b zu viel Verkehr und Hektik (*You would write*, … weil es zu viel …)
c Mietpreise hoch

4 Herr Pleines

Rostock gefällt ihm …

a Arbeitsplatz dort
b Haus dort
c Kinder und Enkelkinder

7

Now use the information about Frau Stabenow and the others given in Activities 1 and 2. Write short statements in German about why these four people enjoy living where they do, using the expressions:

- *Es gefällt ihr/ihm, in ... zu wohnen, weil ...*
- *Er/sie findet es ...*

You might start writing about Frau Stabenow like this:

Frau Stabenow wohnt gern am Stadtrand, weil die Lage ruhig ist.

8

Here is your chance to write about where you live. What are the positive and negative aspects? Read through the list of words below, which you might like to use, and look up the meanings of any words that you don't know. Then write an account of up to 120 words about your own area, giving its advantages and disadvantages from your point of view. You might find it useful to reread the passages in Activities 1 and 5 first.

Here is an example to suggest how you might start off your account:

Ich wohne in einer ziemlich großen Stadt. Es gefällt mir gut, weil ich dort viele Freunde habe. Ich bin in einem Dorf großgeworden, aber für mich ist die Stadt wichtig, weil ich gern ins Kino gehe ...

die U-Bahnstation	die Autobahn	das Theater
die Mietpreise	der Arbeitsplatz	das Kino
das Sportzentrum	die Industrie	das Dorf
Fahrradwege	der Supermarkt	das Schwimmbad
das Freizeitzentrum	Geschäfte	die gute Lage
die Schulen	der Bahnhof	soziale Kontakte
Freunde	die Innenstadt	die Landschaft
der Busbahnhof	der Kindergarten	die Fußgängerzone
der Park		

9

This poem is by Theodor Storm (1817–88), who was born in Husum, on the North Sea coast. He was a lyric poet who also wrote some of Germany's finest short stories or *Novellen*. This poem is about his native town – it brings out the bareness and monochrome nature of the area. Listen to it in *Hörabschnitt 15* and read the transcript out loud a few times.

der Strand *sea shore*
der Nebel *fog*
eintönig *monotonously*
schlagen *here: to sing (of birds)*
ohne Unterlaß *without ceasing*
wehen *wave, sway*
der Jugend Zauber für und für *the eternal magic of (my) youth*
lächelnd *smilingly*

Lerneinheit 9 Aus den Zeitungen

In the final *Lerneinheit* of *Teil 3* you will read two newspaper articles about housing. The first article reflects the changes that have taken place as the quality of accommodation in eastern Germany has been raised towards that in the west. The second article highlights the problem of homelessness, a new problem in the east.

The first topic is *Johannes Pietrowski – from Chemnitz to Leipzig*, the second topic is *Finding out more about a hostel for the homeless*. Besides learning new vocabulary from these articles, you will work on responding to questions in an interview.

STUDY CHART

Topic	Activity and resource	Key points
Johannes Pietrowski – from Chemnitz to Leipzig	1 **Text**	reading a newspaper article
	2 ***Übungskassette***	taking part in a dialogue
Finding out more about a hostel for the homeless	3 **Text**	reading an article and checking you've understood
	4 ***Übungskassette***	answering questions about the new hostel for the homeless
	5 ***Übungskassette***	transcribing parts of an audio excerpt
	6 **Text**	taking part in an interview about the hostel

Here is an article in which Johannes Pietrowski, an inhabitant of Leipzig, talks about where he lives now and where he used to live. Read through it, making notes as you do so. Use these headings for your notes.

Wo er früher wohnte

- die Lage
- was für eine Wohnung oder ein Haus
- Zimmer
- negative Aspekte
- positive Aspekte

Wo er jetzt wohnt

- die Lage
- seit wann
- was für eine Wohnung oder ein Haus
- Zimmer
- positive Aspekte

ehemalig *previous, former*

lud ... ein *(from* einladen) *invited*

der Rentner (-) *pensioner*

gebürtig *born in, native of*

teilen *to share*

das Treppenhaus (¨-er) *staircase*

das Gemeinschaftsgefühl *community feeling/spirit*

Unser Leipzig

„Ich wohne gern hier!“ Johannes Pietrowski (68)

Biennitz ist ein Stadtteil im Norden von Leipzig und ist typisch für so viele ehemalige DDR-Wohngebiete: Es gibt dort vor allem Hochhäuser und Plattenbausiedlungen. Die *Leipziger Nachrichten* wollten wissen: Wie lebt man dort? Johannes Pietrowski (68) lud die *Leipziger Nachrichten* in seine Wohnung ein.

„Guten Tag, da sind Sie ja!“ Johannes Pietrowski öffnet die Wohnungstür. „Kommen Sie doch ins Wohnzimmer – ich bringe gleich den Kaffee!“ Der Rentner (er war früher Polizist) lebt allein in der sonnigen Zwei-Zimmer-Wohnung: Seine Frau Ilse starb vor drei Jahren. Bei Kaffee und Kuchen erzählt er: „Ich wohne seit 1970 in Leipzig-Biennitz – in einem Hochhaus in einer Plattenbausiedlung.“ Johannes Pietrowski hat eine kleine Wohnung im sechsten Stock mit einem kleinen Wohnzimmer – dort hat er auch seine Kochecke, ein Schlafzimmer, ein Badezimmer und einen kleinen Balkon. „Im Sommer sitze ich den ganzen Tag auf dem Balkon – ja, mein Balkon ist mein zweites Wohnzimmer,“ lacht er.

Wo wohnte Johannes Pietrowski früher? „Also, ich bin nicht gebürtiger Leipziger. Ich stamme aus Rostock. Früher habe ich mit meiner Frau in Karl-Marx-Stadt gewohnt, dem heutigen Chemnitz,“ erzählt er. „Wir hatten dort nur eine kleine Zwei-Zimmer-Wohnung ohne Komfort und Luxus – also, Heizung gab es natürlich nicht. Die Küche mußten wir uns mit den anderen Mietern teilen, und Bad und Toilette waren im Treppenhaus – aber es war sehr schön damals. Wir hatten ein gutes Gemeinschaftsgefühl. Man traf sich auf der Straße oder im Hof, die Kinder konnten überall spielen, und es gab wenig Verkehr. Man lebte dort wie in einem Dorf.“

Doch jetzt gefällt ihm das Leben in einer Großstadt: „Ich wohne lieber in Leipzig – hier habe ich alles, was ich brauche: Es gibt einen Supermarkt um die Ecke, die Sparkasse und die Post sind auch ganz in der Nähe, und wenn ich mal in die Stadt fahren will, dann kann ich mit dem Bus fahren – die Haltestelle ist direkt vor dem Haus. Biennitz ist meine Heimat – mir gefällt es hier aber gut!“

2

Using the notes you made in Activity 1, take on the role of Johannes Pietrowski as he is interviewed by the local radio station. The questions you will be asked are given below. Read through them and draft your answers. Then listen to the interviewer in *Hörabschnitt 16* and answer according to the English prompts on the cassette. The interviewer's questions are as follows:

- Guten Tag, Herr Pietrowski. Sie wohnen seit vielen Jahren hier in der Gegend. Können Sie uns zuerst sagen, wo genau Sie wohnen?
- Wohnen Sie gerne hier?
- Wo haben Sie früher gewohnt?
- Und haben Sie auch dort gerne gewohnt?
- Was hat Ihnen dort nicht gefallen?
- Es gefällt Ihnen hier also besser?

Now read this article about the new *Haus für Wohnungslose* in Leipzig and answer the questions below in English. Don't worry about understanding every bit of the text as the activities which follow will help you to explore the text in more detail.

Leipziger Anzeiger 23.12.1994

Neues Heim für Obdachlose ist mehr als ein Nachtquartier

Über 1 200 Menschen ohne Wohnung registriert

Über 1 200 Menschen sind in unserer Stadt als obdachlos registriert. Jedoch gibt es seit gestern ein neues Haus für Wohnungslose. Die Funktion dieses Hauses ist es, Obdachlosen die Chance zu geben, ein normales Leben zu führen. Jetzt können 59 Wohnungslose ohne eigene vier Wände dort eine Unterkunft finden.

Das Haus wurde 1991 eröffnet und dann ein Jahr später durch einen Brand zerstört. Für 1,1 Millionen Mark wurde das zerstörte Haus vollständig rekonstruiert und erweitert. Ein Jahr später wurde das Gebäude wiedereröffnet.

Es gibt keine Spuren des Brandes mehr, der das Haus 1992 zerstörte. Das Haus hat mehr die Atmosphäre einer Pension als die eines Heims. Es hat eine Rezeption, Etagenküchen, Aufenthaltsräume und Zweibettzimmer. Das wurde mit Absicht gemacht, denn in den anderen Unterkünften für Obdachlose gibt es nur Übernachtungsmöglichkeiten. Hier in diesem Haus können Wohnungslose mit guten Integrationschancen rund um die Uhr bleiben.

erweitert *(from erweitern) extended*

der Aufenthaltsraum (¨-e) *recreation room*

1. What is the purpose of this project?
2. What was done to the hostel after the fire?
3. How many can it accommodate?
4. When was the hostel first opened and when did it burn down?
5. What features does the new hostel have?
6. How many hours per day are the homeless people allowed to stay there?

4

Now you will hear two people talking about the new hostel: the warden and a resident. Before listening to *Hörabschnitt 17* read the questions below. Then listen to the cassette and write down the answers in English.

Jürgen Schmidt, Leiter des Hauses

1. How many people have already moved in?
2. Do most of them have jobs?
3. What do people do in the evenings?

Heiko Schimmel, Bewohner

4. Is this hostel better than others?
5. What is the negative aspect?

5

Now listen to *Hörabschnitt 17* once more and fill in the gaps in the transcript below.

Jürgen Schmidt, Leiter des Hauses

„Ja, meine Funktion also – ich bin Leiter des Hauses. Leider __________

__________ __________ __________ __________ mit Obdachlosigkeit

in Leipzig, und so war nach dem Brand dieser Wiederaufbau dringend notwendig. Es haben

bereits 42 __________ __________ __________ Quartier bezogen, und das

sind grundsätzlich Leute mit guten Integrationschancen. __________ __________

__________ __________ __________ __________ , gehen also einer

geregelten Arbeit nach und __________ __________ __________

__________ , wo sie dann __________ __________ __________

__________ __________ __________ . __________ __________

__________ sind auch Fernseher, und Fernsehen ist natürlich eine beliebte

Beschäftigung am Abend."

6

Imagine that you are warden of the hostel and that you are preparing for a radio interview. You have been given a list of topics by the journalist. Go back to the article you read in Activity 3 and prepare your answers (in German). Then read the interview questions below and answer from your notes.

- Darf ich Ihnen einige Fragen stellen, bitte? Wie viele Obdachlose wohnen jetzt schon hier?
- Ist die maximale Kapazität erreicht?
- Wie viele Menschen sind in Leipzig als obdachlos registriert?
- Wie ist das „Haus für Wohnungslose" eingerichtet?
- Wie viele Personen sind in einem Zimmer?
- Wie lange ist das Heim offen?
- Was hat der Neubau gekostet?

Checkliste

By the end of *Teil 3* you should be able to

- ○ recognise and use prepositions with the dative and/or accusative, as appropriate, and the articles *der, die, das,* and *ein, eine, ein.* (*Lerneinheit* 7, Activities 3–4) Seiten 46–47
- ○ describe a flat or house more fully (*Lerneinheit* 7, Activity 6) Seite 47
- ○ use the third person singular and plural dative personal pronouns, and third person possessive adjectives, as appropriate (*Lerneinheit* 8, Activities 3, 4 and 7) Seiten 52 & 5
- ○ give reasons using *weil* (*Lerneinheit* 8, Activity 6) Seite 54

Teil 4

Wiederholung

Teil 4 concentrates on revision of much of what you have covered in *Teile 1–3*. In *Lerneinheit 10, Willkommen in Südstadt*, you will learn about the conversion of the former French barracks in Tübingen into a housing development. In *Lerneinheit 11, Aspekte des Wohnens*, there is revision of language to do with how you live, and some more details of life in Südstadt.

By the end of *Teil 4*, you should have gained confidence in talking and writing about the whole area of housing. You should also be able to arrange to meet people, describe people's circumstances and give reasons.

Lerneinheit 10 Willkommen in Südstadt

In *Lerneinheit 10* you will read about how it feels to live in the new Südstadt development and how people are involved in making decisions about their community.

The first topic, *Exploring Südstadt*, gives some idea of the background to the project; the second topic is called *Revising making arrangements to meet.*

Lerneinheit 10 will help you to revise a wide range of language to do with housing.

STUDY CHART

Topic	Activity and resource	Key points
Exploring Südstadt	**1 Text**	reading an article about a redevelopment
	2 Text	practising *weil*
	3 Text	finding out about the local *Bürgerinitiative*
	4 Text	writing about another Tübingen estate
Revising making arrangements to meet	**5 Text**	arranging to meet another resident
	6 Text	practising making arrangements

Here is an article from a local newspaper about the Südstadt development on the outskirts of Tübingen. Read through it and answer the questions below in English.

Tübingen: Südstadt

entsteht *(from entstehen) is coming into being*

ehemalig *former*

die Kaserne (-n) *barracks*

die Grünanlage (-n) *green area, park*

der Umweltschutz *environmental protection*

schneidet … ab *(from abschneiden) cuts off*

beeinflussen *to influence*

günstig *favourable, reasonable*

Südstadt – Planung geht weiter

Wie beurteilen die ersten Einwohner den Rahmenplan?

Bauboom in Tübingen: Südlich der Stadt entsteht zur Zeit ein neues Wohnviertel mit modernen Eigentums- und Mietwohnungen: Die ehemalige französische Kaserne wird umgebaut. Was plant die Stadt – und was wünschen sich die Anwohner?

Einig sind sich alle: Es soll eine verkehrsfreie Umgebung entstehen mit Grünanlagen und Innenhöfen, Geschäften in der Nähe, und größeren Parkplätzen nur am Rande der Siedlung – und ein klares Nein zur Umweltverschmutzung und Ja zum Umweltschutz. Gute Verkehrsverbindungen bringen die „Südstädter" schnell und bequem in die Innenstadt Tübingens – was will man mehr? Einen großen Nachteil gibt es jedoch für die Einwohner: Die vielbefahrene Umgehungsstraße B 27 schneidet die Südstadt von Tübingen ab. Eine Bürgerinitiative „Südstadt" existiert bereits, um die Planung zu beeinflussen.

Doch wie denken die Bewohner der Südstadt über ihr Wohnviertel? Gefällt es ihnen – oder nicht? Heike Reus und ihr Ehemann Peter haben zwei kleine Kinder und wohnen gern in der Südstadt: „Für Kinder ist die Südstadt ideal," erklärt Heike Reus. „Es gibt einen Kinderspielplatz in der Nähe, und unsere Straße ist verkehrsfrei. Das finden wir gut!" Helga Reuchert und Kurt Jankowski sind jedoch anderer Meinung: „Wir sind nicht zufrieden," sagt Helga Reuchert. Kurt Jankowski erklärt: „Wir haben nämlich eine Wohnung direkt an der B 27. Dort gibt es zuviel Lärm und Umweltverschmutzung!" Die Seniorin Rosa Heck hat andere Probleme: „Mir gefällt es hier nicht – ich habe keinen Wagen, und meine Wohnung ist ziemlich weit von der Bushaltestelle entfernt." Erna Meier versteht solche Klagen nicht: „Ich fühle mich hier sehr zu Hause. Es gibt ein gutes Gemeinschaftsgefühl in unserem Wohnblock, und die Mieten sind günstig – das ist für mich als Rentnerin sehr wichtig!"

1. What sort of housing is there on the new estate?
2. The local people want a number of things. What are they? (seven points)
3. What is the big disadvantage of Südstadt?

WISSEN SIE DAS?

Eine Bürgerinitiative is a citizens' action group, set up to solve a local problem or to influence local policies.

2 In the newspaper article you have just read, four different opinions were given on living in Südstadt. Write down what the people feel about living there and give their reasons, using the conjunction *weil*. Here is an example:

Helga Reuchert und Kurt Janowski sind nicht zufrieden, weil sie an der B 27 wohnen und weil es dort zu viel Lärm und Verschmutzung gibt.

3 The *Bürgerinitiative* in the Südstadt is very active.The organisers try to involve as many people as possible, as you can see from this invitation. Read it, then answer in English the questions overleaf.

Die Bürgerinitiative Südstadt lädt ein:

Wir brauchen Ideen

7000 EinwohnerInnen mehr in der Südstadt! Wie sollen wir denn diesen zusätzlichen Verkehr verkraften? Wo werden Parkhäuser gebaut? Welche AnwohnerstraBen werden verkehrsfrei? Brauchen wir dann nicht auch ein Bürgerhaus? Wo sollen neue Kinderspielplätze entstehen? Wo treffen sich die Jugendlichen? Wie wär's mit einer Seniorenbegegnungsstätte? Haben die Planer auch an Freizeit- und Sporteinrichtungen gedacht? Bekommen wir ein Hallenbad? Bleiben bei der Verstädterung unseres Stadtviertels noch ein paar ruhige Ecken zum Verschnaufen?

Fragen über Fragen. Sie werden derzeit bei den Treffen der Bürgerinitiative Südstadt gestellt. Wollen Sie mithelfen, sie zu beantworten? Die Ideen der SüdstadtbewohnerInnen sollten frühzeitig in die Planung aufgenommen werden - damit wir nachher nicht etwas serviert bekommen, was uns nicht schmeckt. Kommen Sie doch einfach einmal zu einem Treffen der Bürgerinitiative.

Die nächsten Termine: **Dienstag, 9. Februar, 20 Uhr und Dienstag, 2. März, 20 Uhr**, jeweils im neuen Veranstaltungsraum, **Paulinenstraße 25.**

Bringen Sie ruhig alle Ihre Ideen mit!

zusätzlich *additional*

verkraften *to cope with*

brauchen *to need*

das Bürgerhaus (¨-er) *community centre*

der Senior (-en) *senior citizen (male)*

die Seniorin (-nen) *senior citizen (female)*

die Begegnungsstätte (-n) *meeting place, centre*

die Einrichtung (-en) *facility*

das Hallenbad (¨-er) *swimming pool*

die Verstädterung (-en) *urbanisation*

verschnaufen (*colloquial*) *to take a breather*

Fragen über Fragen *question after question*

gestellt (*from* stellen) *put (here: a question)*

aufgenommen (*from* aufnehmen) *adopted, taken up*

serviert bekommen *get served up*

schmecken *to taste*

der Veranstaltungsraum (¨-e) *hall (for performances)*

1 List the main concerns that are spelt out in the 10 questions in the first part of the invitation.
2 Why are the organisers of the *Bürgerinitiative* keen for people to express their opinions and give ideas?
3 What are you asked to bring with you to the meeting?

You probably noticed that the word used in the invitation to residents, *EinwohnerInnen*, is spelt with a capital letter in the middle. This is a recent and not yet fully accepted innovation, indicating that the word in the plural refers to both men and women. Here's how this works with another word:

der Journalist *journalist (male)*
die Journalistin *journalist (female)*

die Journalisten *journalists (male)*
die Journalistinnen *journalists (female)*
die JournalistInnen *journalists (male and female)*

Now imagine that you live in Südstadt and want to get involved in the *Bürgerinitiative*. In order to make a useful contribution to the discussion, you decide to visit another older estate, Waldfried. In Waldfried many of the questions raised by the *Bürgerinitiative* in Südstadt have already been dealt with or discussed. The solutions adopted in Waldfried and the problems that remain are given below. You are to write a short report of 150 words in German. This will be handed round at the next meeting of the *Bürgerinitiative*, to pass on details of what you learned in Waldfried.

Before doing this activity, you might like to revise the language you will need by listening to *Hörbericht 1, Kein Platz für Autos*, again and looking over the work you did in *Teil 2, Lerneinheit 6*.

These are the questions you asked the people in Waldfried:

- Wo befinden sich die Parkplätze?
- Welche Straßen sind verkehrsfrei?
- Haben Sie ein Bürgerhaus?
- Wo gibt es Kinderspielplätze?
- Gibt es eine Seniorenbegegnungsstätte?
- Welche Sporteinrichtuungen haben Sie?
- Gibt es ruhige Ecken?
- Wie ist die Atmosphäre in der Siedlung?
- Welche Probleme haben Sie?

This is the information they gave you:

The car parks are all on the edge of the estate and there are plenty of them. Streets in the middle of the estate are free of traffic. There is a community centre that they find very good. Children can play in the courtyards between the houses and they have had a youth centre for a year. A meeting place for the elderly has been built. They have a sports centre, but no swimming pool. There are two small parks. There is a good community spirit and most people feel at home there. Problems are that the public transport is not good enough; they need more 4-roomed flats for large families and 1-roomed flats for younger people; they have no shops nearby.

5

When you decided to visit Waldfried you rang a friend, Heidrun, and asked her to go along with you. In this activity you have to supply both halves of the conversation.

In preparation for Activities 5 and 6, look back over the work you did in *Lerneinheit 3* on arranging to meet someone. You could also listen once more to the dialogues in *Hörabschnitt 4*. Fill in the gaps in the telephone conversation given below. Then check your version against the *Lösungen* and record the whole conversation on cassette. The beginning of the dialogue is provided for you.

Heidrun	*Hallo. Hier Bauer.*
Sie	Hallo Heidrun, hier ist ... (*Ihr Name*). Nächste Woche ist ein Treffen der Bürgerinitiative Südstadt. Ich werde vorher vielleicht nach Waldfried in Pfäffingen gehen, um einige Fragen zu stellen. Ich möchte wissen, wie es dort zugeht.
Heidrun	*Gute Idee.*
Sie	(Would you like to come?)
Heidrun	*(Yes, certainly. When do you want to go?)*
Sie	(How about Thursday?)
Heidrun	*(At what time?)*
Sie	(In the evening. 7 o'clock?)
Heidrun	*(No, that won't do. Unfortunately I've got something else on.)*
Sie	(How about Wednesday evening?)
Heidrun	*(Yes, that's OK. Shall we say 7 o'clock?)*
Sie	(Yes. Where shall we meet? At my place or yours?)
Heidrun	*(I don't mind. Let's meet at your place.)*
Sie	(OK. See you on Wednesday.)
Heidrun	*(Yes. See you then. 'Bye.)*

6

You have decided to go to the meeting of the *Bürgerinitiative*, and to ask another new resident, Herr Rach, if he would like to go with you.

Make up a telephone dialogue inviting him. He replies that he is interested in the meeting and asks where and when the meeting is. It is at 8pm on Tuesday 9th February, and you agree to meet at his place. As you do not know him well, you will use the more formal *Sie* form when you talk to him. The opening of the dialogue has been provided for you.

Sie Herr Rach. Guten Abend. Mein Name ist ... (*Ihr Name*) und ich bin Mitglied der Bürgerinitiative Südstadt. Es gibt in der nächsten Woche ein Treffen und ich habe gehört, daß Sie sich dafür interessieren.

Herr Rach (Yes. That interests me a lot.)

Lerneinheit 11 Aspekte des Wohnens

Lerneinheit 11 has two topics – *Finding out what residents think*, where you will hear some opinions about Südstadt, and *Looking at Swiss advertisements*, for a final round-up of vocabulary to do with housing.

In *Lerneinheit 11* you will revise the language describing where people live and why, and practise some basic grammar.

STUDY CHART

Topic	Activity and resource	Key points
Finding out what residents think	**1 Text**	reading two articles on what residents think about Südstadt
	2 Text	practising the use of *weil*
	3 Text	practising the use of the articles *ein, der, kein*
	4 Text	practising talking about where you live
Looking at Swiss advertisements	**5 Text**	analysing Swiss housing advertisements
	6 Text	using housing vocabulary

Here is an article from a Tübingen newspaper about Silvia Kiefer, who lives in Südstadt, and a report of the views of her neighbour, Hamida Aziz, on public transport there. Answer the questions on page 67 in German.

am Anfang *in the beginning*
die Schwierigkeit (-en) *difficulty*

Silvia Kiefer, 36 Jahre, alleinerziehende Mutter mit einem Kind, teilt sich mit ihrer Freundin, auch alleinerziehend mit einem Kind, eine 4-Zimmer-Wohnung in der Stuttgarter Straße. „Am Anfang war ich sehr skeptisch," sagt sie. Zuerst wollte Frau Kiefer hier nicht wohnen. Südstadt liegt am Rande der Stadt, und es gibt keine Kinos und keine großen Geschäfte. „Jetzt aber fühle ich mich eigentlich sehr wohl hier, in der Wohnung wie auch im Wohnblock, durch die B 27 sind wir allerdings immer noch etwas von der Stadt abgeschnitten. Auf dem privaten Wohnungsmarkt hatte ich Schwierigkeiten. Ich bin nicht in der Lage eine Wohnung zu kaufen, und ich finde es ja richtig, daß die Mieten günstig sind."

bestehend
existing
lächerlich
laughable

Frau Aziz findet es ist ein Nachteil, daß sie unbedingt ein Auto braucht.

Die Überlegungen zum Autoverkehr innerhalb des Quartiers findet sie gut: „Am liebsten wäre mir alles ohne Auto." Doch bei den bestehenden Busverbindungen brauche sie ihr Auto: „Die Linie 4 ist schrecklich – dreimal in der Stunde. Am Samstag vielleicht zweimal und am Sonntag kann man das fast vergessen. Die Linie 1 fährt nur einmal in der Stunde – wirklich lächerlich."

1. Wohnt Frau Kiefer alleine?
2. Wie viele Kinder hat Frau Kiefer?
3. Wohnt sie in einem Haus?
4. Ist sie verheiratet?
5. Warum war sie am Anfang skeptisch?
6. Wie fühlt sie sich jetzt im neuen Viertel?
7. Welchen Nachteil hat es aber, dort zu wohnen?
8. Warum hat sie eine Wohnung gemietet?

Are these remarks *richtig* or *falsch?* Put a cross in the appropriate box.

		RICHTIG	FALSCH
9	Frau Aziz hätte gern ein Auto.	❑	❑
10	An Wochentagen fährt die Linie 4 mindestens dreimal in der Stunde.	❑	❑
11	Die Linie 1 fährt öfter.	❑	❑

2

This activity will help you to revise the use of *weil*. There are three statements based on the articles in Activity 1. Under each statement there are three possible endings for a sentence which has got *weil* in the middle. Decide which two alternatives fit best with the statement and write out the complete sentences, paying attention to the word order.

1. Frau Kiefer wohnt mit einer Freundin zusammen, weil ...
   - **a** Es ist billiger, eine Wohnung zu teilen.
   - **b** Sie sind beide alleinerziehende Mütter.
   - **c** Sie hat keine Kinder.
2. Frau Kiefer war am Anfang skeptisch, weil ...
   - **a** Südstadt liegt am Stadtrand.
   - **b** Es gibt keine großen Geschäfte.
   - **c** Die Wohnungen sind wirklich sehr schön.
3. Frau Aziz ist nicht sehr zufrieden, weil ...
   - **a** Sie ist sehr skeptisch.
   - **b** Sie würde lieber keinen Wagen besitzen.
   - **c** Die Busverbindungen sind schlecht.

Several words have been left out of the following passage. Most of them are articles (*ein*, *der*, *kein*). Fill the gaps so that the text makes sense.

Frau Kiefer beschreibt ihre Situation

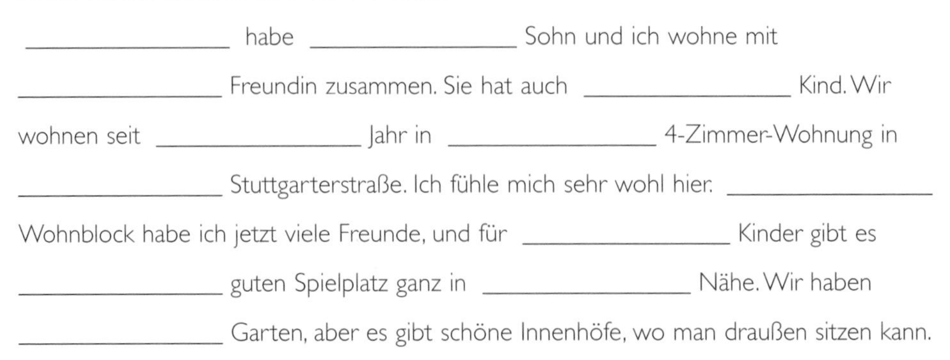

________ habe ________ Sohn und ich wohne mit ________ Freundin zusammen. Sie hat auch ________ Kind. Wir wohnen seit ________ Jahr in ________ 4-Zimmer-Wohnung in ________ Stuttgarterstraße. Ich fühle mich sehr wohl hier. ________ Wohnblock habe ich jetzt viele Freunde, und für ________ Kinder gibt es ________ guten Spielplatz ganz in ________ Nähe. Wir haben ________ Garten, aber es gibt schöne Innenhöfe, wo man draußen sitzen kann.

4

In this dialogue another resident, Frau Uhland, talks to a friend, Frau Schneider, about where she lives. Before doing this activity, look back at *Teil 2*, particularly *Lerneinheiten 4–5*, where the audio extracts will also be helpful to you, and *Lerneinheit 9*, Activity 2. Fill in the answers in German, and check your version against the model in the *Lösungen*. Then record your dialogue on tape.

Frau Schneider: Seit wann wohnen Sie hier, Frau Uhland?

Frau Uhland: *(I've lived here for a year. I like it. Social contacts are good.)*

Frau Schneider: Sind die Wohnungen groß?

Frau Uhland: *(In this block they are about 100 m². Some have a balcony.)*

Frau Schneider: Das ist sicher groß genug für Sie?

Frau Uhland: *(Yes. I have a nice kitchen, two bedrooms and a living room with a dining area.)*

Frau Schneider: Wie finden Sie die Mietpreise?

Frau Uhland: *(The rents are very reasonable here. I'm not in a position to buy a flat. It's really fantastic having a flat here.)*

Frau Schneider: Es gibt also Platz genug für Sie und die Familie?

Frau Uhland: *(Yes. Table and chairs are in the corner and I also have a big sofa and a television. With my work and two children I am exhausted in the evenings, and I watch a lot of TV!)*

Frau Schneider: Ja, das mache ich auch.

Frau Uhland: *(How about a coffee at my place?)*

Frau Schneider: Gerne. Danke sehr … Und wie sind die Busverbindungen?

Frau Uhland: *(The bus services are not very good in Südstadt. I travel mostly by car.)*

These advertisements come from a Swiss newspaper. This is why the rents are given in *Franken*. The word *Chiffre* (box number) is common in Germany as well as in Switzerland. Read the advertisements, then the statements given below. These statements were made by people who live in the flats or houses. About which flat or house would the statement be made? Write **a, b** or **c** against each one.

das Sockelgeschoß *(Swiss German) basement*

basteln *to 'do it yourself', do handicrafts*

a

In Arlesheim vermieten wir in zentraler, ruhiger Lage
2-Zimmer-Dachwohnung
mit Balkon an der Sonnenseite
Wohnfläche 90 m²
hoher Ausbaustandard
WM/Trockner
mit zusätzlichem Atelier/Hobbyraum mit WC/Dusche (20 m²) im Keller

Miete Fr. 2100.– exk. NK

Anfragen unter Chiffre X300–202758
An SERENAWOHNEN, Postfach, 3012 Bern.

b

Ab 1. April Erstvermietung in Bellach
4½-Zimmer-Doppel Einfamilienhaus

mit Garten, inkl. Garage + Abstellplatz, einmalige Lage. Fr. 3300.– exk.

Zuschriften unter Chiffre H 002-358641 an SERENAWOHNEN, Postfach, 3018 Bern.

c

Zu vermieten in Möhlin,
4-Zimmer-Wohnung
3. OG, Lift, Wohnfläche 92m², mit allem Komfort, wie Geschirrspülmaschine, Bad, sep. Dusche; Einstellhalle vorhanden.

Mietzins Fr. 1950.–
+ NK Fr. 172.–

Auskunft und Vermietung:
G. Baumgärtner, Möhlin
Telefon 819 83 61

1. Die Kinder haben einen Raum im Keller, wo sie basteln können.
2. Er ist an der Südseite des Wohnblocks. Am Abend sitzen wir oft draußen.
3. Ein Wäschetrockner ist vorhanden und steht im kleinen Zimmer neben dem Badezimmer.
4. Ja, hier wohnen wir praktisch mitten im Dorf.
5. Die Lage des Hauses ist besonders schön.
6. Es ist ein großer Vorteil, daß es hier eine Garage gibt.
7. Nein, leider gibt es keinen Lift.
8. Hier im dritten Stock hat man eine sehr gute Aussicht.
9. Dusche und WC sind hier nebenan.
10. Nein, es gibt auch eine Dusche. Hier ist nur ein Bad.

Before buying or renting you need to interpret what advertisements say. How would you interpret these descriptions? Match the claims of the advert (listed on the left) to the corresponing more realistic interpretation on the right.

ausgesprochen *exceptional*
vorbeisausen *to rush by*
wegen (*+dat*) *on account of*

1 Bahnhof in der Nähe.
2 Zentrale Lage.
3 Nähe Autobahnkreuz.
4 Schöne Aussicht über die Stadt.
5 Interessanter Innenausbau.
6 Supermarkt in unmittelbarer Nähe.
7 Bushaltestelle in Gehweite.
8 Ausgesprochen ruhige Lage.
9 Schöne Lage – dort wo andere Urlaub machen.

a Die Wohnung ist im 11. Stock.
b Der Eigentümer ist enthusiastischer Heimwerker.
c Man muß mindestens eine halbe Stunde zum Bus laufen.
d Wegen Lärm und Verschmutzung müssen die Fenster das ganze Jahr über zu bleiben.
e Lieferwagen Tag und Nacht.
f Im Sommer muß man wegen der vielen Touristen wegfahren.
g Autos sausen Tag und Nacht vorbei.
h Man kann vor Zügen kaum schlafen.
i Mitten im Wald ohne gute Straße.

Thema 2

Menschenbilder

Menschenbilder, the second *Thema* of this book, looks at many ways of describing people. The four *Teile* will help you to learn how to talk about people's origins, their personalities, their families and friends, and their lives in their communities. In the process you will meet a wide variety of people, most of whom live in Leipzig and Tübingen.

In *Teil 1*, *Zur Herkunft*, you will hear how people describe their origins. You will be working on an audio feature about *Heimat*. *Teil 2*, *Zur Person*, will help you to describe appearance, character and personality. You will also be studying the audio drama, *Begegnung in Leipzig*, where Bettina and Thomas revive their friendship. In *Teil 3*, *Lokalpatriotismus*, you will hear people talking about their homes. *Teil 3* also takes a look at regionalism in Germany and, in particular, the area near the river Rhein (Rhine). *Teil 4*, *Wiederholung*, aims to help you revise the work you have done so far.

By the end of *Thema 4*, you should be able to talk about your origins and past, about your family and some issues to do with citizenship, which are of importance in the Germany of today. You will also have practised using the language you need to help you to describe your own and other people's appearance and character. You will be able to recognise and use the appropriate formal and informal language needed to make invitations and enquire after people.

Teil 1

Zur Herkunft

In *Teil 1* you will hear people talking about their past and present lives and where they feel they belong. *Lerneinheit 1, Wo komme ich her?*, introduces you to people who talk about their origins and how they feel about them. *Lerneinheit 2, Familienbilder*, concentrates on the concept of *Heimat.* This word means not only home, it also covers the idea of native country, or region. *Lerneinheit 3, Heimat*, develops this theme and discusses the status of immigrants in Germany.

By the end of *Teil 1*, you should be able to talk about your origins and have gained a good understanding of the concept of *Heimat.* You will have worked with family trees and be able to talk about what country people come from.

Lerneinheit 1 Wo komme ich her?

In *Lerneinheit 1* you will find out why people live where they do and how they feel about their home area. In the first topic, *Talking about your origins*, you will work on a wide range of personal accounts to help you learn the language needed to describe where you come from. The second topic, *Talking about the past*, will provide you with the grammar you need to do this, and the third topic, *Putting yourself in someone else's shoes*, gives you the opportunity to practise the language and grammar you have just studied.

STUDY CHART

Topic	Activity and resource	Key points
Talking about your origins	**1 Text**	reading about the people you will see on the video
	2 Video	watching a video about people's origins
	3 Text	completing sentences about people's origins
	4 Text	answering questions about people who have come to Germany from abroad
	5 Text	matching statements to people you've read about
Talking about the past	**6 Text**	practising forming past participles
	7 Text	practising forming past participles of separable and inseparable verbs
	8 Text	translating into German and practising forming the perfect tense
	9 *Übungskassette*	answering questions on an account of a Silesian childhood
	10 *Übungskassette*	noting down examples of past participles and their auxiliary verbs
	11 *Übungskassette*	answering questions about a person's youth
Putting yourself in someone else's shoes	**12 *Übungskassette***	answering questions about a person's life

1

Overleaf are some descriptions of people you will meet in the first part of the video. Read through them, then look at the following statements. Are they *richtig* or *falsch?* Indicate which you think is the correct answer by putting a cross in the appropriate box. Then rewrite the false statements correctly in German.

ist großgeworden *(from großwerden) grew up*

ist ... geboren *was born*

der Schwabe (-n) *Swabian (male)*

stammt aus *(from stammen) comes from*

hat ... verbracht *(from verbringen) has spent*

die Schwäbin (-nen) *Swabian (female)*

die Erzieherin (-nen) *nursery nurse*

gebürtig *by birth*

ist ... umgezogen *(from umziehen) moved*

der Ökobauer (-n) *ecological farmer*

die Kindheit *childhood*

der Glaser (-) *glazier*

Dr. Wilfried Setzler ist in Pforzheim großgeworden und ist als Student nach Tübingen gekommen.

Hans-Peter Baumeister ist in Norddeutschland geboren. Er arbeitet an der Universität von Tübingen.

Walter Utz ist Schwabe und stammt aus Tübingen. Er ist jetzt Rentner und hat sein ganzes Leben in Tübingen verbracht.

Renate Baumeister ist geborene Schwäbin. Sie ist durch ihren Beruf als Erzieherin nach Tübingen gekommen und ist nicht dort geboren.

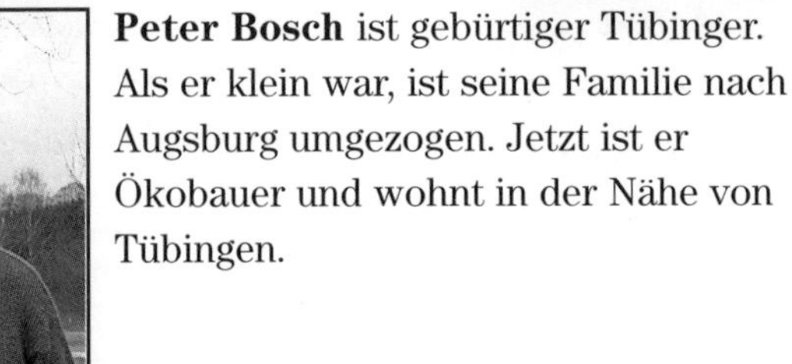

Peter Bosch ist gebürtiger Tübinger. Als er klein war, ist seine Familie nach Augsburg umgezogen. Jetzt ist er Ökobauer und wohnt in der Nähe von Tübingen.

Alice Kurz kommt aus dem Nordschwarzwald. Sie hat ihre Kindheit in Calw verbracht.

Tanja Lindl ist in Heilbronn geboren.

Wolfgang Fritz ist Schwabe. Er ist im Dorf Drejesingen geboren. Er arbeitet als Glaser in Tübingen.

Sultan Braun wohnt in Tübingen Südstadt. Sie ist in der Türkei geboren und ist mit neun Jahren nach Deutschland gekommen.

		RICHTIG	FALSCH
1	Dr. Wilfried Setzler ist in Tübingen aufgewachsen.	❑	❑
2	Hans-Peter Baumeister stammt aus Norddeutschland.	❑	❑
3	Walter Utz ist gebürtiger Tübinger und ist dort altgeworden.	❑	❑
4	Renate Baumeister ist Schwäbin und ist in Tübingen geboren.	❑	❑
5	Peter Bosch ist kein geborener Tübinger.	❑	❑
6	Alice Kurz hat ihre Kindheit im Schwarzwald verbracht.	❑	❑
7	Tanja Lindl ist in Calw geboren.	❑	❑
8	Wolfgang Fritz ist in der Stadt Drejesingen geboren.	❑	❑
9	Wolfgang Fritz ist in Schwaben großgeworden.	❑	❑
10	Sultan Braun stammt aus Griechenland.	❑	❑

14:00–18:54

Now watch the first part of the video for this *Thema* to hear what else these people say about their origins. Towards the end of this video extract you will also get a chance to see Sultan Braun's new flat in Südstadt – the estate on the edge of Tübingen which you heard about at the end of *Thema 1*. Concentrate only on the part of the video that shows her in her flat: 18:12–18:40. When you have watched the video, answer the questions below in English.

der Ureinwohner (-) *original inhabitant*

der zweite Weltkrieg *the Second World War*

es ist … entstanden (*from* entstehen) *it came about*

ein gutes Klima *good climate*

eine künstliche Industriestadt *an artificial(ly created) industrial town*

die Herkunft *origin*

teils … teils *partly … partly*

die Sehnsucht (¨-e) *homesickness, longing*

der Urlaub (-e) *holiday*

1. What does Dr. Setzler say about the original inhabitants of Tübingen?
2. What three words does he use to describe Tübingen? Give the German words and their translation.
3. What three nationalities does he mention that you can meet in Tübingen?
4. Where was Hans-Peter Baumeister born?
5. When does he say that his home town was founded?
6. Where was Walter Utz born?
7. Where did Renate Baumeister grow up?
8. What sort of place did she grow up in?
9. What words does Peter Bosch use to describe where he comes from?
10. Alice Kurz says she came from Calw. What is this?
11. Where does Tanja Lindl come from in relation to Tübingen?
12. Wolfgang Fritz mentions two places apart from Tübingen – Drejesingen and Hagelloch. What happened in each place?

13 Where did Sultan Braun grow up?

14 What does she say about her feelings of longing or homesickness?

3 This activity will help to bring together expressions you have come across in the first two activities. Using the factual information from the video and the expressions in the short biographies (from Activities 1 and 2) complete the sentences below. In some cases more than one answer is possible. In most sentences you will need the perfect tense.

1 Dr. Setzler fühlt sich als ____________ , aber er ____________ nicht in Tübingen ____________ . Er ____________ als Student nach Tübingen ____________ .

2 Hans-Peter Baumeister ____________ kein ____________ wie seine Frau. Er ____________ ____________ dem Norden.

3 Herr Utz ____________ ____________ Tübinger, und ____________ sein ganzes Leben dort ____________ .

4 Frau Baumeister ____________ nicht aus Norddeutschland, wie ihr Mann. Sie ist Schwäbin und ____________ in einem Dorf in der Nähe von Stuttgart ____________ .

5 Peter Bosch ____________ ____________ .

6 Alice Kurz ____________ ____________ dem Schwarzwald.

7 Wolfgang Fritz ____________ in Hagelloch ____________ .

8 Frau Braun ist nicht in Deutschland ____________ . Sie ____________ aus der ____________ .

German nationality is defined by a law of 1913, which stipulates that you are German either by birth or by having nationality granted to you. Children born in wedlock are German, provided that one parent is of German nationality.

To obtain citizenship, a foreigner must satisfy several conditions, which include:

- a secure means of livelihood
- an assured place of residence
- a certain level of competence in German
- absence of a criminal record or of charges
- awareness of the German constitution.

At present (1996), dual nationality is very rarely allowed by the German authorities; this deters many foreigners from applying for German citizenship. Children born in Germany of foreign parents may apply for German citizenship at the age of 18.

The people you have met so far in this book were nearly all born in Germany. Here are some descriptions of people who didn't start life as German citizens. Read them and answer the questions overleaf. These texts are mainly in the imperfect tense, rather than the perfect tense, which you used in the last activity. The imperfect is used frequently in newspapers and magazine articles. These descriptions have been adapted from an article in *Stern*, a German current affairs magazine.

Chaya Mettananda

Sie wurde vor 25 Jahren in Deutschland geboren. Ihre Eltern kamen als politische Flüchtlinge aus Sri Lanka. Chaya, inzwischen deutsche Staatsbürgerin, lebt in Würzburg und hat gerade ihr Studium an der Musikhochschule beendet. Sie hat schon zahlreiche Engagements und Auszeichnungen bekommen – vor ihr liegt eine Karriere als Konzertpianistin.

Cem Özdemir

Als 18jähriger bekam er die deutsche Staatsbürgerschaft: Seine Eltern, die vor 30 Jahren aus der Türkei als Gastarbeiter ins schwäbische Bad Urach kamen, erhielten ihre Staatsbürgerschaft am 14. Oktober 1994 – zwei Tage, bevor ihr Sohn für die Bündnisgrünen in den Bundestag gewählt wurde.

Nadja Masri

Nadja hat eine deutsche Mutter und einen libanesischen Vater: Sie wurde in Flensburg geboren, lebte aber mit ihren Eltern im Libanon, bis der Bürgerkrieg begann. Heute wohnt die 23jährige in Berlin, studiert Publizistik und Geschichte. Nebenbei jobbt sie bei einer Fotoagentur. In diesem Jahr will sie mit ihrem Vater in den Libanon reisen, um von diesem Land, an das sie sich kaum erinnert, einen Eindruck zu bekommen.

der Flüchtling (-e) *refugee*

inzwischen *in the meantime*

die Staatsbürgerin (-nen) *citizen (female)*

die Auszeichnung (-en) *award, prize*

die Staatsbürgerschaft *state citizenship*

der/die Gastarbeiter/in *guest worker (a term formerly used to describe workers of non-German origin who do not have German citizenship; the term used nowadays is* ausländische Mitarbeiter*)*

erhielten *(from* erhalten*)* *received*

der Bundestag *German Parliament*

gewählt *(from* wählen*)* *here: elected*

der Bürgerkrieg (-e) *civil war*

die Publizistik *journalism*

nebenbei *in addition*

jobben *to work now and then in order to earn some extra money, to take casual jobs*

an das sie sich kaum erinnert *that she can hardly remember*

um ... einen Eindruck zu bekommen *in order to get an impression*

1. Why did **Chaya's** parents leave Sri Lanka?
2. What is her nationality now?
3. What has she recently finished?
4. What part of Germany did **Cem's** parents come to?
5. What nationality are his parents?
6. What is his job?
7. Why did **Nadja** leave the Lebanon?
8. What is she doing in Berlin at present?
9. What are her plans for this year?

The *Bündnisgrünen* (as at 1996) are a political party formed from an alliance of the *Bündnis 90*, an east German civil rights group, and *Die Grünen*, the former west German Green Party.

These statements could have been made by the people you have just read about. Link them to the right person by writing the person's name against the appropriate statement. You will notice that the statements are all in the perfect tense.

1. Meine Eltern haben die Staatsbürgerschaft nach dreißig Jahren Aufenthalt in der Bundesrepublik erhalten.
2. Ich bin gebürtige Norddeutsche, habe aber mit meinen Eltern lange Zeit in der Heimat meines Vaters gelebt.
3. Als die Probleme im Land angefangen haben, sind wir nach Deutschland zurückgekommen. Manchmal weiß ich nicht, wo ich zu Hause bin.
4. Ich habe gerade die Musikhochschule beendet und will jetzt eine Existenz als Pianistin aufbauen. Ich habe auch schon Engagements bekommen.
5. Ich fühle mich seit langem als Schwabe. Aber meine Eltern haben die deutsche Staatsbürgerschaft erst letztes Jahr erhalten.

6 Ich bin hier geboren und habe immer hier gelebt. Meine Eltern fühlen sich hier weniger zu Hause.

FORMING the perfect tense

In *Thema 1, Lerneinheit 3* you learned that verbs take either *haben* or *sein* as auxiliary verbs in the perfect tense. The majority of verbs take *haben*, and of those that take *sein*, many are to do with movement or transition. Here are two examples:
Wir sind in die Stadt gegangen. This means both *We went into town* and *We have been into town*.
Wir haben viel gekauft. *We bought lots of things* and *We have bought lots of things*.

You will also know that most past participles are formed by adding *ge-* to the beginning of the stem of the verb, as in the examples above. (The stem of the verb is the main part of the verb minus the *-en* ending.)

Verbs are divided into three groups. You need to know which group a verb belongs to, because this will affect the way you form the past participle. The groups are **regular**, **irregular** and **mixed** verbs. The past participles of irregular and mixed verbs do not follow a regular pattern, so you have to learn them individually. You will, however, find lists of these past participles in grammar books and dictionaries.

1 Regular verbs

The stem of the verb does not change and the past participle ends in *-t*.
machen
Ich habe einen Sprachkurs gemacht. *I have done a language course./I did a language course.*

Verbs that end in *-ieren* do not add *ge-* to the stem.
studieren
Ich habe in Tübingen studiert. *I have studied in Tübingen/I studied in Tübingen.*

2 Irregular verbs

The stem usually changes and the past participle ends in *-en*.
werden
Sie ist in Leipzig großgeworden. *She has grown up in Leipzig./She grew up in Leipzig.*

Laufen is an example of an irregular verb that does not change its stem.
Er ist 5 Kilometer gelaufen. *He has run 5 kilometres./He ran 5 kilometres.*

3 Mixed verbs

The stem changes and the past participle ends in *-t*.
wissen
Cem hat immer gewußt, daß er Politiker werden wollte. *Cem has always known that he wanted to be a politician./Cem always knew that he wanted to be a politician.*

6

This activity will help you to practise forming past participles for the three groups of verbs described on page 79. Use your grammar book if you need to. In each of the sentences below, give the past participle of the bracketed verb, then write out the English translation of each sentence. When translating the sentences, note how the perfect tense in German is put into English. It may not necessarily be a straight conversion using 'has' or 'have', as you can see from the examples on page 79.

1. Er ist gestern (kommen).
2. Ich habe in Dresden (wohnen).
3. Wir sind gestern nach Tübingen (fahren).
4. Uschi ist hier in Hagelloch (bleiben).
5. Gestern bin ich sehr früh ins Bett (gehen).
6. Das Buch hat mich sehr (interessieren).
7. Klaus hat absolut nichts (machen).
8. Ah! Da ist das Telefonbuch. Ich habe es überall (suchen).
9. Vorige Woche haben wir Spielbergs neuen Film (sehen).
10. Brigitte hat dieses Paket heute (bringen).

FORMING the past participle of separable and inseparable verbs

Some verbs have a prefix, which is added to the beginning of the verb in order to change the meaning in some way. There are separable and inseparable prefixes. **Separable** prefixes are complete words such as *an, auf, ein, mit, um*. An example of a verb with a separable prefix is *anfangen* (to begin). **Inseparable** prefixes include *be-, emp-, ent-, er-, ver-, zer-*. An example of a verb with an inseparable prefix is *erhalten* (to receive).

Separable verbs form the past participle by adding -ge- after the prefix and before the main part of the verb:

Der Film hat schon *angefangen*. *The film has already begun.*

Inseparable verbs form the past participle without adding *ge-*:

Er hat einen Paß 1993 *erhalten*. *He obtained a passport in 1993.*

Now practise forming the past participles of separable and inseparable verbs. Replace the bracketed infinitive with the correct form of the past participle.

1. Die Miete war mir zu hoch. Ich habe 800 DM im Monat (bezahlen).
2. Wann beginnt der Film? Hat er schon (anfangen)?
3. Meine Kindheit habe ich in Schlesien (verbringen). Ich bin dort im Hause meiner Großmutter (großwerden).
4. Die Wohnung war schon in Dezember fertig. Wir sind im Januar (einziehen).

5 Was ich gestern abend gemacht habe? Ich habe nur (fernsehen).
6 Am Wochende habe ich Freunde in Bremen (besuchen). Wir sind (spazierengehen).

8

Now translate the following sentences into German. They contain a range of verbs in the perfect tense.

1 Frank has gone shopping.
2 Uschi moved house yesterday.
3 They played tennis.
4 She studied in Berlin.
5 He spent the whole day in bed.
6 I have found the address.
7 We have rented a flat.
8 I went by car.
9 They came at 11 o'clock.
10 I didn't stay long.

9

Listen to *Hörabschnitt 1* on the *Übungskassette*. You will hear Frau Mayerhofer talking about her connections with Schlesien (Silesia), which is on the German-Polish border. You will notice that she uses the perfect tense a number of times. First, study the vocabulary, then answer the questions below in English.

der Verwandte (-n) *relation (male)*
das Bauerngut (¨-er) *farm*
die Landschaft *countryside*
die Landwirtschaft *farming, agriculture*
der Krieg (-e) *war*
mitgeholfen (*from* mithelfen) *helped*
empfunden (*from* empfinden) *felt*

1 When did Frau Mayerhofer spend time in Schlesien?
2 What did her relatives do for a living?
3 What three things does she mention enjoying?
4 What did she do during the Second World War?
5 Where did she also like being?
6 Why did she like it there?

10

This activity helps to prepare you for Activity 11, where you will use the perfect tense in speech.

Listen to *Hörabschnitt 1* again. This time, note down the past participles and the auxiliary verb that goes with each one. There are six pairs in all. The first pair is *bin … gewesen.*

In this activity you will respond to questions about Frau Mayerhofer. Listen to *Hörabschnitt 2* on the *Übungskassette* and answer the questions. Prompts in English are given on the cassette, and you will also need to use the information and expressions you learned in Activities 9 and 10.

12

In this activity you will describe the origins and background of an imaginary relation born in France. Use the information about him given below and answer the questions in *Hörabschnitt 3* in the gaps provided.

Der Lebenslauf von Felix Helt

geboren 1924 in Frankreich

Kindheit Sachsen

Kriegszeit Frankreich bei Verwandten

Studienzeit 5 Jahre Berlin

Beruf Geschichtslehrer in Paris

Lerneinheit 2 Familienbilder

Lerneinheit 2 deals with what people regard as their home town or area, and families – both traditional and modern. There are three topics. In the first, *What is Heimat to me?*, you will hear people from Tübingen and Leipzig talking about their homes. The second topic, *Describing families*, will help you with the language and grammar you will need to do this; and the third topic, *Changing families*, looks at how traditional family structures are changing in Germany. *Lerneinheit 2* will help you practise writing and talking about families, using the genitive case and analysing statistics.

STUDY CHART

Topic	Activity and resource	Key points
What is *Heimat* to me?	**1 Video**	picking out useful language from the video
	2 Video	checking you've understood the video
	3 Text	writing about your own *Heimat*
Describing families	**4 Text**	working on your family tree
	5–6 Text	practising using the genitive case
Changing families	**7–8 Text**	reading about demographic changes

23:46–28:28

The third part of the video shows people talking about their roots and what *Heimat* means to them. Watch this part of the video once right through, then watch it a second time concentrating on Rudolf Kost, Rudolf Dobler, Wilfried Setzler and Hans-Peter Baumeister.

For each of these people, make notes about their reasons for considering a particular place to be their *Heimat* and how they express these reasons in German. Then complete the sentences below in German, using the information provided.

Note the following construction, which you should use in the first three sentences:

Er betrachtet ... als seine Heimat, weil ... *He regards ... as his home, because ...*

Er bezeichnet ... als seine Heimat, weil ... *He characterises ... as his home, because ...*

Er beschreibt ... als seine Heimat, weil ... *He describes ... as his home, because ...*

hier kenne ich mich aus *(from* sich auskennen) *I know my way about here*

machen etwas von Heimat aus *make up* Heimat

unterschiedlich *various*

nicht ... sondern *not ... but (Note that after a negative statement* sondern *is used rather than* aber *to translate 'but'.)*

Herr Kost ist Rentner und sein Hobby ist die Stadtgeschichte Tübingens. Er wurde in Tübingen geboren, wo seine Familie seit Jahrhunderten ansässig ist.

Herr Dobler ist in Tübingen geboren. Früher war sein größtes Hobby segelfliegen. Er geht sehr gern wandern.

1 **Rudolf Kost** betrachtet ..., weil ...
Gründe: Dort geboren und Familie seit vielen Jahrhunderten ansässig

2 **Rudolf Dobler** bezeichnet ..., weil ...
Gründe: Großvater und Vater aus Schwaben; ihm gefällt Tübingen

3 **Dr. Wilfried Setzler** beschreibt ..., weil ...
Gründe: Freunde; sich auskennen; sich wohlfühlen

4 Für **Hans-Peter Baumeister** ist Tübingen Heimat, weil ....
Gründe: Familie; soziale Kontakte; Arbeitsstelle

25:00–27:40

In this activity you will answer questions about the other people in the third part of the video. Watch this extract once more, paying particular attention this time to Tanja Lindl, Ruth Stabenow, Thomas Walter and Dorothea Vogel. Then answer the following questions in German.

Dorothea Vogel ist in Rostock an der Ostsee geboren und hat in Leipzig an der Hochschule für Musik studiert. Sie arbeitet seit 1990 als Geigerin in dem Gewandhaus-Orchester.

Thomas Walter wohnt mit seiner Frau und seiner kleinen Tochter in der Nähe von Leipzig. Er arbeitet als Bauingenieur beim Neubau der Leipziger Messe mit.

1. Wo ist **Tanja Lindls** Heimat?
2. Stammt **Ruth Stabenow** aus Leipzig?
3. Wie beschreibt sie sich?
4. Was betrachtet **Thomas Walter** als seine Heimat?
5. Warum?
6. Was bedeutet ihm besonders viel?
7. Kamen Dorothea Vogels Eltern aus der gleichen Gegend?
8. Warum sind sie jetzt in Rostock ansässig?
9. Wo ist sie aufgewachsen?
10. Als was bezeichnet sie sich?

der Kreis (-e) *circle, here: district council*

die Umgebung (-en) *surroundings*

ich nicht mal … dem Wunsch meiner Kinder nachgekommen bin *I haven't responded to the wish of my children (Note when you are listening to Frau Stabenow that she uses* nicht … sondern, *as Hans-Peter Baumeister did.)*

in einem anderen Land heimisch zu werden *to become at home in another country*

nicht an diesen Begriff … gebunden *not tied to this concept*

was mir … viel bedeutet *what matters a lot to me*

die Wurzel (-n) *root*

die Zugehörigkeit *belonging*

mich geprägt hat *has left an impression on me*

Now it's your turn to write a few sentences (no more than 50 words) giving your reasons for regarding somewhere as your *Heimat.* Watch the video again, if you wish, and look at the words and expressions that you have encountered in *Lerneinheiten 1–2* before you start writing.

4 In common with others on the video, Hans-Peter Baumeister identifies his family as an element in defining *Heimat*. Here is Renate's and Hans-Peter's family tree. To help you to learn or revise the words for members of a family, look at the family tree, then make up your own, using the words here. The relationships here are given from Max Baumeister's point of view.

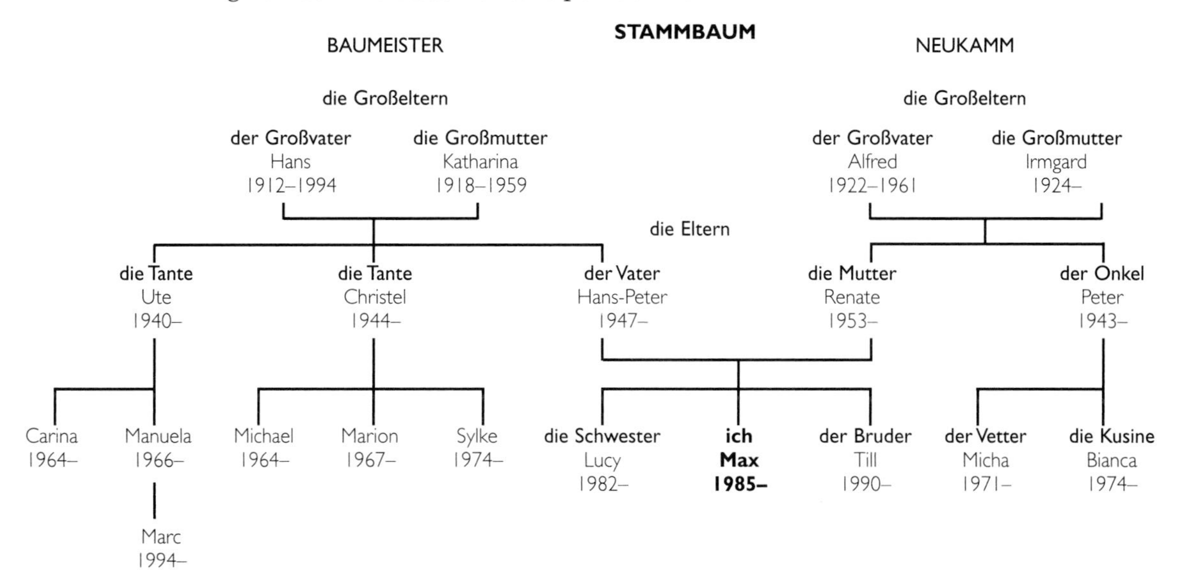

5 To practise the genitive case, pretend you are Max Baumeister, and complete the sentences below. The first is done for you. Note the emboldened endings of the definite article and the possessive adjectives in these sentences. They show how the genitive case is formed.

1 Die Schwester mein**es** Vater**s**. Das ist meine Tante.

2 Die Tochter **der** Schwester mein**es** Vater**s**. Das ist ______ ______.

3 Die Mutter mein**es** Vater**s**. Das ist ______ ______.

4 Der Sohn **des** Bruder**s** mein**er** Mutter. Das ist ______ ______.

5 Die Tochter mein**er** Eltern. Das ist ______ ______.

6 Der Bruder mein**er** Mutter. Das ist ______ ______.

And now a riddle:

7 Es ist nicht meine Schwester und nicht mein Bruder, aber es ist das Kind meiner Eltern, wer ist es? Das ist ______.

INDICATING possession

The genitive case

The genitive case normally indicates possession as in „*Das Haus* **meines Großvaters** *liegt in Hamburg*".

Here are the endings for the nominative and genitive cases of definite and indefinite articles and possessive articles:

	Singular			Plural
	Masculine	**Feminine**	**Neuter**	*(same for all 3 genders)*
Nominative	der Bruder ein Bruder mein Bruder	die Schwester eine Schwester meine Schwester	das Kind ein Kind mein Kind	die Verwandten meine Verwandten
Genitive	des Bruders eines Bruders meines Bruders	der Schwester einer Schwester meiner Schwester	des Kindes eines Kindes meines Kindes	der Verwandten meiner Verwandten

Note that -es or -s are added to masculine and neuter nouns in the singular.

Here are the possessive adjectives with their pronouns:

ich	**mein-**	*my*
du	**dein-**	*your (used informally)*
er	**sein-**	*his*
sie	**ihr-**	*her*
es	**sein-**	*its*
wir	**unser-**	*our*
ihr	**euer- eur-**	*your (used informally – see also the grammar note below)*
Sie	**Ihr-**	*your*
sie	**ihr**	*their*

USING familiar forms of address

As you know, when talking to someone formally you use *Sie* for 'you' and the possessive adjective *Ihr-*, meaning 'your'. These are used when you are talking to one person or a number of people.

Möchten Sie mit uns essen gehen, Frau Eltges?
Would you like to go out for a meal with us, Frau Eltges?

Guten Morgen, Frau Braun. Guten Morgen, Herr Braun. Hatten Sie eine gute Reise? Ist das Ihr Gepäck?
Hello, Frau Braun. Hello, Herr Braun. Have you had a good journey? Is that your luggage?

Wo ist Ihr Vater geboren?
Where was your father born?

CONTINUED

When you talk to one person informally, *du* is used for 'you' and *dein* for 'your'. When you talk or refer to more than one person, *ihr* is used for 'you' and *euer* for 'your'.

Here are some examples where someone is talking to more than one person whom they know well:

Ich habe mehrmals versucht anzurufen. Ist euer Telefon kaputt?
I've tried to ring several times. Is your telephone out of order?

Kommt ihr aus Wien? Und sind eure Eltern auch dort geboren?
Do you come from Vienna? And were your parents born there as well?

Here is a short activity to help you practise using the genitive case. Write descriptions of Baumeister family members as though you were Frau Baumeister, using her family tree. In each case, use the genitive and base your description on the information given below and in the family tree. The first one has been done for you.

1. Vater/mein Mann/Name → Der Vater meines Mannes hieß Hans.
2. jüngere Schwester/mein Mann/Geburtsjahr
3. Tochter/mein Bruder/Name
4. Mann/meine Mutter/Geburtsjahr
5. Ältester/Vetter/meine Kinder/Name
6. Nichte/mein Bruder/Name

In Germany, traditional family structures are changing. The birth rate is declining and an increasing proportion of the population lives alone. The article overleaf is about these significant demographic changes.

Read through it, then answer the questions in English. Note these uses of the genitive in the article:

line 1: **die Zahl *der* Single-Haushalte** – *the number of single households*
line 8: **die Zahl *der* Ein-Personen-Haushalte** – *the number of one person households*
line 9: ***aller* 35,7 Millionen Privathaushalte** – *of all 35.7 million private households*
line 11: **50 Prozent *der* Haushalte** – *50% of households*

nach dem neuesten Stand *according to the latest situation*

teilte ... mit *(from mitteilen) informed, said*

das Bundesamt (¨-er) *Federal Office*

der Zuwachs *growth*

knapp *just*

binnen Jahresfrist *within a year*

mittlerweile *in the meantime*

gezählt *counted*

wie etwa *such as, for example*

nach Angaben *according to information supplied*

der Wirtschaftsbereich (-e) *economic sector*

Nahrungsmittel *(pl) foodstuffs*

nach Einschätzung *according to estimates*

In Deutschland gibt es immer mehr Singles

Wiesbaden (AFP/dpa/taz) – Die Zahl der Single-Haushalte hat in den neuen Ländern deutlich zugenommen. In Ostdeutschland leben nach dem neuesten Stand (Mai 1992) mittlerweile 1,9 Millionen Menschen alleine in ihrer Wohnung, teilte das Statistische Budesamt am Dienstag in Wiesbaden mit.

Mit diesm Zuwachs um knapp zwei Prozent binnen Jahresfrist ist in den neuen Ländern mittlerweile mehr als jeder vierte Haushalt (28,1 Prozent) ein Single-Haushalt. Auch in der alten Bundesrepublik wurden wieder mehr Singles gezählt. In ganz Deutschland erreichte die Zahl der Ein-Personen-Haushalte im Mai 1992 erstmals die Zwölf-Millionen-Marke, das sind mehr als ein Drittel (33,7 Prozent) aller 35,7 Millionen Privathaushalte.

In Großstädten wie etwa Berlin werden schon heute mehr als 50 Prozent der Haushalte von nur einer Person bewohnt. Nach Angaben des Amtes ist dieser Trend seit Anfang der 80er Jahre ungebrochen. Er werde in zunehmendem Maß Konsequenzen für alle Wirtschaftsbereiche vom Wohnungsbau bis zur Narhungsmittelindustrie und den Freizeitsektor haben. Im Jahre 2010 wird nach Einschätzung des Bundesamtes fast jeder zweite Haushalt (40 Prozent) ein Single-Haushalt sein.

Paragraph 1

1 Where are the *neue Länder?*
2 What has happened there?
3 Who has published this information?
4 What exactly do the statistics tell us?

Paragraph 2

5 What is the consequence of the 2% growth?
6 Describe the trend in the *alte Länder*.
7 What is the overall position in Germany as a proportion of the total?

Paragraph 3

8 What is happening in Berlin?
9 Can you describe the trend?
10 Which three economic sectors are mentioned?
11 What will be the position in 2010?

8

The main reason for the trend described in the article in Activity 7 is that the number of single parents in Germany is rising. The following diagram presents some statistics about this. Study the diagram, then choose the correct figures given below to complete the short text. Note that the genitive is used in this text in the same way as in the previous article.

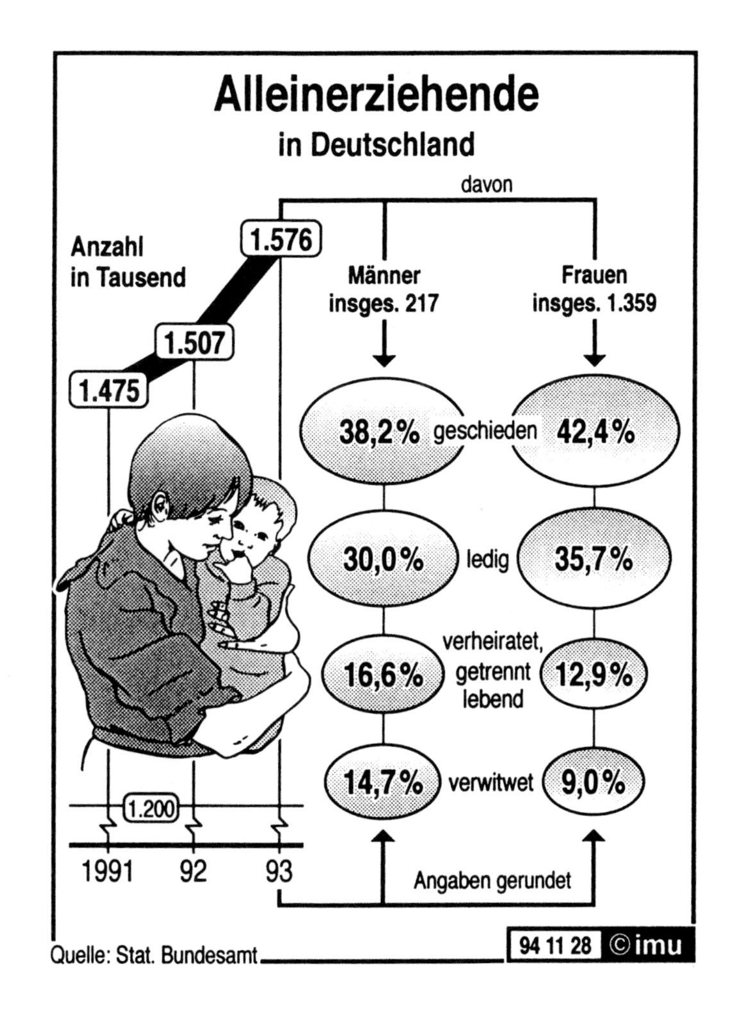

1,3 Millionen   ein Drittel   0,2 Millionen   40   100 000

1993 haben in Deutschland rund ____________ Frauen und etwa ____________ Männer ihre Kinder allein erzogen. Die Zahl der Alleinerziehenden ist zwischen 1991 und 1993 um rund ____________ Personen gestiegen. Etwa ____________ Prozent der alleinerziehenden Männer und Frauen sind geschieden. Ungefähr ein ____________ der Männer und Frauen sind ledig.

Lerneinheit 3 Heimat

The first topic of *Lerneinheit 3* is devoted to the *Hörbericht* on *Heimat*. You will hear people talking about what makes a place special to them and others explaining how they have integrated themselves into their new communities. There are two other topics, *Immigration into Germany*, where you will interpret statistics, and *A particular example: Ong and Gunthea*. You will also practise describing what countries people come from.

STUDY CHART

Topic	Activity and resource	Key points
Working on the *Hörbericht: Heimat*	1 ***Hörbericht***	checking you've understood the feature overall
	2 ***Hörbericht***	checking understanding in detail
	3 ***Hörbericht***	writing about a person from the *Hörbericht*
	4–5 ***Hörbericht***	more checking understanding in detail
Immigration into Germany	6 **Text**	reading about immigration
	7 **Text**	interpreting statistical information
	8 ***Übungskassette***	identifying words to do with nationality
	9 **Text**	working on words denoting nationality
A particular example: Ong and Gunthea	10 **Text**	reading about two Cambodian orphans
	11 **Text**	picking out relevant vocabulary
	12 ***Übungskassette***	answering questions about Ong and Gunthea

Hörbericht 2

Hörbericht 2, *Heimat*, has four sections. Here are some details:

Part 1 Three people from Leipzig and Tübingen talk about where they live.
Part 2 An itinerant musician reflects on his lack of *Heimat*.
Part 3 The villagers from the Swabian village of Jettenburg are not all Swabians, nor even German by birth. Many men belong to the *Gesangverein* (choral society), which gives them a strong sense of community.
Part 4 Clubs like the *Gesangverein* play a significant rôle in village life.

First study the vocabulary, then listen to *Hörbericht 2* and answer the following questions in English. There is one question for each of the four parts of *Hörbericht 2*.

Part 1

der Ort (-e) *place*

auch wenn ich … wegzieh' *(from* wegziehen*) even when I go away*

kennengelernt *(from* kennenlernen*) got to know, became acquainted with*

Part 2

die Harfe (-n) *harp*

ständig *always*

unterwegs auf Reisen *travelling, on a journey*

Part 3

der Bekannte (-n) *acquaintance*

der Verein (-e) *club, association*

nett *nice (of people)*

der Stammgast (¨-e) *regular (of a pub)*

der Gastwirt (-e) *publican, landlord*

Part 4

die Weihnachtsfeier (-n) *Christmas celebration*

das Fest (-e) *celebration*

die Gemeinde (-n) *parish*

… hat ihm geholfen *(from* helfen *+dat) has helped him*

ins Gespräch kommen *to get into conversation*

1. What are the first three people talking about?
2. Riccardo Delfino mentions three countries he has lived in – which are they?
3. Where do the two people come from who are interviewed in Jettenburg?
4. What important point is made by Professor Bausinger about clubs and villages? How is this confirmed by what Herr Winter says?

Hörbericht 2

Activities 2–5 will deal with parts 1–4 of *Hörbericht 2* in detail.

In part 1 of *Hörbericht 2* Frau Lotzmann, the young woman in the pub, and Herr Mayerhofer all give reasons why their town is their *Heimat*. Listen to part 1, then complete these sentences. To do this, you will need to use the German for 'she', 'he', 'her', 'his'. You can check these by looking back at *Thema 1, Lerneinheit 8*.

1. Frau Lotzmann liebt ihre Stadt, weil … .
2. Auch wenn sie wegzieht, betrachtet die junge Frau im Gasthaus Tübingen als ihre Heimat, weil …, weil …, weil … und weil … .
3. Herr Mayerhofer bezeichnet Leipzig als seine Heimat, weil er dort viele Schul-, Studien- und andere Freunde hat, weil …, weil …, weil …, weil … und weil … .

Hörbericht 2

Listen to part 2 of the *Hörbericht* about Riccardo Delfino and write a passage of up to 50 words about him, building on these key words:

- Beruf
- Geburtsort
- Vater
- Wohnorte
- Lebensweise
- was er als Heimat betrachtet

Hörbericht 2

In part 3 of the *Hörbericht*, which is based in Jettenburg, you will hear Herr Naber and Herr Thassioulis talking about themselves. Answer the following questions in German.

1 Wo liegt Jettenburg?
2 Welche zwei Vereine gibt es dort?
3 Woher kommt Herr Naber?
4 Seit wann wohnt er im Dorf?
5 Was ist Deutschland für ihn?
6 Was mag er in Deutschland und was nicht?
7 Woher kommt Herr Thassioulis?
8 Seit wann lebt er in Deutschland?

Hörbericht 2

laut *according to*

Now listen to part 4, the last section of the *Hörbericht* and answer the following questions.

1 Was hat man, laut Professor Bausinger, früher immer gesagt?
2 Wann treffen sich die Männer des Gesangvereins?
3 An welchen Festen singen sie, laut Herrn Winter?
4 Wie hat der Gesangverein Herrn Winter geholfen?

bereits *already*

die Rückkehr *return*

schlechter dastehen *be in a worse situation*

die gesamte Wirtschaftsleistung (-en) *the total industrial output*

die Milliarde (-n) *thousand million*

erarbeiten *to create (wealth), to produce*

Here is an article about the place of non-German workers in the German economy. Read it and answer the questions below in German.

Ausländer in Deutschland – wie lange sie schon hier sind

Für viele der mehr als sechs Millionen Ausländer ist Deutschland zu einer zweiten Heimat geworden. 61 von Hundert Ausländern wohnen bereits seit mehr als zehn Jahren hier. An Rückkehr denken viele nicht mehr. Sie sind hier verheiratet, ihre Kinder sind hier aufgewachsen und gehen zur Schule. Das Heimatland ihrer Eltern kennen viele nur noch von Urlaubsreisen. Ohne die ausländischen Mitbürger würde die Wirtschaft schlechter dastehen. 1,9 Millionen ausländische Männer und Frauen arbeiteten 1991 in den alten Bundesländern. Von der gesamten Wirtschaftsleistung in Westdeutschland des Jahres 1991 (2 200 Milliarden Mark) erarbeiteten die ausländischen Mitbürger ein Zehntel.

1 Was ist Deutschland für viele Ausländer?
2 Seit wie vielen Jahren wohnt die Mehrheit der Ausländer schon in Deutschland?
3 Welches Land kennen viele nur als Urlauber?
4 Wieviel tragen sie zur deutschen Wirtschaftsleistung bei?

7

Hörabschnitt 4 on the *Übungskassette* gives the numbers of foreigners by country living in Germany in 1994. Listen to *Hörabschnitt 4* and write down the numbers against the appropriate country in the list below.

beitragen zu
(+dat) to contribute to

Ausländer in Deutschland ______________	Österreich ______________
Türkei ______________	Rumänien ______________
Ex-Jugoslawien ______________	Spanien ______________
Italien ______________	Niederlande ______________
Griechenland ______________	USA ______________

Now listen to *Hörabschnitt 4* again and write down the German words for the following nationalities. Then classify them into groups according to their endings. Put nationalities ending in *-er* in the plural into the first group and those ending in *-en* in the plural into the second.

Italians Greeks Austrians Rumanians
Spaniards Americans Turks Kurds

DESCRIBING nationality

Nouns

With a few exceptions, all the names for nationality fall into the same two groups as you have just listed in Activity 8. The words there were in the masculine plural form. Here is the complete set of masculine and feminine forms with plurals:

Group 1	Male	Female
Singular	*der Italiener*	*die Italienerin*
Plural	*die Italiener*	*die Italienerinnen*

Afrikaner, Engländer, Jordanier, Schweizer and *Waliser* (Welsh) all belong in this group.

Group 2	Male	Female
Singular	*der Brite*	*die Britin*
Plural	*die Briten*	*die Britinnen*

Chinese, Ire (Irish), *Pole, Russe* and *Schotte* all belong in this group. The feminine version of *der Franzose* is *die Französin*. All the masculine forms are weak masculine nouns – they behave like *der Herr* and require an *-n* at the end of the word in the accusative, genitive and dative cases and in the plural.

CONTINUED

The word for 'German' is formed like this:

	Male	Female
Singular	*der Deutsche*	*die Deutsche*
Plural	*die Deutschen*	*die Deutschen*

Adjectives

Adjectives of nationality are normally formed by adding *-sch* to the stem of the word for the nationality. Here are some examples:

der Afrikaner ***afrikanisch*** **der Brite** ***britisch*** **der Niederländer** ***niederländisch***

There are a few irregular forms: **der Engländer** ***englisch*** **der Franzose** ***französisch*** **der Pole** ***polnisch*** **der Schweizer** ***schweizerisch***

Adjectives referring to countries take a small letter as adjectives and a capital as the name of the language: **die deutsche Sprache** ***ich spreche Deutsch***

When you say what nationality a **person** is, you should use the noun and not the adjective:
Wir haben eine neue Sekretärin. Ist sie Deutsche oder Französin?

For **things,** you can use the adjective:
Du hast ein neues Auto. Ist es ein deutsches oder ein französisches?

Countries

Most countries are neuter and no article is used:
Ich komme aus China und wohne in Sri Lanka.

However, there are a few countries which are feminine; they all take the definite article:
Er kommt aus der Schweiz.
Wir fahren in die Türkei.
Ich reise in die Bundesrepublik Deutschland.

Complete the following sentences with a noun describing the person's nationality.

1 Ein Mann aus Polen ist ein ______________ .

2 Eine Frau aus Großbritannien ist eine ______________ .

3 Leute aus Amerika sind ______________ .

4 Eine Frau aus Frankreich ist eine ______________ und ein Mann ist ein ______________ .

5 Ein Mann aus der Schweiz ist ein ______________ und eine Frau ist eine ______________ .

6 Eine Frau aus Italien ist eine ______________ .

7 Ein Mann aus Spanien ist ein ______________ .

8 Eine Frau aus der Türkei ist eine ______________ und ein Mann ist ein ______________ .

10

This article, abridged from the German weekly magazine *Der Spiegel*, is about two adopted children, Ong and Gunthea. Read the article and answer the questions below in English.

das Waisenkind (-er) *orphan*

hatten … verloren (*from* verlieren) *lost*

weltoffen *liberal-minded, cosmopolitan*

der/die Austausch-schüler/in *exchange …*

die Zukunft *future*

die Kranken-gymnastin (-nen) *physiotherapist*

der Tischler (-) *carpenter*

selbständig *self-employed*

wuchsen (*from* wachsen) *grew*

Zwei Waisenkinder aus Kambodscha in Deutschland

Ong und Gunthea waren elf und zehn Jahre alt, als sie zur deutschen Familie Dietrich kamen. Sie hatten ihre Eltern, fünf Brüder und drei Schwestern im Krieg verloren.

In Wewelsfleth, einem Dorf in Norddeutschland, wuchsen die Kinder in einem weltoffenen Mikrokosmos auf. Ihr neuer Vater, Peter Dietrich, hatte Freunde in der ganzen Welt, die regelmäßig zu Besuch kamen. Im Haus waren oft Gäste aus drei Kontinenten, dazu Austauschschüler und auch Kinder aus Tschernobyl. Die Kinder aus Kambodscha lernten so das tolerante Deutschland kennen. Es wurde ihre zweite Heimat und das Land ihrer Zukunft. Heute ist Gunthea 23 Jahre alt und Krankengymnastin. Ong ist 24 und möchte sich als Tischler selbständig machen. Mit den Dietrich-Söhnen Matthias und Johannes wuchsen Ong und Gunthea eng zusammen. Alle vier sehen sich als Geschwister.

1. Where did Ong and Gunthea come from?
2. Why did they come to the Dietrich family?
3. What is Ong's ambition?

11 Now go through the article again. Find and underline the German equivalents for the following phrases.

1 they had lost their parents
2 friends all over the world
3 guests from three continents
4 the country of their future
5 it became their second home
6 close together
7 all four see each other as brothers and sisters

12 In this activity, imagine that you are being interviewed about Ong and Gunthea. Answer the questions following the prompts you are given on the cassette in *Hörabschnitt 5*.

Checkliste

By the end of *Teil I* you should

- ○ be able to talk about people's origins (*Lerneinheit 1*, Activity 3) — Seite 76
- ○ be able to use the perfect tense (*Lerneinheit 1*, Activities 6–10) — Seiten 80–81
- ○ be able to use the genitive case (*Lerneinheit 2*, Activities 5–6) — Seiten 85 & 87
- ○ be able to handle higher numbers (*Lerneinheit 2*, Activity 8; *Lerneinheit 3*, Activities 6–7) — Seiten 89; 92–93
- ○ have practised word order using *weil* (*Lerneinheit 3*, Activity 2) — Seite 91
- ○ be able to understand and use nouns and adjectives of nationality (*Lerneinheit 3*, Activities 8–9) — Seiten 93–94

Teil 2

Zur Person

The first *Lerneinheit* of *Teil 2* is called *Ich gebe eine Party.* This contains the second episode of the *Hörspiel, Begegnung in Leipzig,* where Bettina renews her acquaintance with Thomas. An invitation to a party in Leipzig provides a link to work on party invitations and how to greet and ask after people. *Lerneinheit 5, Wie sieht sie aus?,* covers a wide range of ways in which you can describe people's physical appearance. *Lerneinheit 6, Kleider machen Leute,* concentrates on people's clothing.

By the end of *Teil 2,* you should have gained some cultural insights into the way Germans write and respond to invitations and the way in which they greet each other. You should be able to describe people's characters, physical appearance and clothing.

Lerneinheit 4 Ich gebe eine Party

The first topic of *Lerneinheit 4, Listening to the audio drama,* will give you listening and writing practice. The second topic, *Working on party invitations,* will help you to revise and practise the use of personal and possessive pronouns as well as looking at how to formulate invitations. The final topic is *Making conversation.*

By the end of *Lerneinheit 4,* you should have gained confidence in social skills in German – greeting people and enquiring after their health. You should also have a better sense of informal and formal language.

STUDY CHART

Topic	Activity and resource	Key points
Listening to the audio drama	**1–2 *Hörspiel***	checking you've understood the drama
	3 Text	writing a report of what happened in the drama
Working on party invitations	**4 Text**	checking you've understood *du* and *ihr*
	5 Text	assessing degrees of formality in invitations
	6 Text	reading a poem about party-type gossip
Making conversation	**7 *Übungskassette***	completing dialogues
	8 Text	selecting phrases from the dialogues
	9 Text	correcting inappropriate language
	10 *Übungskassette*	practising greetings and enquiries

Hörspiel, Folge 2

Before listening to *Folge 2* of the *Hörspiel*, study the vocabulary. Then listen to the drama and answer the questions below in English.

aufregend *exciting*

mich ... eingewöhnt (*from* sich eingewöhnen) *got used to*

undiszipliniert *undisciplined*

ich kenne jemanden *I know someone*

Darf ich dir ... vorstellen? *May I introduce ...?*

kleinbürgerlich *provincial, petty bourgeois*

erledigen *to do something, sort something out*

die Einladung (-en) *invitation*

das Datum (Daten) *date*

fast *almost*

verdienen *to earn*

die Moritzbastei *a popular café in Leipzig*

auftreten *to appear, perform*

der Veranstaltungsraum (¨-e) *room for functions*

erzählen *to tell, recount*

1. Before they order coffee, what does Bettina say to Thomas about how well she knows Leipzig?
2. After the coffee comes, what do they talk about?
3. What does Orhan tell Thomas?
4. After Orhan has gone, Bettina hears more about Thomas's personal life. What does she learn?
5. Thomas is currently still a student, but he has ambitions to do what?
6. Before they say goodbye, what does Thomas do?
7. Bettina goes back and sees Sonja. What is Sonja's reaction to what Bettina tells her?

WISSEN SIE DAS?

Bettina says in the drama that she works in a *Hauptschule*. In Germany there are five types of secondary school. First, there are *Sonderschulen* (special schools) for children with learning or other difficulties and *Gesamtschulen* (comprehensive schools) mainly found in the northern *Länder* and catering for a relatively small percentage of young people. Then there are three types of school based on selection and parental choice. These are the

- *Gymnasium*, a grammar school for aged 10–19 attended by about 35% of the school population.
- *Realschule*, a school for pupils aged 10–16, attended by another 35%.
- *Hauptschule*, a school for pupils aged 10–15/16, preparing for training in skills and crafts. The percentage of the school population (currently less than 30%) attending is decreasing.

Children start school at the age of 6 in Germany, when they all attend the *Grundschule*. All young people in Germany must remain in some form of education, vocational or other, until the age of 18.

Hörspiel, Folge 2

2 Read through these questions, then listen to the *Hörspiel* again and answer the questions in German.

1. Wo im Café sitzen Bettina und Thomas?
2. Seit wann ist Bettina in Leipzig?
3. Seit wann ist Thomas in Leipzig?
4. Was ist Bettina von Beruf?
5. Wie findet sie die Schüler?
6. Wo wohnt sie zur Zeit?
7. Was für eine Wohnung möchte sie haben?
8. Warum hat sie Tübingen verlassen?
9. Woher kommt Orhan?
10. Wie alt is Kai?
11. Ist Thomas verheiratet?
12. Wohnt sein Sohn bei ihm?
13. Warum macht Thomas Straßenmusik?
14. Was ist die Moritzbastei?
15. Thomas lädt Bettina ein. Für wann?

3 Imagine that Sonja had been more sympathetic and interested in what Bettina had been doing and that Bettina had told her all about her coffee with Thomas. Give a report of the meeting, using the points provided below. Your text should be written in the perfect tense and be no more than 100 words long.

- in ein Café gehen
- über die Arbeit sprechen
- was Thomas macht
- wie und warum er Geld verdient
- türkischer Freund kommt vorbei
- Einladung zur Party
- die Familie von Thomas
- Einladung für morgen abend

4 When an invitation is given in German it can be formal or informal in the way it addresses people and can, of course, refer to one or more people. On the following page you will see Orhan's invitations – he uses two versions, depending on who he is writing to. Read them and say which version Thomas would get and why (remembering what Orhan said in the café). Give the reasons for your choice.

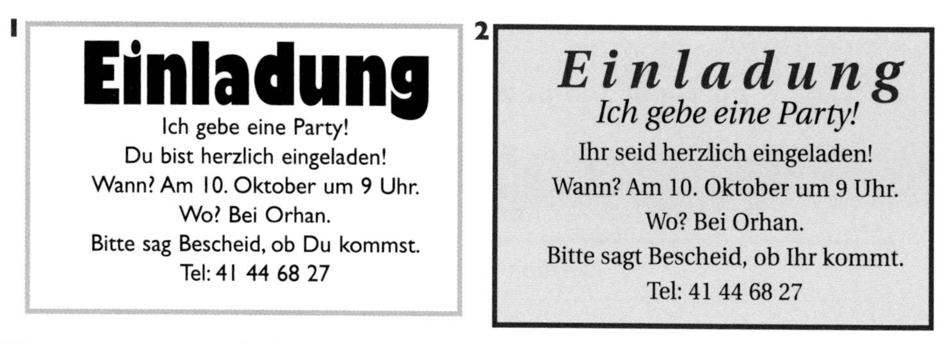

1

Einladung

Ich gebe eine Party!
Du bist herzlich eingeladen!
Wann? Am 10. Oktober um 9 Uhr.
Wo? Bei Orhan.
Bitte sag Bescheid, ob Du kommst.
Tel: 41 44 68 27

2

Einladung

Ich gebe eine Party!
Ihr seid herzlich eingeladen!
Wann? Am 10. Oktober um 9 Uhr.
Wo? Bei Orhan.
Bitte sagt Bescheid, ob Ihr kommt.
Tel: 41 44 68 27

5 Here are some more invitation cards – to a house warming, *eine Einweihungsfete* or *ein Einweihungsparty.* These are the kinds of invitations that Sultan Braun, whom you met in the first part of the video for *Thema 2*, might have sent out when the Südstadt housing project was finished.

Read the invitation cards below and decide which is the formal version, which is addressed to an individual, and which to more than one person. Give the reasons for your choice.

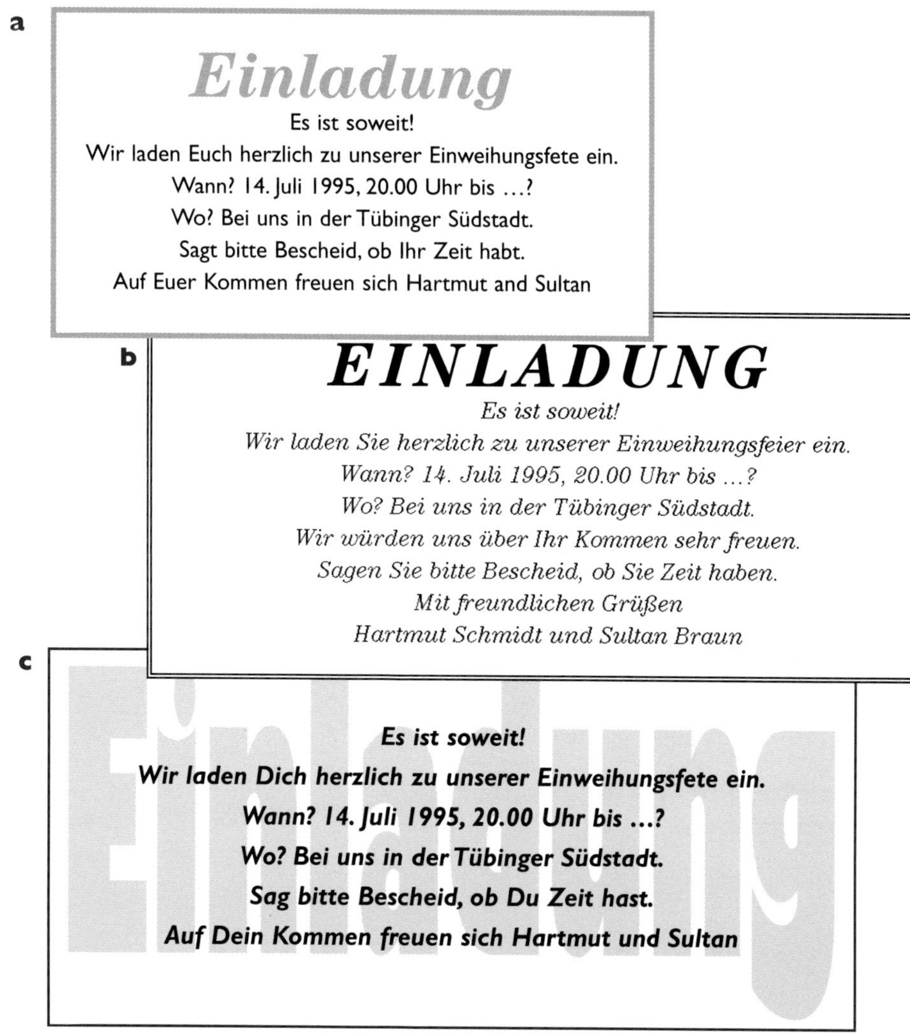

a

Einladung

Es ist soweit!
Wir laden Euch herzlich zu unserer Einweihungsfete ein.
Wann? 14. Juli 1995, 20.00 Uhr bis ...?
Wo? Bei uns in der Tübinger Südstadt.
Sagt bitte Bescheid, ob Ihr Zeit habt.
Auf Euer Kommen freuen sich Hartmut and Sultan

b

EINLADUNG

Es ist soweit!
Wir laden Sie herzlich zu unserer Einweihungsfeier ein.
Wann? 14. Juli 1995, 20.00 Uhr bis ...?
Wo? Bei uns in der Tübinger Südstadt.
Wir würden uns über Ihr Kommen sehr freuen.
Sagen Sie bitte Bescheid, ob Sie Zeit haben.
Mit freundlichen Grüßen
Hartmut Schmidt und Sultan Braun

c

Einladung

Es ist soweit!
Wir laden Dich herzlich zu unserer Einweihungsfete ein.
Wann? 14. Juli 1995, 20.00 Uhr bis ...?
Wo? Bei uns in der Tübinger Südstadt.
Sag bitte Bescheid, ob Du Zeit hast.
Auf Dein Kommen freuen sich Hartmut und Sultan

USING personal and possessive pronouns

When you are writing letters and invitations, and asking how people are, you will almost certainly use the various forms of personal and possessive pronouns. Here is a complete list of the personal pronouns:

	Nominative	Accusative	Dative
I	ich	mich	mir
you (familiar)	du	dich	dir
he	er	ihn	ihm
she	sie	sie	ihr
it	es	es	ihm
we	wir	uns	uns
you (pl. fam.)	ihr	euch	euch
you (sing. or pl. formal)	Sie	Sie	Ihnen
they	sie	sie	ihnen

You will need to use the dative form in these phrases:
Wie geht's dir? *How are you? (informal)*
Wie geht's Ihnen? *How are you? (formal)*
Wie geht's euch? *How are (the two or more of) you? (informal)*
Es geht mir gut *I'm fine.*
Wie geht's deinem Vater/deiner Mutter? *How's your father/mother?*
Es geht ihm/ihr gut. *He's/She's fine.*

Here is a poem called 'Gossip on Sunday Morning' by Horst Bienek. It shows how the definite article can be used in a variety of ways. Read through and check that you understand it.

ohne Gewähr *without commitment, on timetables: subject to change*
am Klavier *at the piano*

Klatsch am Sonntagmorgen

Wer mit wem?
Die mit dem!
Der mit der?
(Ohne Gewähr)
Sie und er?
Der und er??
Wer ist wer?

Wir mit ihr?
Sie mit dir!
(Am Klavier)
Du mit ihm!
Sie mit ihm!
Ich und du?
Who is who?

Horst Bienek

7

Hörabschnitt 6 on the *Übungskassette* contains two conversations which took place at the house-warming party in the Südstadt. The conversations are transcribed below, with some gaps. Listen to *Hörabschnitt 6* and fill in the gaps, using phrases from the list provided. Each gap represents one expression or phrase.

der Nachbar (-n) *neighbour (male)*
die Nachbarin (-nen) *neighbour (female)*

Dialog 1

Hartmut Hallo, Bernd und Sonia. Schön, daß ihr da seid. ____________ ?

Bernd Hallo. ____________ . Mir geht's eigentlich immer gut, wenn Parties gefeiert werden. Und ____________ ? ____________ ?

Hartmut Tja, danke, gut. Aber komm doch erst mal 'rein.

Bernd Mensch, das ist ja toll geworden. Wie lange wohnt ihr jetzt schon hier?

Hartmut Seit Januar. Ah – Ülkü, ____________ ? Bernd, ____________ .

Ülkü Hallo, Bernd. ____________ .

Bernd Freut mich auch.

Hartmut Was möchtet ihr denn trinken, ihr zwei?

Dialog 2

Frau Braun Guten Abend, Herr Holzner. Schön, daß Sie kommen konnten.

Herr Holzner ____________ . Das Projekt ist endlich fertig. ____________ im neuen Haus?

Frau Braun Sehr gut, vielen Dank. ____________ ? Sibylle, das ist Herr Holzner vom *Tübinger Tageblatt.*

Herr Holzner ____________ .

Frau Braun Und das ist mein Partner Hartmut, und das sind Bernd und Ülkü, unsere Freunde. ____________ ?

Alle Hallo, guten Abend.

Hartmut ____________ ? Das ist doch einfacher.

Herr Holzner Ja, gern.

Wie geht es Ihnen denn jetzt | Guten Abend, Frau Schneider, freut mich
Darf ich euch Herrn Holzner vorstellen | Freut mich, dich kennenzulernen
Wollen wir uns nicht alle duzen | was ist mit deiner Mutter | Mir geht's gut
darf ich dir meinen Freund Bernd vorstellen | Geht es ihr wieder besser
Wie geht's euch | das ist Ülkü, eine Freundin von Sultan
Darf ich Ihnen meine Nachbarin, Frau Schneider, vorstellen | 'n Abend, Frau Braun

Now listen to *Hörabschnitt 6* again or work from the complete texts given in the transcript booklet and pick out the phrases which belong under the headings below. An example of each category is given. Add to the lists any other suitable phrases with which you are familiar.

Greetings	**Introductions and responses**	**Enquiring how someone is, and responding**
Hallo!	*Darf ich dir meinen Freund Bernd vorstellen?*	*Wie geht's euch?*

9

The *Bürgermeister* (mayor) of Tübingen is the guest of honour at the house-warming party. Read this conversation between him and Frau Braun. There is something wrong – they are using informal instead of formal language, and the greetings they are using do not fit the situation. Replace the inappropriate phrases with better ones. You may find it useful to refer back to Activity 7.

Frau Braun	Hallo, Herr Bürgermeister. Wie geht's?
Bürgermeister	Gute Nacht, Frau Braun. Sehr gut, danke. Und dir?
Frau Braun	Auch gut, danke. Schön, daß du gekommen bist. Komm doch 'rein. Darf ich dir Sibylle Schneider, meine Nachbarin, vorstellen?
Bürgermeister	Hallo, Sibylle. Freut mich, dich kennenzulernen.
Frau Schneider	Guten Abend, Herr Bürgermeister. Schön, daß Sie kommen konnten.

Now it's your turn to practise giving greetings, responding and asking after people. Take part in the four dialogues in *Hörabschnitt 7*, following the prompts given.

Lerneinheit 5 Wie sieht sie aus?

In *Lerneinheit 5* there are three topics. In the first topic, *Describing what people look like*, you will watch the video and describe the people who appear on it. In the second topic, *Other people's characteristics*, you will eavesdrop on gossip about how people look and behave. Finally, in *Summing people up*, you will work on lonely hearts advertisements as a useful way of describing people.

STUDY CHART

Topic	Activity and resource	Key points
Describing what people look like	**1 Video**	filling in gaps in descriptions of people from the video
	2 Video	correcting descriptions of people from the video
	3 Text	practising adjectival endings
Other people's characteristics	**4 *Übungskassette***	checking you've understood comments about people
	5 *Übungskassette*	writing descriptions of people
Summing people up	**6 Text**	checking you've understood lonely hearts adverts
	7 *Übungskassette*	taking part in conversations about prospective partners

23:44–28:28

In this activity, the video will be used to help you to describe people. The descriptions below are of the people in the third part of the video. Some words have been omitted for you to fill in. Using the video and the vocabulary, complete all the descriptions.

Rudolf Kost geht spazieren. Wegen der Kälte hat er rote Backen. Er hat graue Haare und er trägt eine Brille.

Rudolf Dobler ist auch im Freien. Er ist glattrasiert und grauhaarig. Er lächelt, während er spricht.

Wilfried Setzler ist zwischen fünfzig und fünfundfünfzig Jahre alt. Er hat einen graumelierten Bart und einen Schnurrbart. Er trägt ____________ ____________ und er ____________ , während er ____________ . Wie Herr Kost und Herr Dobler ist er ____________ ____________ .

Tanja Lindl hat lange, rötliche ____________ , ein rundes ____________ und sie trägt ____________ ____________ .

Ruth Stabenow hat blonde, kurze, wellige ____________ . Sie trägt ____________ ____________ und Ohrringe.

Thomas Walter hat einen kleinen Schnurrbart und braune Haare. Er hat ein schmales Gesicht. Er ____________ nicht, sondern sieht ernst aus.

Dorothea Vogel sieht auch ____________ aus. Sie hat ein blasses ____________ und eine hohe Stirn.

Hans-Peter Baumeister lächelt ein bißchen. Seine Haare sind fast weiß aber er hat schwarze Augenbrauen. Er hat einen ____________ und einen ____________ , und er trägt ____________ ____________ . Er ist Mitte vierzig. Seine Frau, **Renate**, sitzt neben ihm. Sie hat dunkelbraune Augen und glatte, ____________ Haare. Sie trägt ____________ . Sie ist Anfang vierzig.

die Backe (-n) *cheek*
wegen der Kälte *on account of the cold*
die Brille (-n) *spectacles*
im Freien *in the open air*
glattrasiert *clean shaven*
lächelt (*from* lächeln) *smiles*
während *whilst, during*
graumeliert *greying*
der Bart (¨-e) *beard*
der Schnurrbart (¨-e) *moustache*
kurz *short*
wellig *wavy*
schmal *narrow*
das Gesicht (-er) *face*
er sieht ernst aus (*from* aussehen) *he looks serious*
blaß *pale*
die Stirn (-en) *forehead, brow*
die Augenbraue (-n) *eyebrow*
dunkelbraun *dark brown*
glatt *flat, straight*
Anfang vierzig *in her early forties*

USING adjectives after *ein-* and *kein-*, with *der*, *die* and *das* and without any article

In the descriptions you have just been working on in Activity 1, the endings of the adjectives vary. This is because they describe masculine, feminine or neuter nouns and because in the examples you have just read, they are in the accusative case.

In *Lerneinheit 5* you will mostly be using adjectives with nouns in the accusative and the dative cases. Note that most of the adjectives end in *-en*, so it is easier to learn those that do not end in this way. The complete set of adjectival endings is on page 107:

CONTINUED

Adjectives after *ein-* and *kein-*

	Masculine	Feminine	Neuter	Plural
Nominative	ein grauer Bart	eine runde Brille	ein ovales Gesicht	keine grauen Haare
Accusative	einen grauen Bart	eine runde Brille	ein ovales Gesicht	keine grauen Haare
Genitive	eines grauen Barts	einer runden Brille	eines ovalen Gesichts	keiner grauen Haare
Dative	einem grauen Bart	einer runden Brille	einem ovalen Gesicht	keinen grauen Haaren

The endings of the possessive adjectives (*mein, dein, sein, ihr,* etc.) are the same as *ein-* and *kein-*.

Adjectives after *der, die das* and plural *die*

With *der, die, das* and the plural *die* the adjectival endings are either *-e* or *-en*. Note that the endings differ from the use with *ein-* only in the nominative and accusative cases.

Nominative	der graue Bart	die runde Brille	das ovale Gesicht	die grauen Haare
Accusative	den grauen Bart	die runde Brille	das ovale Gesicht	die grauen Haare

In the genitive and dative cases, adjectival endings are the same as for *ein-*.

Adjectival endings where there is no article

	Masculine	Feminine	Neuter	Plural
Nominative	heißer Tee	warme Milch	kaltes Bier	lange Haare
Accusative	heißen Tee	warme Milch	kaltes Bier	lange Haare
Genitive	heißen Tees	warmer Milch	kalten Biers	langer Haare

LERNTIP

You may find these adjectival endings difficult to remember. The best thing to do is to memorise a certain number of phrases in which they occur and which will give you a mental reference point when you want to use the structure with different words. You could also listen out for the endings used in particular phrases. This will help you to remember them.

14:00–18:54

Now watch the first video extract from the point at which Dr. Setzler speaks. Read the following descriptions of each person and, using the pause button, check the description against the image. Correct the written descriptions where they are wrong.

1 Wilfried Setzler hat einen schwarzen Bart. Er trägt eine Brille.
2 Hans-Peter Baumeister hat weiße Haare und weiße Augenbrauen. Sein Bart ist graumeliert. Er trägt eine runde Brille.
3 Walter Utz ist ein junger Mann. Er hat braune Haare und ist glattrasiert.
4 Renate Baumeister hat rote Ohrringe, wellige, blonde Haare und trägt keine Brille.
5 Peter Bosch hat lange, graue Haare.
6 Alice Kurz: Ihre Haare sind blond und kurz.
7 Tanja Lindl ist eine junge Frau mit kurzen, roten Haaren.
8 Wolfgang Fritz ist ein junger Mann. Er hat lange, blonde Haare.
9 Sultan Braun ist eine alte Frau mit grauen Haaren.

3

This activity will help you practise adjectival endings. Some of these word groups have come up earlier. Others will be new to you, and you may need to look up the adjectival endings in the table on page 107. Complete these descriptions, using the right endings.

Gesine Jüttner ist gebürtig– Leipzigerin. Sie ist Mitte 30. Sie hat schulterlang–, rot– Haare und dunkelbraun– Augen mit schmal– Augenbrauen.

Günter Leypoldt hat ein glattrasiert– Gesicht. Er wohnt in Tübingen im alt– Teil der Stadt.

Sibylle Metzger ist Studentin. Sie trägt groß–, silbern– Ohrringe. Wo wohnt sie? Sie wohnt mit zwei ander– Frauen in einer schön– Wohnung mit einem groß– Balkon in Tübingen.

Daniela Krafak wohnt in Leipzig. Sie teilt eine groß– und schön– Wohnung mit ihrem Freund.

Tanja Lindl wohnt in der sehr schön– Altstadt von Tübingen. Wie sieht sie aus? Sie hat ein rund– Gesicht, eine hoh– Stirn und sie trägt eine rund– Brille.

Ruth Stabenow hat eine klein– Wohnung in einer ruhig– Lage in Leipzig. Sie hat gut– Freunde in ihrem Wohnblock.

Hans-Peter Baumeister wohnt mit seiner Frau und seinen Kindern in einem modern– Haus in Tübingen. Er hat einen graumeliert– Bart, und er trägt eine rund– Brille.

4

In *Hörabschnitt 8* you will hear five sets of comments made about people the speakers saw or met at a party. Study the vocabulary below, then listen to *Hörabschnitt 8* and answer the questions about each conversation in English.

lustig *cheerful*
fröhlich *happy*
aufgeschlossen *open minded*
ich mag sie/ihn *I like her/him*
geschminkt *made up*
ich kann … nicht leiden *I can't stand …*
dumm *silly*
unsympathisch *unpleasant*
sie ist in Ordnung *she's OK, all right*
ruhig *quiet*
dich … gestritten (*from* sich streiten) *quarrelled*
stur *obstinate, pigheaded*
er geht mir auf die Nerven *he gets on my nerves*

Conversation 1

1 How does the first speaker identify the person he is talking about?
2 How does he go on to describe him?
3 What does the woman say about Karl?

Conversation 2

4 Can you describe Sibylle?

Conversation 3

5 Why didn't the man talk to Anna?
6 What is his opinion of her?
7 Can you describe her appearance?

Conversation 4

8 What does the woman ask in her first question?
9 How does the man describe Angelika?

Conversation 5

10 How does the woman feel about Peter?
11 Is he unfriendly towards either of the speakers?
12 What reasons does she give for her attitude to him?

5

Listen to the conversations in *Hörabschnitt 8* again. Make notes about the people who are being discussed and then write a description of each one. You should include the opinions voiced in the conversations.

Here is a description of Karl, the first person to be described, as an example:

Karl ist groß und lustig und er trägt eine runde Brille. Die Frau findet ihn fröhlich und aufgeschlossen.

WISSEN SIE DAS?

Giving someone's height

Height in German is given in metres, e.g. 1,80; you say *ein Meter achtzig* or *eins achtzig*. Weight is given in kilos, e.g. *65 Kilo*.

In the last two activities of *Lerneinheit 5* you will look at other ways of describing people by reading lonely hearts advertisements.

Read through the adverts (*Kontaktanzeigen*) overleaf, check that you have understood all the abbreviations, and then match the statements with the adverts by writing the letter of the advert alongside.

begeisterungsfähig *enthusiastic*
gemeinsam *common*
die Unternehmung (-en) *activity*
die Ehe (-n) *marriage*
die Chiffre (-n) *box number*
die Witwe (-n) *widow*
schlank *slim*
zuverlässig *reliable*
gebildet *educated*
ausgeschlossen *(from ausschließen) excluded*
der Arzt (¨-e) *doctor*
der Unternehmer (-) *entrepreneur*

Weiblich

a Lehrerin, 31/1,65, blond, sportlich-elegant u. sympathisch, mit viels. Interessen: Sprachen, Reisen u. Kunst, freut sich auf begeisterungsfähigen, aufgeschlossenen Partner für gemeinsame Unternehmungen, spät. Ehe mögl. Bildzuschriften bitte unter Chiffre …

b Vitale Witwe, Anfang 60, dunkel u. schlank, sucht liebenswerten und toleranten Lebenspartner bis 65 J. Zuschriften erbeten unter Chiffre …

c Akademikerin, 40 J., gesch. (1 Kind), Nichtraucherin, natürlich und offen mit viels. kulturellen Interessen: Oper, Theater und Literatur, möchte zuverlässigen u. gebildeten Mann für gemeinsame Konzert– u. Theaterbesuche kennenlernen. Spät. Ehe nicht ausgeschlossen. Zuschriften unter Chiffre …

Männlich

d Arzt, 35/1,93, sportlicher Typ, humorvoll, aufgeschlossen und tolerant – aber leider allein! – sucht intelligente, offene Partnerin – ebenfalls mit Sinn für Humor – zwischen 25 u. 30 für gemeinsame Zukunft. Zuschriften (wenn mögl. mit Bild) unter Chiffre …

e Charmanter Single, Mitte 40, sportlich und gutaussehend, möchte sympathische und dynamische Lebensgefährtin bis 35 kennenlernen. Tel. 44 87 26 19–21 Uhr.

f Unternehmer, 50/1,75, verw., Nichtraucher, dynamisch und begeisterungsfähig, interessiert sich für Kultur und gemütl. Zuhause, fühlt sich einsam und möchte gebildete und tolerante Ehepartnerin bis Mitte 40 kennenlernen. Bildzuschriften bitte unter Chiffre …

This is what the abbreviations stand for in the advertisements:

u. = und
viels. = vielseitigen *many sided*
spät. = spätere *later*
mögl. = möglich *possible*
gesch. = geschieden *divorced*
Tel. = Telefon *telephone*
verw. = verwitwet *widowed*
gemütl. = gemütliches *cosy, comfortable*

1 This person can be phoned only in the evening. ❑
2 The advertiser is a single parent interested in cultural activities. ❑
3 This non-smoking businessman has a homely side to him. ❑
4 This person would consider marriage and is looking for a partner who enjoys travel. ❑
5 This person has a sense of humour, and would like to see a photo. ❑
6 This person is widowed. ❑
7 This person is looking for a reliable partner. ❑
8 This person is looking for someone dynamic. ❑
9 This person is dark and slim. ❑
10 This person would like an enthusiastic and open-minded partner. ❑

7

In this activity in *Hörabschnitt 9* imagine that you are working in an introductions agency. Your job is to answer questions put by clients, who have received some details about potential partners and have phoned you to find out more.Take part in the dialogues using the English prompts given on the *Übungskassette*.

First, note the following word: **die Redakteurin (-nen)** *editor (female)*

Lerneinheit 6 Kleider machen Leute

There are two topics in *Lerneinheit 6*: *Describing people's clothes* and *What people like to wear*. You will use the video as a means of practising the language and grammar you need.

By the end of *Lerneinheit 6*, you should be able to describe a wide range of clothing and be able to discuss what you most like wearing.

STUDY CHART

Topic	Activity and resource	Key points
Describing people's clothes	**1 Video**	revising words for clothes and colours, and adjectival endings
	2 Video	completing descriptions of people's clothing
What people like to wear	**3–4 Text**	checking you've understood an article about what people like to wear
	5–6 *Übungskassette*	checking you've understood interviews about what people wear
	7–8 *Übungskassette*	taking part in dialogues about clothing

1

23:44–28:28

This activity aims to help you revise a number of things. First of all, you will be using the German words for colours, so check that you know them. Then you will need to use the words for the different items of clothing worn by the people in the third part of the video – these are given overleaf, though you will have to fill them in from sentence 2 onwards. You will also practise adjectival endings, since all the words for clothing used here are in the accusative case (so you will have to make sure the adjective agrees). For reference, here are all the accusative endings:

der Pullover – Sie hat ein**en** blau**en** Pullover an.
die Krawatte – Er trägt ein**e** grün**e** Krawatte.
das Halstuch – Sie trägt ein bunt**es** Halstuch.
die Pullover (*pl*) – Sie hat zwei blau**e** Pullover an.

der Schal (-s) *scarf*

der Hut (¨-e) *hat*

der Mantel (¨) *coat*

der Schutzhelm (-e) *hard hat, helmet*

die Öljacke (-n) *waxed jacket (literally: oil jacket)*

bunt *brightly coloured*

das Halstuch (¨-er) *scarf, neckerchief*

Now watch the third section of the video (23:44–28:28). Turn the sound down, so that you can concentrate on what people are wearing. Then complete the sentences below.

1 Rudolf Kost trägt eine dunkle Jacke, ein weißes Hemd und einen dunklen, karierten Schal. Er trägt auch eine dunkle Krawatte.

2 Rudolf Dobler trägt eine dunkelblaue ______________ , einen blauen Pullover und einen ______________ Hut.

3 Wilfried Setzler hat einen ______________ Mantel und ein ______________ Hemd an. Er trägt einen gelben ______________ aber keine ______________ .

4 Tanja Lindl trägt einen dunkelgrünen ______________ .

5 Ruth Stabenow hat eine lila Bluse und einen lila ______________ an.

6 Thomas Walter hat einen weißen ______________ auf. Er trägt ein ______________ ______________ und eine ______________ Öljacke.

7 Dorothea Vogel hat zwei blaue Pullover an, einen hellblauen und einen ______________ .

8 Hans-Peter Baumeister hat ______________ ______________ ______________ und ______________ ______________ ______________ an. Seine Frau, Renate, trägt ein buntes Halstuch und ______________ ______________ ______________ .

LERNTIP

Für's Notizbuch

Here are some colloquial German expressions that involve items of clothing. Use a dictionary and guess which German expression goes with which English equivalent.

1 Ich mache mich auf die Socken.
2 Da geht mir der Hut hoch.
3 Jetzt platzt mir aber der Kragen!
4 Wo drückt der Schuh?

a What's on your mind? What's the problem?
b It makes me wild.
c I'm off!
d That's the last straw! I've had enough!

2

14:00–14:30

In this activity use the first few frames of the first section of the video to describe what the people are wearing. You will need to use the pause button, as each sequence is very short. Complete the sentences below using the vocabulary from Activity 1 and that listed below.

der Anorak (-s) *anorak*	**die Jeans** *jeans*	**die Regenjacke (-n)** *waterproof jacket, anorak*
der Handschuh (-e) *glove*	**die Kleider** *clothes*	**der Regenmantel (¨)** *raincoat*
die Hose (-n) *trousers*	**die Lederjacke (-n)** *leather jacket*	**der Schuh (-e)** *shoe*

sich unterhalten *to have a conversation*

Sequence 1

Zwei Frauen sprechen miteinander. Die Frau auf der linken Seite hat ____________ ____________ ____________ an und die andere Frau trägt ____________ ____________ ____________.

Sequence 2

Zwei Senioren stehen auf der Straße und unterhalten sich. Die Frau trägt ____________ ____________ ____________ und ____________, und der Mann trägt ____________ ____________ ____________ und ____________ ____________ ____________.

Sequence 3

Fünf Kinder und eine junge Frau gehen spazieren. Die Kinder habe alle bunte ____________ und ____________ an und die junge Frau trägt ____________ ____________ und ____________ ____________.

Sequence 4

Vier junge Leute unterhalten sich. Zwei stehen und zwei sitzen. Die zwei, die stehen, tragen ____________ und einer von ihnen trägt eine ____________, und der andere trägt eine ____________ ____________. Beide tragen ____________ Schuhe.

Sequence 5

Ein Mann und eine Frau gehen am Marktplatz vorbei. Sie trägt ____________ ____________ ____________, und er hat ____________ ____________ ____________ an.

3

Overleaf there are some some extracts from a survey carried out by a fashion magazine into what people like to wear and when. Read the extracts and then answer the questions on page 115.

Uwe Kürten, 35, Büroangestellter „Bei der Arbeit trage ich meistens Jeans und Hemden und im Winter auch warme, selbstgestrickte Pullover. Nur bei offizielleren Anlässen trage ich Jacketts, feinere Hosen aus Baumwolle oder Wolle und bunte Krawatten. Anzüge kann ich nicht leiden, weil sie mir nicht gefallen und sie viel zu formell aussehen."

Ilse Unterberg, 71, Renterin „Vor kurzem habe ich Leggings entdeckt. Sie sind vielleicht zu modern für eine alte Frau, aber ich mag sie sehr, und im Winter gibt's nichts Besseres. Ich trage am liebsten legere aber warme Kleidung. Wenn ich ausgehe, trage ich einen Rock und einen Pullover."

Eva Reus, 28, Marketingassistentin „Am liebsten trage ich Grün. Diese Farbe paßt zu meinen Augen und zu meinen roten Haaren. Zu besonderen Anlässen trage ich mein schwarzes Kostüm – aber immer mit etwas Grünem dabei – und meine Schuhe mit hohen Absätzen."

Andreas Schiffer, 46, Bauer „Hier an der Nordsee ist es oft kalt und naß, und da ich so oft im Freien bin, hängt das, was ich trage, viel vom Wetter ab. Ich gehe auch gern spazieren – das heißt, ich brauche Stiefel, eine dicke Hose und eine Windjacke. Ich trage selten formelle Kleider. Meine Frau sagt, daß Krawatten mir einfach nicht stehen."

Tanja Polinski, 38, Redakteurin „Was ich trage? Es kommt darauf an, was ich mache oder auf die Jahreszeiten. Ich trage am liebsten legere Kleidung, so ein T-Shirt oder Shorts, wenn möglich. Bei der Arbeit trage ich dann ein Kleid oder eine bequeme Hose. Manchmal einen Jogginganzug. Bei uns beim Radio gibt's keine Vorschriften. In der Freizeit trage ich dieselben Sachen wie bei der Arbeit."

Albrecht Winter, 46, Abteilungsleiter bei Siemens „Im Büro muß ich ordentlich angezogen sein. Da trage ich meistens einen Anzug. Ich habe oft mit Kunden zu tun. Graue Anzüge sind allerdings nicht mein Geschmack und ich trage lieber bunte Jacketts. Wenn ich nach Hause komme, ziehe ich mich sofort um – dann ist es ein Hemd und Jeans."

selbstgestrickt *hand knitted*
bei offizielleren Anlässen *on more official occasions*
das Jackett (-s) *jacket*
aus Baumwolle *made of cotton*
die Wolle *wool*
der Anzug (¨-e) *suit*
ich mag sie (*from* mögen) *I like them*
leger *informal*
der Rock (¨-e) *skirt*
... paßt zu (*from* passen) *goes with, suits*
besonders *special*
Schuhe mit hohen Absätzen *high-heeled shoes*
naß *wet*
es hängt vom Wetter ab *it depends on the weather*
der Stiefel (-) *boot*
dick *thick*
Krawatten stehen mir nicht *ties don't suit me*
es kommt darauf an *it all depends*
das Kleid (-er) *dress*
bequem *comfortable*
die Vorschrift (-en) *regulation, instruction*
angezogen (*from* anziehen) *dressed*
ich habe mit Kunden zu tun *I have contact with customers*
der Geschmack *taste*
ziehe ich mich um (*from* sich umziehen) *I change*

1 Was trägt Uwe Kürten meistens bei der Arbeit?
2 Wann trägt Ilse Unterberg Leggings?
3 Warum trägt Eva Reus gern Grün?
4 Warum hängt das, was Andreas Schiffer trägt, vom Wetter ab?
5 Warum trägt er selten Krawatten?
6 Trägt Tanja Polinski in der Freizeit etwas anderes als bei der Arbeit?
7 Warum trägt Albrecht Winter meistens einen Anzug im Büro?

SAYING what you like or prefer

You have probably come across the following expressions. They help you to say what you like and express a preference.

ich mag *I like*
ich trage gern ... *I like wearing ...*
ich trage nicht gern ... *I don't like wearing ...*
ich trage lieber ... *I prefer wearing ...*
am liebsten trage ich ... *most of all I like wearing ...*
... kann ich nicht leiden *I can't stand ...*
... sind nicht mein Geschmack *... are not my thing, are not to my taste*
... steht mir nicht *... doesn't suit me*

LERNTIP

Für's Notizbuch
In the extracts in Activity 3 people used a number of expressions of time. Keep a note of these as you will need some of them in later activities.

immer *always*
meistens *mostly*
manchmal *sometimes*
oft *frequently, often*
selten *seldom*
sofort *immediately*
vor kurzem *a little while ago*

4

Read through the extracts in Activity 3 again. In the statements below, there are factual errors. Write out corrected versions.

1. Herr Kürten mag Pullis, Jeans und T-Shirts.
2. Jacketts mag er nicht.
3. Frau Unterberg trägt nicht sehr gern Leggings.
4. Zum Ausgehen trägt sie ein Kleid und einen Pullover.
5. Frau Reus trägt bei besonderen Anlässen ein grünes Kostüm.
6. Sie trägt nie Schuhe mit hohen Absätzen.
7. Am liebsten trägt Herr Schiffer formelle Kleider.
8. Bei schlechtem Wetter trägt er eine Windjacke und Stiefel.
9. Am liebsten trägt Frau Polinski etwas Legeres.
10. Im Büro gibt es neue Vorschriften.
11. Bunte Jacketts sind nicht Herrn Winters Geschmack.
12. Er trägt Jeans, wenn er mit Kunden zu tun hat.

5

In *Hörabschnitt 10* you will hear two short interviews with people who tell an interviewer from a fashion magazine what they like or dislike wearing. They discuss what they wear for work, in their leisure time and on special occasions.

First, study this list of vocabulary, then listen to the interviews and answer the questions below in English.

weit *wide*
eng *tight, narrow*
das Sweatshirt (-s) *sweatshirt*
schick *smart*
selten *seldom*
die Gelegenheit (-en) *occasion, opportunity*
Klamotten *slang for clothes*
die Kombination (-en) *suit, two-piece*
das Oberteil (-e) *upper part*
das Jäckchen (-) *little jacket*
die Wahl (-en) *choice*

Interviewee 1

1. What does she like to wear with leggings?
2. Why doesn't she like wearing tight clothes?
3. What sort of clothes does she like to wear at work?
4. What does she like to do on special occasions?

Interviewee 2

5. Why does he say he has no choice about what he wears?
6. What does he wear at work?
7. What type of clothes does he wear at the weekend?
8. What sort of trousers does he mention?

6 Listen to *Hörabschnitt 10* again and then fill in the gaps below to complete the descriptions of each person.

1 Diese Lehrerin braucht keine ____________ Kleidung zu tragen. Bei ____________ Arbeit trägt sie meistens ____________ Kleidung. Zu besonderen ____________ gibt sie gern viel Geld ____________ und kauft sich schöne ____________ .

2 Dieser Mann ist Manager ____________ einer Bank und ____________ viel mit wichtigen ____________ zu tun. Deshalb trägt er ____________ dunklen Anzug und ein ____________ Hemd.

7 In *Hörabschnitt 11* you are asked to take part in a conversation with a friend, who has asked you what your colleagues wear, in order to form a picture of what they are like. Take part in the conversation, following the prompts in English.

8 The final activity in *Lerneinheit 6* is a dialogue in *Hörabschnitt 12* in which you should imagine that you are talking to a friend who has a wholesale fashion business. Your friend has asked your opinion of the latest range. Take part in the dialogue following the prompts given in English on the cassette.

Checkliste

By the end of *Teil 2* you should be able to

- ○ understand invitations (*Lerneinheit 4*, Activity 5) — **Seite 101**
- ○ use personal pronouns in formal and informal registers (*Lerneinheit 4*, Activity 7) — **Seite 103**
- ○ extend greetings, make introductions and make an enquiry about another person (*Lerneinheit 4*, Activities 7–10) — **Seiten 103–104**
- ○ describe another person's appearance (*Lerneinheit 5*, Activities 1–5) — **Seiten 105–109**
- ○ use adjectives before nouns (*Lerneinheit 5*, Activities 1–5 and 7) — **Seiten 105–109, 11**
- ○ describe another person's nature (*Lerneinheit 5*, Activities 4, 5 and 7) — **Seiten 108–9, 111**
- ○ describe clothes (*Lerneinheit 6*, Activities 1–2 and 5–8) — **Seiten 111–113, 116–117**
- ○ understand and express likes and dislikes (*Lerneinheit 6*, Activity 5) — **Seite 116**

Teil 3

Lokalpatriotismus

In *Teile 1–2* of *Thema 2* you have concentrated on people. Now you will get the chance to find out more about places in Germany. *Lerneinheit 7, Wo bin ich zu Hause*, concentrates on German towns and cities; *Lerneinheit 8, Regionale Aspekte*, concentrates on various aspects of regionalism seen through the eyes of one person, and *Lerneinheit 9, Der Rhein und die Elbe*, concentrates on these rivers.

By the end of *Teil 3*, you should be able to talk about why people live where they do and have practised recounting events from the past.

Lerneinheit 7 Wo bin ich zu Hause?

In *Lerneinheit 7* you will hear local people talking about the places where they live, in Germany and elsewhere in Europe, and why they feel at home there. In the first topic, *My home and its importance*, several Leipzigers explain what their city means to them. The second topic provides a discussion of *Germany's position in Europe*.

The work in *Lerneinheit 7* will expand your knowledge of the language and vocabulary needed to talk about your local area and give you a sense of how Germany relates to the rest of Europe.

STUDY CHART

Topic	Activity and resource	Key points
My home and its importance	**1–2 Video**	checking you've understood the video
	3 Video	writing about a person from the video
Germany's position in Europe	**4 Video**	checking you've understood the video
	5 Text	reading about Germany's position in Europe
	6 *Übungskassette*	listening to statistics about Germany
	7 *Übungskassette*	answering questions about Germany

18:56–23:42

In the next three activities you will work on the second video sequence, in which Frau Jüttner, Herr Rübling and Professor Rotzsch talk about why they like the place they live in. Be prepared to deal with language that is quite difficult at times. First, check that you understand the vocabulary, then watch the part of the video, which concentrates on Gesine Jüttner (18:58–20:35) and answer the questions below.

die Eigenart (-en) *characteristic*

alles Fremde *anything foreign, new, different*

das Vorurteil (-en) *prejudice*

mit Vorurteilen aufräumen *to get rid of prejudices*

anhaften *here: to be inherent in, to mark out*

berühmt sein als (die Stadt des Buches) *to be famous for being (the city of books)*

Spuren hinterlassen *to have an impact, have left an impression*

prägen *to shape*

viel tun für etwas *to do a lot for something*

der Menschenschlag *a certain type of people*

ausgesprochen *definite, real, emphatically*

1 Where does Frau Jüttner come from?

2 What, according to her, is the typical attitude of the people of her town towards anything new?

3 How does she finally sum herself up?

4 Leipzig has the oldest ______ ______ in ______ .

5 The town is famous for ______ , ______ and ______ .

6 The town has the ______ ______ ______ in Germany.

7 It has fine ______ .

18:56–23:42

Now concentrate on Herr Rübling. Watch the video from 20:35–21:48, then answer the questions below.

ehemalig *former*

das Grundstück (-e) *property*

wir besaßen (*from* besitzen) *we owned*

wir entschlossen uns (*from* entschließen) *we decided*

beabsichtigen *to intend*

einziehen *to move in*

ohnehin *anyway*

verputzen zu lassen *to have plastered*

1 How long has Herr Rübling lived in Leipzig?
2 What four reasons does he give for considering Leipzig his home town?
3 Where did he use to live?
4 Why did the Rüblings decide to build a house on their plot of land?
5 When are they planning to move in?

20:35–21:48

Watch the section of video about Herr Rübling again, then write about 50 words about Herr Rübling's reasons for considering Leipzig his *Heimat* and about the plans that he and his wife have. It may be useful to refer to *Lerneinheit 2*, Activity 1 where you learned how to use expressions like *er betrachtet/ bezeichnet/beschreibt* and revised giving reasons using *weil*.

21:49–23:42

In the final section of this part of the video Professor Rotzsch talks about where he feels at home. Study the vocabulary, then watch the video and answer the questions below.

das Land erschließen *to explore the country*

der Status dieser Städte *here: the (good) state those cities are in*

im Verhältnis zu *compared to*

der Verfall unserer Städte *the decay of our cities*

leiden *to suffer*

gepflegt werden *to be looked after*

ein Schatten der Schuld lag auf mir *a shadow of guilt lay on me*

spüren *to feel*

überall *everywhere*

die Verbindung (-en) *connection, contact*

Brücken schlagen *to forge links, build bridges*

Professor Rotzsch wurde in Meissen geboren. Er hat in Leipzig Medizin studiert und ist Professor für klinische Chemie und Laboratoriumsdiagnostik sowie Leiter des Seniorkollegs an der Universtität Leipzig.

1. Which important event in the recent history of Germany is he talking about?
2. This event brought about many changes for the inhabitants of the former DDR. Which change is Professor Rotzsch particularly happy about?
3. What does he say about the state of the cities in the eastern part of the country (in comparison to those in the west)?
4. Where does Professor Rotzsch feel at home?
5. How old was he at the end of the war?
6. Why is he particularly pleased about Germany's links with France and Great Britain?

5

Professor Rotzsch mentioned the links between Germany, France and Great Britain. Read the article on page 122 about Germany's position in the heart of Europe, then answer the questions in German.

der Mittelmeerraum *the area round the Mediterranean*

das Durchgangsland *transit country*

Ein Land in der Mitte Europas

Deutschland liegt in der Mitte, man könnte auch sagen im Herzen Europas. Kein anderes europäisches Land hat so viele Nachbarstaaten wie Deutschland: Insgesamt sind es neun – Dänemark im Norden, die Niederlande, Belgien, Luxemburg und Frankreich im Westen, die Schweiz und Österreich im Süden und die Tschechische Republik und Polen im Osten. Deutschland verbindet Nordeuropa und den Mittelmeerraum einerseits und West- und Osteuropa andererseits. Es wird deshalb auch als Durchgangsland bezeichnet. Gleichzeitig ist Deutschland als Mitglied der Europäischen Union und der NATO eine Brücke zu den osteuropäischen Staaten.

1. Wo liegt Deutschland?
2. Wie viele Nachbarstaaten hat es?
3. Warum wird Deutschland als Durchgangsland bezeichnet?
4. Bei welchen Organisationen ist Deutschland Mitglied?
5. Welche Funktion hat es als Mitglied dieser Organisationen?

6

In *Hörabschnitt 13* you will hear facts and figures concerning the size of Germany in relation to its European neighbours. First check that you understand the vocabulary, then listen to *Hörabschnitt 13* several times and fill in the missing figures below.

Quadratkilometer (km^2) *square kilometers*

die Luftlinie *as the crow flies*

die Grenze (-n) *border*

Deutschland

Größe ______________ km^2

Norden – Süden ______________ km

Westen – Osten ______________ km

Grenzen ______________ km lang

Einwohner rund ______________

Italien Einwohner ______________

Großbritannien Einwohner ______________

Frankreich Einwohner ______________

Frankreich Größe ______________ km^2

Spanien Größe ______________ km^2

7

Now imagine that you have been asked to provide statistical information about Germany to an enquirer. Using the information you completed in Activity 6, answer the questions in *Hörabschnitt 14*.

Lerneinheit 8 Regionale Aspekte

Lerneinheit 8 concentrates on regional aspects of Germany and provides much audio work. The first topic is *Harald Winck's story* – a not untypical tale of a refugee childhood, followed by adulthood settled in Tübingen. In the second topic, *Aspects of regionalism*, Harald Winck defines the special Swabian character. By the end of *Lerneinheit 8*, you should have a better idea of the huge variety of regions in Germany and will have practised recounting past events.

STUDY CHART

Topic	Activity and resource	Key points
Harald Winck's story	**1 *Übungskassette***	listening to a refugee's story
	2 *Übungskassette*	matching events with dates
	3 *Übungskassette*	retelling Herr Winck's life story
Aspects of regionalism	**4 *Übungskassette***	checking you've understood an anecdote about regionalism
	5 *Übungskassette*	defining what makes Swabians different

1

In *Hörabschnitt 15*, Harald Winck, a refugee from Poland after the war, tells you his life story. Look at the vocabulary, then listen to the cassette and trace Herr Winck's movements on the map below.

ursprünglich *originally*

wir wurden evakuiert *we were evacuated*

eine Fahrt quer durch Deutschland *a journey right across Germany*

wir wurden umgesiedelt *we were relocated*

ich wurde entlassen *here: I was demobilised*

lauter Schwaben *Swabians only*

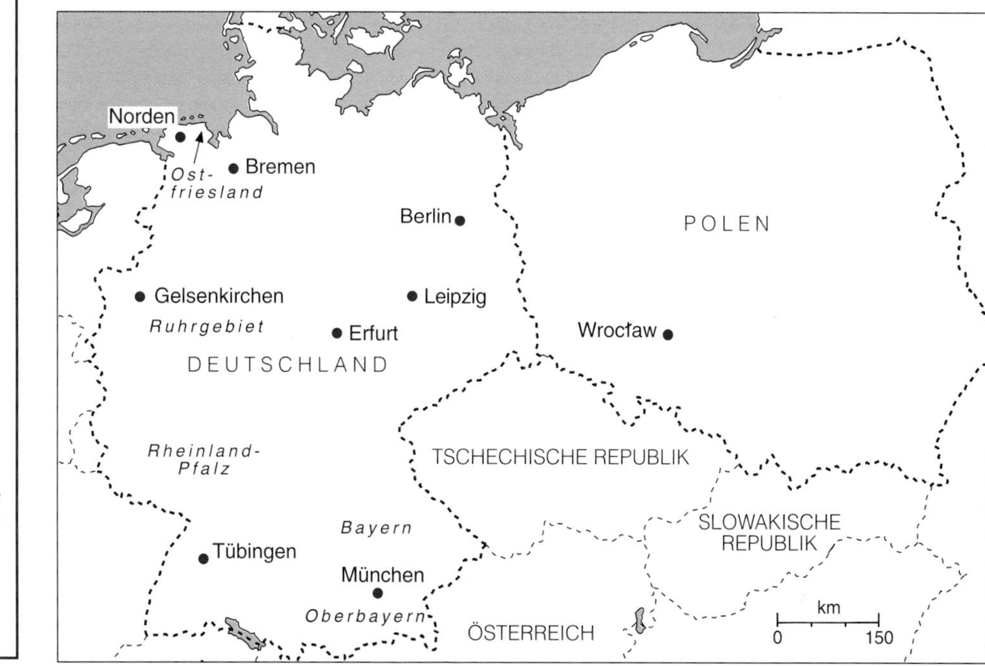

Now listen to *Hörabschnitt 15* again and match the details in the left-hand column to the events in the right-hand column.

1	Breslau (Wrocław)	**a**	zwei Jahre Bundeswehr
2	1946	**b**	die ersten drei Schuljahre
3	Ostfriesland	**c**	Geburt
4	Gelsenkirchen	**d**	Beginn des Studiums
5	Oberbayern	**e**	evakuiert
6	Tübingen	**f**	Gymnasium und Abitur

A friend has asked you about Harald Winck's past. Listen to *Hörabschnitt 15* and use the prompts listed below to recount Herr Winck's story in about 50–60 words. You will notice that the prompts are given in the perfect tense, so use the perfect tense to tell the story. Remember to use the correct auxiliary verb (*sein* or *haben*).

- in Polen geboren
- 1946 nach Ostfriesland gekommen
- dort drei Jahre in die Schule gegangen
- ins Ruhrgebiet gezogen
- dort aufs Gymnasium gegangen und Abitur gemacht
- dann für zwei Jahre zur Bundeswehr nach Oberbayern gegangen
- in Tübingen studiert

im Lauf *in the course of*

der Stamm *tribe*

zusammenwachsen *to grow together*

weiterleben *to continue to exist*

WISSEN SIE DAS?

Read this description of the German regions – above is some vocabulary to help you.

Regionale Unterschiede

Im Lauf der letzten tausend Jahre ist das deutsche Volk aus verschiedenen deutschen Stämmen wie den Franken, Sachsen, Schwaben und Bayern zusammengewachsen. Heute existieren diese alten Stämme natürlich nicht mehr, aber die Dialekte und Traditionen der Stämme leben in den Regionen weiter. Die Regionen Deutschlands sind jedoch nicht immer mit den Bundesländern identisch.

Each region in Germany has well-known characteristics as far as its people and culture are concerned. In the second extract of Herr Winck's story he demonstrates how the idea of regionalism manifests itself in everyday life. He recalls overhearing a conversation in an inn in Mannheim, where a few older men were talking about their youth. Listen to *Hörabschnitt 16* and decide whether the statements on page 125 are *richtig* or *falsch*, putting a cross in the appropriate box. Then answer the final question in English.

die Wirtschaft (-en) *inn*

die Hochsprache *(also called* Hochdeutsch) *standard German as opposed to dialect*

ein Gefühl vermitteln *to give a certain feeling*

die Regionalabtrennung (-en) *regional differences*

in zweiter Hinsicht *here: the fact that one is German comes second*

die Konkurrenz *competition*

	RICHTIG	FALSCH
1 Herr Winck was a student when he overheard the conversation.	❑	❑
2 The men in the inn were in their mid-sixties.	❑	❑
3 One of the men mentioned his travels to other countries.	❑	❑
4 He talked about his time in the army and his fellow conscripts from other German regions.	❑	❑
5 He perceived the group as being international.	❑	❑

6 How does Harald Winck define regionalism?

5

selbst *here: even*

der Schwabe akademischer Bildung *the Swabian with an academic education*

regional verwurzelt bleiben *to remain rooted in one's region*

mit dem Hintergedanken *with the thought at the back of one's mind*

Finally, Herr Winck comments on the characteristics of the Swabians as he sees them. First look at the vocabulary and listen to the whole of *Hörabschnitt 17* once. Then read through the phrases below: there are three alternative endings to each sentence. Listen to the extract again and choose the ending which matches what Herr Winck says.

1 „Das ist eine Eigenart eigentlich auch des Schwaben ..."
- **a** ohne akademische Bildung
- **b** mit akademischer Bildung
- **c** selbst akademischer Bildung

2 „... daß er ..."
- **a** stark regional verwurzelt ist
- **b** sehr stark regional verwurzelt bleibt
- **c** sehr stark regional verwurzelt ist

3 „Er ist ..."
- **a** sehr tolerant, sehr weltoffen
- **b** tolerant, weltoffen
- **c** nicht sehr tolerant, nicht sehr weltoffen

4 „... aber immer mit dem Hintergedanken: Bei mir zu Hause ist es ..."
- **a** gemütlich
- **b** schön
- **c** am schönsten

Lerneinheit 9 Der Rhein und die Elbe

Lerneinheit 9 introduces you to *The Rhein and other German rivers.*

By the end of *Lerneinheit 9*, you will have covered vocabulary to do with rivers and flooding, revised prepositions and practised the perfect tense.

STUDY CHART

Topic	Activity and resource	Key points
The Rhein and other German rivers	**1 Text**	picking out prepositions from a description of the Rhein
	2–3 Text	filling in appropriate prepositions
	4 Text	identifying words to do with rivers
	5 Text	working on a text about the river Elbe
	6–7 Text	reading an article about flooding

On page 127 there is a passage about one of Germany's greatest rivers, the Rhein. Read it once to check that you understand it, then go through it again, picking out all the prepositions that are used (twelve different ones in all). Label each preposition with the case it takes – the accusative, genitive or dative. Don't forget that some prepositions take either the accusative or the dative, according to whether movement or rest is involved.

Der Rhein ist einer der wichtigsten Wasserwege Europas und verbindet insgesamt sechs Länder. Er fließt durch die Schweiz, Deutschland und die Niederlande und entlang den Grenzen von Österreich, Liechtenstein und Frankreich. Der Rhein entspringt im Schweizer Kanton Graubünden, fließt dann durch den Bodensee und über den berühmten Rheinfall bei Schaffhausen nach Basel. Von dort fließt er über Straßburg, Karlsruhe, Mannheim und das Ruhrgebiet Richtung Norden, bis er bei Rotterdam in die Nordsee mündet.

Bis Ende des 19. Jahrhunderts war der 1 300 km lange Rhein für große Transportschiffe allerdings nur bis Ludwigshafen/Mannheim schiffbar. Heute aber ist der Rhein die größte Binnenwasserstraße Europas. Der Gütertransport ist von der Nordsee bis zum Mittelmeer und, über den Rhein-Main-Donau-Kanal, bis zum Schwarzen Meer möglich. Der Ausbau des Rheins hat in den letzten Jahren aber auch viele Flutkatastrophen ausgelöst, und es gibt oft Überschwemmungen am Niederrhein.

Der Rhein ist nicht nur wirtschaftlich, sondern auch historisch von großer Bedeutung. Viele Orte im Rheintal stammen aus der Römerzeit, und überall am Rhein stehen heute noch große Burgen, Schlösser und Kirchen, die von der wichtigen politischen und geschichtlichen Bedeutung des Rheins zeugen.

Das Hagen-Denkmal in Worms

Der Rhein steht auch im Mittelpunkt berühmter deutscher Sagen und Legenden, wie zum Beispiel des Nibelungenlieds. In Worms siedelten im 5. Jahrhundert die Burgunden. Nach der Nibelungensage, die um 1200 entstand, heiratete Siegfried die burgundische Königstocher Kriemhild. Hagen ermordete Siegfried und warf ihr Gold, den Nibelungenhort, in den Rhein.

verbinden *to link*
entspringen *to have its source*
fließen *to flow*
münden *to flow into*
schiffbar *navigable*
die Binnenwasserstraße (-n) *inland water way*
das Mittelmeer *Mediterranean Sea*
der Ausbau *development*
auslösen *to trigger off, produce*
die Überschwemmung (-en) *flood*
die Burg (-en) *fortress*
zeugen *to bear witness*
die Sage (-n) *story, legend*
siedeln *to settle*
ermorden *to murder*
werfen *to throw*
der Nibelungenhort (-e) *Nibelungen hoard, treasure*

Now complete the following sentences to practise using the appropriate prepositions.

1 ____________ der Schweiz ____________ in die Nordsee fließt der Rhein ____________ sechs Länder.

2 Von Schaffhausen fließt der Rhein ____________ der Grenze zwischen Deutschland und der Schweiz.

3 Nördlich von Basel fließt der Rhein ungefähr 170 km ____________ der Grenze zu Frankreich.

4 Danach fließt er ______________ das Bundesland Rheinland-Pfalz.

5 ______________ den Rhein-Main-Donau-Kanal ist die Schiffahrt bis zum Schwarzen Meer möglich.

6 Der Mittelrhein ist ______________ 1900 schiffbar.

7 Heute fahren Frachtschiffe bis ______________ Mittelmeer.

8 Wie die Elbe mündet der Rhein ______________ die Nordsee.

9 ______________ den Handel ist der Rhein sehr wichtig.

10 Der Rhein fließt ______________ Rotterdam in die Nordsee.

3 In this activity you will practise using the correct case after prepositions. Complete the following sentences.

1 Von ______________ Rheinquelle in der Schweiz bis zu ______________ Mündung sind es mehr als 1 000 km.

2 Der Rhein fließt zwischen Bregenz und St. Gallen durch ______________ Bodensee.

3 Seit 1900 ist der Fluß zwischen ______________ Stadt Basel in der Schweiz und ______________ deutschen Stadt Mannheim schiffbar.

4 Der Rhein fließt entlang ______________ französischen Grenze.

5 Nach ______________ Ruhrgebiet fließt der Rhein langsamer.

6 Für ______________ Industrie ist der Rhein eine wichtige Verkehrsader.

7 Die Sage der Nibelungen stammt aus ______________ 13. Jahrhundert.

8 Hagen hat das Rheingold bei Worms in ______________ Fluß geworfen.

9 Auf ______________ Niederrhein herrscht reger Schiffsverkehr.

10 Vor Rotterdam fließt der Rhein durch ______________ Landschaft, die sehr flach ist.

4 Read through the passage in Activity 1 again and list all the words that relate to rivers. There are eleven of them.

5 Here is a description of another great German river, the Elbe. A number of words have been omitted from the text, all of which are to do with rivers. Using the list of words from Activity 4, fill in the gaps.

Die Elbe ist der wichtigste ____________ in Norddeutschland. Sie ____________ nördlich von Hamburg in die Nordsee, aber ihre Quelle liegt weit im Süden. Dieser Fluß ____________ in den Bergen der Tschechischen Republik und von dort ____________ er in einer nordwestlichen Richtung durch Deutschland. Die Elbe ist auf ihrer ganzen Länge in Deutschland ____________ . Dann und wann, im Frühling oder im Winter, gibt es in der Nähe von Hamburg ____________ .

Read this newspaper article about flooding and answer the questions overleaf in English.

Die nächste Flutwelle kommt bestimmt

Hamburg (dpa/AP)

Die Menschen in den von Hochwasser und Überschwemmungen betroffenen Regionen Deutschlands können noch nicht aufatmen. Nach neuen heftigen Regenfällen und Schneetreiben hat sich die Lage in Hessen, Rheinland-Pfalz, Baden-Württemberg und Niedersachsen wieder verschärft. Auch in Nordrhein-Westfalen und Bayern hieß es weiter: „Land unter".

Die Region Göttingen erlebt derzeit das schlimmste Hochwasser seit fast 50 Jahren: Die Weser erreichte am späten Dienstagabend den bisherigen Höchststand von 6,21 Metern.

Auch der Rhein stieg nach starken Regenfällen wieder. Aus Köln wird ein bisheriger Höchststand von 8,66 Metern gemeldet. Während einige Vororte bereits unter Wasser stehen, blieb die Altstadt von Köln noch verschont. Doch das Hochwasserzentrum in Mainz warnt bereits vor einer verheerenden Rhein-Flut. Zum Wochenende könnten die Pegelstände vom Dezember 1993 erreicht oder überschritten werden. Ähnlich an der Mosel: Starke Regenfälle haben eine neue Flutwelle ausgelöst; die Höchstwerte von Montag werden heute wohl überschritten. Gut möglich, daß auch hier der Höchststand vom Dezember '93 erreicht wird.

betroffen *struck*	**der Höchststand (¨)** *highest point*	**der Pegelstand (¨e)** *marker level*
aufatmen *breathe again or breathe freely*	**stieg** (*from* steigen) *rose*	**erreichen** *to reach*
sich verschärft *worsened*	**wird … gemeldet** *is announced*	**überschritten** (*from* überschreiten) *exceeded*
hieß es *it was, the situation was*	**verschont** *spared*	**ähnlich** *similar(ly)*
erleben *to experience*	**verheerend** *disastrous*	

1 What does the article say about people living in the affected areas?
2 What caused the floods?
3 How many *Länder* are affected?
4 What is happening in the Göttingen area?
5 Which river is flooding there?
6 Which parts of Köln are flooded and which are not?
7 What is forecast by the Mainz authorities?
8 What could happen at the weekend?
9 What has caused the problem on the Mosel?

Here are some sentences about flooding. Complete them with the past participles of the verbs given below.

1 Göttingen hat das schlimmste Hochwasser seit Jahren ______________ .

2 Am Donnerstagabend hat das Wasser einen Stand von 6,21 Metern ______________ .

3 Auch der Rhein ist wieder ______________ .

4 Die Altstadt von Köln ist verschont ______________ .

5 Das Hochwasserzentrum von Mainz hat vor einer Rhein-Flut ______________ .

steigen erreichen warnen bleiben erleben

By the end of *Teil 3* you should

- ○ have learned the names of a number of countries and certain geographical terms (*Lerneinheit 7*, Activity 6; *Lerneinheit 9*, Activity 1)

Seiten 122; 126

- ○ have improved your ability to describe people's natures (*Lerneinheit 8*, Activity 5)

Seite 125

- ○ have revised the perfect tense (*Lerneinheit 8*, Activity 3; *Lerneinheit 9*, Activity 7)

Seiten 124; 130

- ○ have revised prepositions and cases (*Lerneinheit 9*, Activities 1–3)

Seiten 126–128

Teil 4

Wiederholung

Teil 4 will help you to revise what you have covered so far in *Thema 2*. *Lerneinheit 10, Sie über sich*, looks across German society and focuses on the concept of nationality, and there is a trip to the wine festival in Iggelbach. *Lerneinheit 11, Können Sie das beschreiben?*, looks back at parties and small talk, the lonely hearts agency, people's appearance and, finally, the idea of *Heimat*. By the end of *Teil 4*, you should have revised the perfect tense, summary writing, the use of the genitive case and the way in which you describe nationalities.

Lerneinheit 10 Sie über sich

Lerneinheit 10 has two topics, *Describing people's origins and circumstances* and *The Weinkerwe in Iggelbach.*

STUDY CHART

Topic	Activity and resource	Key points
Describing people's origins and circumstances	1 *Übungskassette*	writing a summary of the *Hörabschnitt*
	2 Text	revising the perfect tense
	3 Text	revising past participles
	4 Text	writing a summary of a story
	5 Text	checking you've understood an article about poverty
	6 Text	revising the genitive case
	7 Text	revising nationalities and adjectival endings
The *Weinkerwe* in Iggelbach	8 Text	reading comprehension
	9 Text	retelling a story and revising the perfect tense

Listen to *Hörabschnitt 18* two or three times and make notes of the main points it covers – some key words are given on page 133 to help you. Then write a summary of what Frau Schmidt says, about 50 words long, covering the points you have just noted and including the verbs given on page 133. You might find it helpful to look back at *Thema 2, Lerneinheit 1* when doing this activity and Activities 2–3.

- Ihr Vater – Herkunft
- Ihre Mutter – Herkunft und Kindheit
- Ihre Eltern – Heirat: Wann?
- Frau Schmidt – Schule; ihr Mann; Heirat

kennenlernen gehen stammen aufwachsen heiraten

In the following account a young Romanian immigrant explains why he feels at home in Germany now.

There are a number of gaps in the text. Choose suitable verbs from those listed below to fill them. Put the verbs into the perfect tense and use the correct auxiliary verb (*haben* or *sein*). Each verb is used only once.

sich heimisch fühlen *to feel at home*

die Hotelfachschule (-n) *hotel management college*

kontaktfreudig *sociable*

es erinnert mich *it reminds me*

Ich fühle mich hier sehr heimisch

Ich bin 31 Jahre alt und komme aus Rumänien. In meiner Heimat __________ ich Abitur __________ , dann __________ ich zum Militär __________ . Danach __________ ich ins Ausland __________ , zunächst nach Griechenland. Da __________ ich eine Hotelfachschule __________ und jetzt bin ich Hotelfachmann.

Nach zwei Jahren __________ ich nach Deutschland __________ , und hier arbeite ich jetzt als Hotelkaufmann.

Ja, mit den Menschen habe ich eigentlich keine Probleme, so gut wie keine Schwierigkeiten. Ich __________ viele Deutsche __________ . Die meisten sind sehr kontaktfreudig und versuchten immer wieder zu helfen, wo etwas zu helfen war.

Also, ich fühle mich hier sehr heimisch. Es ist vieles so wie in meiner Heimatstadt. Es erinnert mich vieles an meine Heimat, die Gebäude, die Straßen, vieles. Ich fühle mich eben ziemlich wie zu Hause. Auch das Klima und die Vegetation und alles. Und die Menschen auch. Deshalb möchte ich auch hier bleiben, ich bleibe in Deutschland, ich gehe nie wieder nach Rumänien.

kennenlernen kommen machen gehen gehen besuchen

3

These sentences sum up the account you have just read. Complete them, inserting the appropriate past participle at the end of each sentence.

1 Er ist in Rumänien __________ .

2 In Rumänien ist er zur Schule __________ .

3 Er hat dort den Militärdienst ______________ .

4 Danach hat er Rumänien ______________ .

5 Er ist nach Griechenland ______________ .

6 Dort hat er eine Ausbildung in einer Hotelfachschule ______________ .

7 Er ist nach Deutschland ______________ .

8 Mit den Menschen hat er keine Probleme ______________ .

9 Er hat die Deutschen sehr kontaktfreudig ______________ .

10 Deutschland hat ihn an seine Heimat ______________ .

How would you retell this young Romanian's story to a friend? Write a short summary of about 60 words in English.

Read this article and then answer the questions below in German.

das dauert noch lange *that will take some time*

von staatlicher Hilfe leben *to be dependent on state benefits*

aufgezogen *(from* aufziehen*)* *brought up*

der Zwilling (-e) *twin*

bis vor kurzem *until recently*

durfte … nicht *was not allowed to*

der Aushilfsjob *temporary job*

„Ich lebe am Rand der Gesellschaft"

Irgendwann, wenn Tom groß ist, möchte er viel Geld verdienen. Dann kauft er einen Computer und einen Videorecorder. Und er fährt ins Disneyland nach Paris. Aber das dauert noch lange.

Neulich war Fasching in der Schule, aber Tom wollte nicht hingehen. Das schönste Kostüm sollte einen Preis bekommen, und Tom dachte, „schön" bedeutet „teuer".

Er ist sieben Jahre alt und eines von vier Geschwistern. Nina Schmitz, die Mutter, lebt seit Toms Geburt von staatlicher Hilfe. Ihre älteren Kinder Tom und Gianni hat sie allein aufgezogen. Der Vater der Zwillinge Karim und Hany ist Ägypter und durfte bis vor kurzem nicht in Deutschland arbeiten. Jetzt hat er für zwei Wochen einen Aushilfsjob. „Ich lebe," sagt die 35jährige, „am Rand der Gesellschaft."

Der Rand der Gesellschaft ist eine 3-Zimmer-Wohnung. Dort wohnen sie seit einem Jahr zu sechst.

1 Warum verdient Tom noch kein Geld?
2 Warum will er nach Paris fahren?
3 Wie viele Geschwister hat er?
4 Seit wann lebt seine Mutter von staatlicher Hilfe?
5 Hat Frau Schmitz alle ihre Kinder alleine aufgezogen?
6 Warum durfte der Vater der Zwillinge in Deutschland nicht arbeiten?

die Dauer *extent*

der Aufenthalt (-e) *stay*

In this activity you will revise the genitive case. Fill in the gaps in each of the sentences by inserting the correct word in the genitive case. You may want to refer to the explanation of the genitive in *Thema 2, Lerneinheit 2.*

Der rumänische Kaufmann

1. Er hat die ersten Jahre ______ Lebens in Rumänien verbracht.
2. Die Dauer ______ Aufenthalts in Griechenland war zwei Jahre.
3. Die meisten ______ Kollegen waren sehr kontaktfreudig.

Tom Schmitz

4. Der Mann ______ Mutter stammt aus Ägypten.
5. Der Preis ______ Kostüms war sehr hoch für die Familie.
6. Der Traum ______ Jungen ist, einen Computer zu kaufen.

This activity will help you to revise adjectives of nationality and adjectival endings. Complete these sentences, using an appropriate adjective of nationality and choosing a suitable noun from the selection given overleaf. You may need to use a dictionary to do this activity. Refer to *Thema 2, Lerneinheit 5,* if you need to check adjectival endings. The first sentence has been completed to help you.

1. Wodka *ist* *ein* *russisches* *Getränk* .
2. Der Parthenon ______ ______ ______ ______ .
3. Edamer ______ ______ ______ ______ .
4. Der Neckar ______ ______ ______ ______ .
5. Paella ______ ______ ______ ______ .
6. Verdi ______ ______ ______ ______ .
7. Baseball ______ ______ ______ ______ .
8. Ein Ferrari ______ ______ ______ ______ .

9 Der Dudelsack ______________ ______________ ______________

______________ .

10 Cricket ______________ ______________ ______________ ______________ .

11 Döner Kebab ______________ ______________ ______________

______________ .

der Fluß der Käse die Spezialität der Sport der Wagen der Komponist

die Spezialität das Instrument der Sport das Getränk das Gebäude

8 The next two activities are based on the programme of the village wine festival in Iggelbach, Rheinland-Pfalz. The events in the *Weinkerwe* programme have been mixed up and written down out of their chronological order. Put the programme back into the right order.

die Kerwe *fair, local festival*

der Umzug (¨-e) *procession*

hinunterziehen *to go down*

die Rede (-n) *speech*

feiern *to celebrate*

das Festzelt (-e) *celebration tent*

die Verlosung eines Schweins *raffle with a pig as first prize*

der Frühschoppen *morning/lunch-time drink*

VIEL SPAß AUF DER IGGELBACHER WEINKERWE!

a Der Kerwe-Umzug beginnt am Sonntag um 14 Uhr auf dem Zimmerplatz und zieht die Dorfstraße hinunter bis zum Kerweplatz. Dort hören alle die Kerwerede.

b Am Wochenende feiert das pfälzische Dorf Iggelbach seine Weinkerwe. Die Kerwe beginnt am Freitagabend.

c Am Samstag feiern die Leute ab 14 Uhr im Festzelt, und ab 20 Uhr spielen die „Pfälzer Musikanten".

d Zur Eröffnung singen die Gesangsvereine von Elmstein und Iggelbach Weinlieder.

e Höhepunkt ist die Verlosung eines Schweins am Sonntagnachmittag.

f Am Dienstag endet die Iggelbacher Kerwe mit einem Heringsessen.

g Der traditionelle Montagsfrühschoppen fängt dieses Jahr um 10 Uhr an.

h Der Bürgermeister eröffnet das Fest und lädt alle zur Weinprobe ein.

9

Imagine you are a tourist who has been to this year's *Weinkerwe* in Iggelbach. You tell a German-speaking friend about it afterwards. Using the information from the *Lösung* to Activity 8, tell your story in the perfect tense. Here is the first sentence:

Am Wochenende hat das pfälzische Dorf Iggelbach seine Weinkerwe gefeiert …

Lerneinheit 11 Können Sie das beschreiben?

Lerneinheit 11 contains five revision topics: *Party talk*, *Describing the ideal partner*, *Describing clothes*, *Defining Heimat*, and *Word Searches*.

STUDY CHART

Topic	Activity and resource	Key points
Party talk	**1 Text**	revising the use of *du* and *Sie*
	2 Text	checking you've understood an account of the difficulties in using *du* and *Sie*
	3 Text	revising personal pronouns
Describing the ideal partner	**4 Text**	drafting lonely hearts adverts
Describing clothes	**5 Text**	writing descriptions of some German sportsmen's taste in clothes
	6 Text	writing descriptions of people's appearances
Defining *Heimat*	**7 Text**	checking you've understood a dialogue
	8 Text	writing a short life history
	9 Text	revising the definite article and possessive adjectives
Word searches	**10–11 Text**	doing word searches

1

Overleaf there is a passage about the uncertainties of using the familiar form *du* or the formal *Sie* in conversation. First, read the passage, then fill in the missing personal pronouns from the selection given overleaf. Before doing this and Activity 3, you may like to refer to *Thema 2*, *Lerneinheit 4*, where personal pronouns are outlined.

So einer wie ich, ich meine: In meinem Alter, ist heute verunsichert. Ein Beispiel: Nachbarn geben eine große Party. Als meine Frau und ich geklingelt haben, öffnet uns die Hausfrau. „Schön, daß ________ kommt," sagt sie. Und ich denke: „Duzen wir uns denn?" Ich weiß es nicht genau, aber eins weiß ich: Wenn ich jetzt sage: „Wir haben ________ diese Blumen mitgebracht," dann klingt das fast frostig. Man sagt heute besser: „Wir haben ________ diese Blumen mitgebracht." Und nach ein paar Gläsern Wein sagen dann sowieso alle „ ________ ". Das ist heute so.

Nur der ältere Herr mit Krawatte sagt den ganzen Abend ganz klar „ ________ " zu allen Gästen und fühlt sich dabei auch wohl.

Die dritte Möglichkeit ist, immer eine ganze Gruppe gleichzeitig anzusprechen, und das universale „ ________ " zu verwenden. Damit macht man bestimmt nichts falsch!

Sie ihr du Ihnen euch

verunsichert *insecure, uncertain*
klingeln *to ring (bell)*
klingen *to sound*
gleichzeitig *simultaneously*
jemanden ansprechen *to address someone*
damit macht man bestimmt nichts falsch *that way you can't go wrong*

2 Now answer the following questions in English.

1 What does this party-goer feel uncertain about?
2 How does he decide to reply to the hostess' welcome?
3 What is likely to happen anyway after a few glasses of wine?
4 Which mode of address does the older gentleman use, formal or informal?
5 What is the third option for our party-goer?

Personal pronouns have been omitted from the following conversations. The first is between people who are meeting for the first time, the second between a mother, her son and his partner. Fill the gaps by inserting the appropriate pronouns. Before doing this activity you may like to refer to *Lerneinheit 4*.

1 – Guten Tag Frau Bauer. Darf ich ________ meinen Mann vorstellen?

– Guten Tag Herr Bowes. Freut mich, ________ kennenzulernen. Seit wann sind ________ in Marburg?

– Ich bin schon eine Woche hier.

– Und gefällt ________ unsere Stadt?

– Ja, sehr.

– Also mein Mann und ich, wir möchten _____________ zu uns einladen. Könnten _____________ morgen abend zu uns kommen?

– Ja. Danke sehr. Um wieviel Uhr?

die Klapperkiste (-n) *old banger*

2 Mutter Da seid _____________ endlich!

Axel Hast _____________ lange warten müssen?

Mutter Ja. Warum seid _____________ so spät?

Axel Naja. Das Auto, _____________ weißt wie es ist.

Mutter Ach. Axel, wie oft habe ich _____________ gesagt, daß _____________ diese alte Klapperkiste verkaufen sollst!

Axel Ja. Ich weiß schon. Also, wie geht's _____________ ?

Mutter Gut danke. Und _____________ beiden?

Britta Einigermaßen. Sag mal, ist deine Enkelin bei _____________ ?

Mutter Ja. Seit gestern. Sie freut sich sehr auf euren Besuch. Auf _____________ besonders, Britta. Aber komm mal 'rein.

4

Imagine that you work at a dating agency and are advising someone on how to write a lonely hearts advert. Help two clients to describe their ideal partner and design their own adverts, using the words given overleaf. Remember that when using adjectives, you need to add the appropriate endings, as underlined in the examples below.

Do you remember the phrases you used in *Thema 2, Lerneinheit 5*, such as *kulturelle Interessen*; *spät. Ehe möglich/nicht ausgeschlossen*; *für gemeinsame Zukunft*? Try to reuse some of them here.

Witwe, Mitte 50, möchte charmant<u>en</u>, liebenswert<u>en</u> Partner kennenlernen. Bildzuschriften bitte unter …

Mann, Ende 30, gutaussehend, sucht dynamisch<u>e</u>, gebildet<u>e</u> Frau für gemeinsam<u>e</u> Unternehmungen. Zuschriften unter Chiffre …

charmant	Akademiker	sucht	aufgeschlossen	Lebensgefährte
begeisterungsfähig	Akademikerin	freut sich auf	begeisterungsfähig	Lebensgefährtin
dynamisch	Mann	möchte kennenlernen	gebildet	Partner
gebildet	Frau		gutaussehend	Partnerin
humorvoll	Lehrer		humorvoll	
	Lehrerin		intelligent	
	Sekretärin		liebenswert	
	Unternehmer		tolerant	
	Witwer		zuverlässig	
	Witwe			

5

How do Germany's top sportsmen dress? Boris Becker, Henry Maske, Matthias Sammer and Michael Schuhmacher have told the German weekly magazine *Stern*. Look at the short description of Boris Becker's preferred clothing. Use the verbs and various clues given below for the three others, and write similar texts about them in German. Refer to *Lerneinheit 5* if you are uncertain about how you might approach this activity or need some more vocabulary.

modebewußt *fashion conscious*

Die Klasse der Meister Wie kleiden sich Deutschlands Top-Sportler?

Boris Becker

Der Wimbledon-Sieger ist sehr modebewußt. Er liebt Kleidung von internationalen Designern. Am liebsten trägt er italienische Mode, weite weiße Hemden und bequeme dunkle Hosen. Aber sein Lieblingsstück ist seine alte braune Lederjacke.

gerne tragen   lieben   gerne haben   am liebsten tragen   mögen

1 **Henry Maske**, der Gentleman-Boxer
- toll (Klamotten)
- sportlich-elegant (Kleidung)
- Hosenträger und Mützen

2 **Matthias Sammer**, Fußballspieler
- bequem (Jeans) und bunt (T-Shirt)
- auch klassisch (das Outfit)

3 **Michael Schuhmacher**, Formel-1-Weltmeister
- sein Renn-Overall (m)
- auch leger (Kleidung)
- weiß, fein (Hemden)

6

Now imagine that you have to describe the two following people who are to be met at the airport. Write two faxes in German about them which would enable someone to recognise them.

1. **Angela Winter** is in her mid 30s and is tall. Has long black hair and wears glasses. Wearing a blue suit, a brightly coloured scarf and a raincoat.
2. **Gerhard Reuter** has short grey hair and a beard. Early 50s. Doesn't wear glasses. Wearing a white suit.

7

Here is an interview in which a German talks about his lack of a sense of *Heimat*. Read through it, then look at the statements overleaf, which paraphrase what he says, and put them back into the right order.

der Reisepaß (¨-) *passport*

auf keinen Fall *here: but never, on no account*

der Bezirk (-e) *here: district in east Berlin*

die waren uns fremd *they were strange to us, they meant nothing to us*

ist ... geflüchtet *fled*

Heimweh haben *to feel homesick*

verbarrikadiert *barricaded, blocked off*

Interviewer Wo sind Sie geboren?

Heinz *Berlin, genauer gesagt: Berlin-Charlottenburg. So steht es in meinem Reisepaß.*

Interviewer Sie sind also Berliner?

Heinz *Richtig.*

Interviewer Berlin ist also Ihre Heimatstadt?

Heinz *Geburtsstadt, nicht Heimatstadt. Nein, auf keinen Fall Heimat.*

Interviewer Und warum?

Heinz *Ich bin in Berlin geboren und aufgewachsen, bin dort zur Schule gegangen bis zum Abitur. Aber das ist alles sehr lange her.*

Interviewer War das in Ostberlin oder in Westberlin?

Heinz *Das war damals Ostberlin. Ich bin aufgewachsen im Bezirk Friedrichshain, nicht weit vom Alexanderplatz.*

Interviewer Wie war das damals?

Heinz *Berlin war damals eine Ruine. Da konnte ich keine Heimatgefühle haben. Wir haben als Kinder in den Ruinen gespielt. Dann standen da neue Häuser, aber die waren uns fremd. Auch das war nicht Heimat.*

Interviewer Und was haben Sie dann gemacht?

Heinz *Dann ist meine Familie in den Westen geflüchtet. Dann kamen das Studium und die Arbeit im Ausland. Ich habe nicht mehr an Berlin gedacht. Ich hatte kein Heimweh nach Berlin, nach dem Haus, wo ich gewohnt habe, keine Heimatgefühle.*

Interviewer Sind Sie nochmal dort gewesen?

Heinz *Einmal, nach 40 Jahren, war ich wieder dort. Ich wollte unsere Straße wiedersehen, die Bäckerei, den Gemüseladen an der Ecke und das Milchgeschäft, naja, die Welt von damals eben.*

Interviewer Und wie war das?

Heinz *Die Straße war verbarrikadiert. Die Menschen waren fremd und gar nicht freundlich. Ich bin nie wieder dorthin gefahren.*

Interviewer Und heute?

Heinz *Ich denke nicht an Berlin, wenn ich an „Heimat" denke. Heimat, das ist wohl doch was anderes.*

a Ich bin in der Nähe vom Alexanderplatz aufgewachsen.
b Ich wollte die Welt meiner Kindheit wiedersehen.
c Berlin-Charlottenburg ist mein Geburtsort, aber nicht meine Heimat.
d Das war das letzte Mal, daß ich dorthin gefahren bin.
e Als Kinder haben wir in den kaputten Häusern gespielt.
f Ich habe studiert und im Ausland gearbeitet.
g Später ist meine Familie in den Westen gegangen.
h Berlin ist nur meine Geburtsstadt.
i Ich habe in Berlin mein Abitur gemacht.

Now use the information given in the interview and statements in Activity 7 to write a short life history in German of Heinz. Write about 70 words and use the headings below to structure your account.

- Geburt
- Schule
- Berlin
- Flucht
- Studienzeit
- Besuch in Berlin
- seine Wünsche
- seine Gefühle über Berlin

Fill in the gaps in this passage about Heinz using the correct German forms for 'his' and 'the'.

In ______________ Reisepaß steht, daß er in Berlin geboren wurde. Zwar hat er ______________ Kindheit dort verbracht und hat dort auch ______________ Gymnasium besucht, aber er betrachtet Berlin nicht als ______________ Heimat. In ______________ großen Ruine die Berlin damals war, waren ihm sogar ______________ neuen Häuser fremd. Mit ______________ Eltern hat er ______________ Stadt verlassen und hat ein neues Leben in ______________ Westen angefangen.

10

Hidden in this word search puzzle are twelve German words for places and sights you might be looking for in a German town. You need to look for them up and down, from right to left and vice versa, and diagonally. List the words and their meanings when you have found them.

S	X	T	S	O	P	G	T	A	C
E	T	Q	F	R	J	R	K	F	Z
P	R	A	T	H	A	U	S	O	T
T	I	S	D	U	X	B	L	H	A
K	K	H	P	T	A	D	V	N	L
I	G	R	L	U	P	G	M	H	P
R	Y	F	A	R	O	L	D	A	K
C	W	M	T	M	M	E	A	B	R
H	B	O	Z	H	Z	B	T	N	A
E	W	D	C	N	E	D	A	L	P

11

To help you to revise the words needed to describe people's clothes, look for the fourteen words in this word search puzzle. You need to work up and down, from left to right and vice versa, and diagonally. List the words and their meanings when you have found them.

S	V	A	E	I	F	P	O	N	K
T	H	P	J	Q	L	P	C	S	H
R	H	U	T	U	A	L	R	U	G
U	Z	L	H	V	H	O	H	K	D
M	K	L	R	C	C	C	O	A	M
P	L	I	O	W	S	B	S	R	E
F	F	Y	C	X	T	D	E	O	H
J	A	C	K	E	Z	P	N	N	H
M	N	D	V	L	E	T	N	A	M
B	A	D	E	A	N	Z	U	G	H

Bilder aus Tübingen ...

Fachwerkhäuser in Tübingen mit dem Neptunbrunnen, der 1617 gebaut worden ist.

Tübinger Studenten vor der alten Aula, die bis 1845 das Hauptgebäude der Universität war.

… und Leipzig

Das Romanushaus, das von 1701 bis 1704 erbaut wurde, steht an der Ecke der Katherinenstraße. Franz Conrad Romanus (1671–1746) hat die Straßenlaterne in Leipzig eingeführt und hat sein eigenes Geld gedruckt, womit er das Romanushaus bezahlen wollte.

Die Grimmaische Straße: Hier hörte Bettina Thomas zum ersten Mal spielen!

Zum Coffe Baum: Bereits 1711 wurde hier „Coffee“ serviert. Goethe, Lessing, Liszt, Wagner und Robert Schumann haben alle als Studenten den „Coffe Baum“ besucht

Das Völkerschlachtdenkmal erinnert an die Schlacht von Leipzig (1813) bei der Napoleon Bonaparte von Armeen aus Österreich, Preußen, Rußland und Schweden besiegt wurde.

Lösungen Thema 1

Lerneinheit 1

1 Here are the answers you should have given.

2 Das Rathaus steht am Marktplatz.
3 *Either:* Die Ammer fließt im Norden der Stadt. *or:* Der Neckar fließt im Süden der Stadt. **4** Das Schloß ist in der Altstadt. **5** Es gibt einen Markt montags, mittwochs und freitags. **6** Die reichen Bürger wohnten früher in den Fachwerkhäusern.

2 Here are the answers, together with extracts from the video, which should have given you the clues you needed.

1. Dr. Setzler gave the number of inhabitants in Tübingen as 80,000. The latest figure available in 1996 was 85,000. *„Sehen Sie, wir haben 80 000 Einwohner ...“*
2. The town was described as being 1,500 years old. (commentary) *„Die Stadt Tübingen ist 1 500 Jahre alt.“*
3. The old university is on top of the hill in Tübingen. (commentary) *„... Oben am Berg, neben der Universität ...“*
4. The manual workers used to live down by the river Ammer. (commentary) *„Die Arbeiter der Stadt bauten ihre Häuser unten an der Ammer.“*
5. Dr. Setzler said that he came to Tübingen originally as a student. *„... ich bin als Student hierher gekommen.“*

3 Quotations from the video have been provided, which should have given you a clue about the answers.

	RICHTIG	FALSCH
1 *„... ich bin nicht hier geboren, ich bin als Student hierher gekommen.“*	❑	☒
2 *„Um 1845 war die Altstadt für die Universität zu klein geworden.“*	☒	❑
3 *„Das neue Universitätszentrum wurde am Stadtrand gebaut.“*	❑	☒
4 *„... 15 000 etwa leben in der Stadt ...“*	❑	☒
5 *„... 10 000 pendeln jeden Tag ein ...“*	❑	☒
6 *„... Hochhäuser und moderne Wohnsiedlungen, Neubaugebiete ...“*	☒	❑
7 *„... eine ruhige, idyllische Stadt mit Kirchen, gemütlichen Ecken und stillen Plätzchen.“*	☒	❑

4 Here are the answers, together with extracts from the tourist brochure, which should have given you the clues you needed.

1. Tübingen had town walls and a market place by the eleventh century. *„Schon im 11. Jahrhundert war Tübingen eine bedeutende Stadt mit Marktplatz and Stadtmauer.“*
2. In Tübingen you can find a theatre, art centre, museums, galleries, concert halls and cinemas. *„Das Landestheater Tübingen und*

die Tübinger Kunsthalle … zahlreiche Museen, Galerien, Konzerthallen und Kinos …"

3 The university is the main employer in Tübingen. *„Die meisten Einwohner Tübingens arbeiten für die Universität."*

4 Tourism is an important industry in Tübingen. *„Auch der Tourismus ist schon seit langem sehr wichtig für die Stadt."*

5 Tübingen liegt in Südwestdeutschland **am** Neckar. Die Stadt ist 1 500 Jahre alt und wurde von den Alemannen gegründet. Tübingen ist eine schöne, **alte** Stadt **mit** einer Universität. Sie hat viele kleine, **enge** Gassen und schöne Fachwerkhäuser. **Im** Jahr 1477, als die Stadt 3 000 Einwohner hatte, wurde die Universität gegründet. Das alte Universitätsgebäude befindet sich in der **Stadtmitte.** Schon im **19. Jahrhundert** war die Altstadt zu klein für die Universität und man hat ein **neues** Universitätszentrum am **Stadtrand** gebaut. Tübingen ist ein kulturelles Zentrum **mit** Theatern, Museen und Galerien.

Die Stadt hat wenig Industrie, aber auch wenig **Arbeitslosigkeit**: Die meisten Einwohner arbeiten für die Universität und ein **Drittel** aller Einwohner sind **Studenten**. Tourismus ist auch eine wichtige Industrie.

Die Stadt hat aber auch einige **Probleme**. Die Verkehrsprobleme sind besonders schlimm: Es gibt zu viele **Autos** und zu wenig **Parkplätze**.

6 **1** Er (*subject*) sucht das Schloß (*object*).
2 Das Hotel Hospiz (*object*) sucht er (*subject*).
3 Am Rande der Stadt gibt es (*subject*) viele Hochhäuser (*object*). **4** Ich (*subject*) möchte etwas (*object*) essen. **5** Den Bahnhof (*object*) suchen Sie? (*subject*) **6** Oben auf dem Berg gibt es (*subject*) ein Schloß (*object*).

7 There are a number of possible questions that you could have asked. Here are some suggestions.

1 Ich möchte etwas essen. Entschuldigen Sie. Gibt es ein Restaurant hier in der Nähe?/Ich suche ein Restaurant.

2 Ich habe Kopfweh und hätte gern ein Aspirin. Entschuldigung. Ich bin hier fremd. Wo gibt es hier eine Apotheke, bitte?

3 Ich möchte einige Bücher kaufen. Entschuldigen Sie. Können Sie mir helfen? Ich suche eine Buchhandlung./Gibt es hier eine Buchhandlung in der Nähe?

4 Ich muß Briefmarken kaufen. Ist hier in der Nähe eine Post?/Gibt es hier eine Post, bitte?/Ich suche die Post.

5 Ich möchte Geld umtauschen. Wo gibt es hier eine Bank?/Ich suche die Bank.

6 Ich möchte parken. Ich suche ein Parkhaus./Gibt es hier ein Parkhaus, bitte?

7 Ich interessiere mich für moderne Kunst. Gibt es hier in der Nähe eine Galerie?/Ich suche die Galerie.

8 Ich fahre mit dem Zug nach Mannheim. Ich suche den Bahnhof.

8 Here is one possible text, with a few variations in brackets.

Tübingen liegt in Süddeutschland und ist eine kleine Universitätsstadt. Tübingen hat ungefähr 85 000 Einwohner. Die Stadt ist 1 500 Jahre alt. Die Universität ist über 500 Jahre alt. Die reichen Leute wohnten früher oben am Berg; die Arbeiter wohnten unten an der Ammer. Ein Drittel der Einwohner sind Studenten. Das neue Universitätszentrum ist am Stadtrand (befindet sich am Stadtrand). Tübingen hat wenig Industrie. In Tübingen gibt es auch viel Verkehr (viele Autos, moderne Wohnsiedlungen, Neubaugebiete, gemütliche oder idyllische Viertel).

Lerneinheit 2

1 Here are the answers, together with extracts from the captions, which should have given you the clues you needed.

1 The Altes Rathaus is in the Marktplatz. *„… steht am Marktplatz."*

2 The Altes Rathaus is used as a museum nowadays. *„Heute dient das Alte Rathaus als Museum …"*

3 The Neue Gewandhaus is the headquarters of the Gewandhaus-Orchester. *„Hier spielt das … Gewandhaus-Orchester."*

4 Before the *Wende*, in 1989, people met at the Nikolaikirche every Monday to pray for peace. *„Hier fanden die Friedensgebete* *und, im Jahre 1989, die Friedensdemonstrationen statt.“*

5 The Neues Rathaus has the highest town hall tower in Germany. *„... und hat den höchsten Rathausturm Deutschlands.“*

2 Here are the answers, with quotations from the *Hörabschnitt*, which should have given you the clues you needed.

1 The Nikolaikirche is described as the biggest and oldest church in Leipzig. *„Die Nicholaikirche ist die größte und älteste Kirche der Stadt.“*

2 It was the point of departure for the demonstrations. *„Im Herbst 1989 war diese Kirche der Ausgangspunkt der großen Montagsdemonstrationen.“*

3 The demonstrations took place on Mondays.

4 The demonstrations took place in the autumn.

5 In the 19th century the Gewandhaus was famous for its orchestra. *„Das Gewandhaus-Orchester war schon im 19. Jahrhundert sehr berühmt.“*

6 Luther preached in the Thomaskirche and brought the Reformation to Sachsen. *„1539 war Martin Luther hier in dieser Kirche. Damit kam die Reformation nach Sachsen.“*

7 Bach died in Leipzig. *„Bach ... ist hier gestorben.“*

8 Bach was director of the Thomanerchor. *„Er war ... Leiter des Thomanerchors.“*

9 The old town hall was built in the market place. *„... am Alten Rathaus, das 1556 am Marktplatz errichtet wurde.“*

3

1 Die Nikolaikirche wurde **im 12. Jahrhundert** gebaut.

2 Die Revolution war im Jahre **1989**.

3 Das Neue Gewandhaus wurde **1981** eröffnet.

4 Das Gewandhaus-Orchester war schon **im 19. Jahrhundert** berühmt.

5 Luther hat **1539** in der Thomaskirche gepredigt.

6 Der Thomanerchor stammt aus **dem 13. Jahrhundert**.

7 Das Alte Rathaus wurde **1556** errichtet.

5 Quotations from the original text have been provided, which should have given you a clue to the answers.

		RICHTIG	FALSCH
1	*„Leipzig hat 1165 die Stadtrechte bekommen ...“*	❑	☒
2	*„Die Stadt entstand am Kreuzpunkt von zwei großen Handelsstraßen ...“*	☒	❑
3	*„Der Buchdruck ist seit dem 16. Jahrhundert von großer Bedeutung für die Stadt.“*	❑	☒
4	*„... im 19. Jahrhundert entwickelte sich die Metall- und die Elektroindustrie.“*	☒	❑
5	*„Leipzig ist noch heute eine wichtige Drehscheibe für den Ost-West-Handel.“*	❑	☒

6 Note that the figure given by Frau Schmidt for the population of Leipzig is 508,000. The population in 1996 was 500,234.

1 Johanna Schmidt wohnt **seit 69 Jahren** in Leipzig.

2 Sie ist **Gästebetreuerin** von Beruf.

3 Leipzig ist ungefähr **850 Jahre** alt.

4 Wo Leipzig sich befindet, kreuzten sich zwei alte Handelsstraßen. Sie waren **die Königsstraße** und **die Reichsstraße**.

5 Eine der Handelsstraßen führte von **Spanien** bis **Rußland**.

6 Die andere Handelsstraße führte von **Skandinavien** nach **Italien**.

7 Die Oper ist **300** Jahre alt und das Gewandhaus ist **250** Jahre alt.

8 Felix Mendelssohn-Bartholdy gründete **1843** die Musikhochschule.

9 Johann Sebastian Bach, der Komponist, lebte **27** Jahre in Leipzig.

10 Johann Wolfgang von Goethe, der Dichter, **studierte** in Leipzig.

11 In der Zeit der Wende erhielt Leipzig den Namen **Heldenstadt**.

12 Während der Revolution von 1989 fanden die Friedensgebete **in der Nikolaikirche** statt.

13 Die Bürger versammelten sich auf dem **Karl-Marx-Platz**.

7

1. Seit der Wende ist es hier viel **besser**.
2. Die vielen Bäume machen die Stadt viel **schöner**.
3. Das Neue Rathaus ist viel **größer als** das Alte.
4. Im 14. Jahrhundert war die Stadt nicht **so reich wie** im 16. Jahrhundert.
5. Die Universität von Leipzig ist **älter als** die Universität von Tübingen.
6. Die Messestadt Frankfurt ist eines der Finanzzentren Europas, aber als Industriemessestadt ist Leipzig vielleicht **bedeutender**.

8 Model answers are provided in *Hörabschnitt 2*, and the written version is in the transcript booklet.

9 Model answers are provided in *Hörabschnitt 3*, and the written version is in the transcript booklet.

10 Here are two suggested passages, which describe Leipzig and compare it to Tübingen.

Leipzig
Leipzig ist ungefähr 850 Jahre alt. Es hat 1165 die Stadtrechte bekommen. Leipzig liegt am Kreuzungspunkt von zwei alten Handelsstraßen und ist heute eine wichtige Messestadt mit 500 234 Einwohner. Es ist auch eine wichtige Industrie- und Handelsstadt. Der Buchdruck und die Metall- und Elektroindustrie sind von großer Bedeutung für die Stadt. Leipzig hat eine lange Kulturgeschichte. Es ist eine bedeutende Musikstadt. Bach lebte 27 Jahre in Leipzig.

Leipzig und Tübingen
Tübingen liegt in Südwestdeutschland; Leipzig liegt nördlicher von Tübingen (im Nordosten). Die Stadt is älter als Tübingen. (Tübingen ist nicht so alt wie Leipzig.) Die Universität von Leipzig ist auch älter als die Universität von Tübingen. Leipzig ist viel größer als Tübingen. (Tübingen ist viel kleiner als Leipzig.) Es ist eine Industriestadt. Tübingen hat wenig Industrie und der größte Arbeitsgeber ist die Universität. (Die Universität ist der größte Arbeitsgeber in Tübingen.)

Lerneinheit 3

1 Here are the answers, together with extracts from *Hörabschnitt 4*, which should have given you the clues you needed.

1. The suggested activity is going out for a meal. *„... weil meine Frau und ich heute abend essen gehen."*
2. At 8 o'clock. *„Wie wäre es mit acht Uhr?"*
3. They arrange to meet outside the restaurant. *„Am besten direkt vor dem Restaurant."*
4. The restaurant is in the market square, opposite the town hall. *„... am Marktplatz ... gegenüber vom Rathaus."*
5. Frau Schaan suggests a trip to the theatre. *„... hätten Sie Lust, ins Theater zu gehen?"*
6. Herr Finkler has something on already. *„Ich bin schon verabredet."*
7. Frau Schaan suggests that Herr Finkler come for lunch and that they could then go for a walk. *„... vielleicht könnten Sie bei uns zu Mittag essen? ... könnten wir spazierengehen."*
8. At 12 noon. *„... sagen wir um zwölf bei uns?"*
9. Karin, the second speaker, is having a rest; she is staying in and watching TV. *„Ich bleibe zu Hause und sehe fern. Ich muß mich mal ausruhen."*
10. Klaus suggests that they go to the cinema. *„... hast du keine Lust ins Kino zu gehen?"*
11. Karin refuses because she is dead tired and wants to go to bed early. *„Ich bin todmüde und ich will früh ins Bett gehen."*
12. Karin then suggests going tomorrow. *„Wie wäre es mit morgen?"*
13. They arrange to meet at 7.40. *„... um zwanzig vor acht ..."*
14. They will meet in front of the Olympia cinema *„... vorm Olympia."*

2 These are the expressions of time from the conversations.

Dialog 1 guten Abend; heute abend; wie wäre es mit 8 Uhr?; um acht Uhr; bis heute abend
Dialog 2 morgen abend; um zwölf; am Nachmittag
(You may have written down zu Mittag *as an expression of time. Unfortunately it isn't, it means 'for lunch'.* Zu Abend essen *means to eat an evening meal.)*
Dialog 3 heute abend; morgen; um 19.45 Uhr (*spoken as* neunzehn Uhr fünfundvierzig) und um 21.45 Uhr; zwanzig vor acht; bis morgen

3 **A 1** *leider* **k** unfortunately
2 *ich bin schon verabredet* **i** I'm already booked up
3 *Wie wäre es mit …?* **d** How about …?
4 *Was würden Sie am liebsten machen?* **l** What would you most like to do?
5 *bei Ihnen* **j** at your place
6 *Wo treffen wir uns?* **b** Where shall we meet?
7 *Geht das?* **e** Is that OK?
8 *ich weiß, wo …* **c** I know where …
9 *Hätten Sie Lust?* **a** Would you like to?
10 *Wissen Sie, wo …?* **g** Do you know where …?
11 *bis 8 Uhr* **f** see you at eight
12 *ja, gerne* **h** yes, I'd like to

B 1 I'm sorry *es tut mir leid*
2 at 8 *um 8 Uhr*
3 Are you acquainted with …?/Do you know …? *Kennen Sie …?*
4 that's not possible *das geht nicht*
5 at your place *bei Ihnen*
6 I'm resting *ich ruhe mich aus*
7 I don't feel like it *ich habe keine Lust*
8 perhaps *vielleicht*

4 Model answers are provided in *Hörabschnitt 5*, and the written version is in the transcript booklet.

5 Here are three possible dialogues – yours may be different. If so, check how you have conveyed your meaning against the phrases you have been given. Look at your word order as well, since even if you have used different words from those in the dialogues here, the word order might be the same.

1 – *Hätten Sie Lust heute abend ins Kino zu gehen?/Möchten Sie … gehen?*
– Ja. Das wäre schön./Ja gerne. Um wieviel Uhr?
– *Acht Uhr.*
– Und wo treffen wir uns?
– *Wie wäre es mit halb acht bei mir?*
– Ja, gut.
– *Bis halb acht also.*
– Ja. Bis halb acht. Tschüs.

2 – *Hätten Sie Lust am Dienstag mit mir einkaufen zu gehen?*
– Ja. Gerne. Um wieviel Uhr?
– *Um 14.00 Uhr. Geht das?*
– Ja. Wo treffen wir uns?
– *Wir könnten uns bei Ihnen treffen.*
– Ja. Das geht. Bis Dienstag.
– *Ja. Tschüs.*

3 – *Hätten Sie Lust heute abend essen zu gehen?*
– Leider kann ich nicht. Ich bin schon verabredet.
– *Schade. Wie wäre es mit morgen abend?*
– Ja. Das geht. Um wieviel Uhr?
– *Um halb acht?/Um neunzehn Uhr dreißig? Essen Sie gerne Griechisch?*
– Ja. Sehr.
– *Treffen wir uns also im Restaurant am Marktplatz?*
– Ja, gut, bis morgen abend.
– *Bis dann. Auf Wiederhören./Tschüs.*
– Auf Wiederhören./Tschüs.

6 **1** They went for a long walk along the Ammer.
2 He watched TV and went to bed early.
3 With Claudia and Claudia's boyfriend.
4 They went to a pub. **5** Claudia sends her best

wishes/greetings. **6** They did nothing apart from eating. **7** Oliver Förster went to the cinema at the weekend. **8** He had gone shopping. **9** They went shopping to buy things for the new flat.

The infinitives in each letter were as follows:
Hans Drössers Brief: spazierengehen*; entlanglaufen*; bleiben*; fernsehen; gehen*
Christine Launers Brief: spielen; gehen*; kommen*; essen; machen
Oliver Försters Brief: sehen; gehen*; einkaufen gehen*; kaufen

7 Here are some suggestions.

1. Am Freitag abend bin ich mit Karla ins Kino gegangen. Wir haben einen Film von Spielberg gesehen. Am Samstag bin ich einkaufen gegangen, und am Sonntag habe ich nichts gemacht.
2. Nein. Ich bin zu Hause geblieben, habe ferngesehen und bin früh ins Bett gegangen.
3. Okay. Am Samstag habe ich Tennis gespielt. Am Abend haben wir (habe ich) Italienisch gegessen. Am Sonntag haben wir (habe ich) einen Ausflug gemacht und sind (bin) im Sachsenwald spazierengegangen.

Lerneinheit 4

1

	RICHTIG	FALSCH
1 *Die Szene spielt in **Leipzig** auf der Straße.* Besides the clue in the title of the *Hörspiel* you might have picked up clues from the places mentioned.	❑	☒
2 You will have guessed this from what Sonja said „*… wir haben … viel zu tun, sonst gibt es dieses Wochenende nichts zu essen.*"	☒	❑
3 *Es ist Freitag.* Bettina said „*Heute morgen war die Klasse ziemlich friedlich. Gott sei Dank ist es Wochenende.*"	❑	☒
4 You could have guessed this from question 3.	☒	❑
5 This can be assumed since Sonja is showing Bettina the sights of Leipzig.	☒	❑
6 *Bettina ist todmüde und möchte einen Kaffee trinken.*	❑	☒
7 She says, „*Die finde ich toll!*"	☒	❑
8 As she leaves Bettina, Sonja asks her, „*Findest du den Weg zur Wohnung?*"	☒	❑

2

1. Sie treffen sich um **vier** Uhr **nach** der Arbeit.
2. Sonja würde gern am Wochenende **ins Kino oder ins Theater** gehen.
3. Bettina möchte sich **zu Hause mit einem Glas Wein ausruhen**.
4. Richtig.
5. Vor dem Einkaufen möchte Sonja einen **Kaffee** trinken.
6. Sonja kennt ein Café gegenüber **dem Rathaus**.
7. Bettina interessiert sich für die **Grimmaische Straße**.
8. Richtig.
9. Bettina und der Straßenmusikant waren Studenten in **Tübingen**.
10. Bettina und der Straßenmusikant gehen **Kaffee trinken**.

3 Here is a summary with some variations.

Es ist Freitag. Nach der Arbeit treffen sich Bettina und Sonja um vier Uhr in der Stadt. (Bettina und Sonja treffen sich um vier Uhr in der Stadt.) Sonja möchte am Wochenende ins Kino oder ins Theater gehen. Aber Bettina hat keine Lust dazu. Sie möchte sich ausruhen. Jetzt müssen sie einkaufen gehen. Sie haben nichts für das Wochenende. Bettina ist todmüde und hätte gern einen Kaffee. Sie suchen ein Café. In der Grimmaischen Straße hören sie einen Straßenmusikanten. Sonja möchte nicht länger bleiben und fährt nach Hause. Bettina spricht mit dem Straßenmusikanten (mit ihm). Er singt das Tübingenlied. Sie kennt ihn aus Tübingen, wo er Student war. Sie waren zusammen auf der Universität. Sie gehen zusammen Kaffee trinken.

4 **1 d** Haus am Waldrand **2 b** Gemeinsame Küche **3 a** Balkon **4 b** Gartenbenutzung **5 a** Altbauwohnung **6 b** Dachgeschoßwohnung **7 d** *This is the only advert which doesn't mention central position or good public transport.* **8 b** Nähe Bahnhof und Bushaltestelle **9 a** Nähe Uni **10 d** Haus am Waldrand or **c** Ruhige Lage

5 Here are the completed questions with suggested answers.

1. Wohin kommt der Sessel? *Ins Wohnzimmer.*
2. Wohin kommt das Doppelbett? *Ins große Schlafzimmer.*
3. Wohin kommt die Waschmaschine? *In die Küche/In den Keller.*
4. Wohin kommt die Stereoanlage? *Ins Wohnzimmer.*
5. Wohin kommt das Klavier? *Ins Eßzimmer.*
6. Wohin kommt der Herd? *In die Küche.*
7. Wohin kommt der Kleiderschrank? *Ins große Schlafzimmer.*
8. Wohin kommt das Bett? *Ins kleine Schlafzimmer.*
9. Wohin kommt die Spülmaschine? *In die Küche.*
10. Wohin kommen die Stühle? *Ins Eßzimmer.*
11. Wohin kommt der Wäschetrockner? *In den Keller.*
12. Wohin kommt das Bücherregal? *Ins kleine Schlafzimmer.*

6 **1** Frau M. *„Landschaftlich schöne Lage. Intensive Begrünung."* **2** Herr W. *„Altstadt 5 Min."* **3** Herr W. *„Badezimmer mit neu installierter Dusche, Toilette, Waschbecken."* **4** Herr W. *„Altbauwohnung"* **5** Frau M. *„Grüne Innenhöfe mit Spielplätzen"* **6** Herr W. *„sonnige Lage"* **7** Herr W. *„Wohnzimmer mit … Tür zum Garten"* **8** Frau M. *„nördlich von Leipzig"*

7 **Herr Wagners Wohnung**

Lieber Karl,

wir sind vor drei Wochen umgezogen. Die neue Wohnung ist eine Altbauwohnung/in einem Altbau mit Garten. Sie liegt im Erdgeschoß. Sie hat Parkettboden. Die Miete beträgt DM 945/die Wohnung kostet DM 945,– Miete. Die Wohnfläche beträgt/ist 79 m^2. Die Wohnung hat drei Zimmer: Das Wohnzimmer hat eine Küchenzeile und eine Tür zum Garten. Das Wohnzimmer ist weiß und sehr schön. Das Badezimmer hat eine neuinstallierte Dusche, Toilette und Waschbecken. Die Lage ist ruhig, sonnig und zentral. Es sind nur 5 Minuten bis zur Altstadt. Einkaufsmöglichkeiten und Bushaltestelle sind in unmittelbarer Nähe. Es ist sehr schön, hier zu wohnen.

Viele Grüße,

Ulrike

Note: This model answer includes the phrase es sind … *i.e. a singular subject with a plural verb. This expression is the equivalent of 'there are' in English.*

Frau Mühlens Wohnung

Liebe Christine und lieber Hans-Peter,

die Neubauwohnung ist komfortabel und liegt in Lindental am nördlichen Stadtrand von Leipzig in landschaftlich schöner Lage. Sie kostet DM 1 200 pro Monat und ist 104 m^2 groß. Sie hat fünf Zimmer: Das Wohnzimmer mit Kamin hat Zugang zum Balkon. Das Eßzimmer hat einen Durchgang zur komplett eingerichteten Küche. Es gibt drei Schlafzimmer und ein Luxus-Badezimmer. Die Wohnung hat Fußbodenheizung und eine Tiefgarage. Die Siedlung ist begrünt, und es gibt grüne Innenhöfe mit Spielplätzen. Die Verkehrsverbindungen sind sehr gut. Es sind nur fünf Autominuten zum Bahnhof und 20 Minuten mit dem Zug zum Leipziger Hauptbahnhof.

Viele Grüße,

Holger

Lerneinheit 5

1 Here are the answers, together with extracts from *Hörabschnitt 6,* which should have given you the clues you needed.

1. It is very expensive. *„… die Gegend hier … die teuerste Gegend Deutschlands ist. Hier*

sind die Häuser praktisch doppelt so teuer …"

2 They own the flat. *„Wir haben hier eine Eigentumswohnung gekauft …"*

3 The flat is about 120 m². *„… ungefähr 120 m²."*

4 Four families live in the building. *„… in diesem Hause … sind wir vier Parteien."*

5 The families share the utility room, the bike cellar and a few other things. *„… man hat … die Waschküche zusammen, und man hat den Fahrradkeller zusammen, und es gibt noch ein paar andere Dinge, die man zusammen … hat."*

6 Some families also have a loft conversion/attic space. *„… einige haben noch einen Dachboden …"*

7 Herr Hartmann lives outside Tübingen. *„Ich wohne außerhalb …"*

8 The population of Nähren is 3,600. *„… mit 3 600 Einwohnern, in Nähren, …"*

9 This is a one-family house. *„… in einem Einfamilienhaus …"*

10 The house has 140 m². *„… von rund 140 m² …"*

11 The garden is very big. *„… und einem riesengroßen Garten."*

12 The plot of land is 1,200 m². *„Das sind etwa hier 1 200 m² …"*

13 The one-family house was made into a two-family house. *„… dieses frühere Einfamilien-, heute Zweifamilienhaus …"*

14 The house was built in the thirties. *„… in den dreißiger Jahren errichtet wurde."*

15 Frau Storr has a semi-detached house. *„… es ist also eine Doppelhaushälfte …"*

16 Her house has 4 rooms. *„… wir haben vier Zimmer …"*

17 It has 3 floors (including the attic floor). *„… auf zwei Stockwerken, und ein Dachgeschoß …"* (A more usual word used for attic living space is *Dachboden*.)

18 Ground floor: living room, kitchen, lavatory. First floor: 2 children's rooms, the parents' room and a bathroom. Attic floor: office. *„Es besteht aus einem Wohnzimmer, einer Küche im Erdgeschoß und einer Toilette, und im ersten Stock zwei Kinderzimmer und das Schlafzimmer und's Bad." „… und ein Dachgeschoß, das Büro."*

19 Frau Patzwahl describes the three flats or houses she has lived in as: *„… eine Zweizimmerwohnung … eine Dreizimmerwohnung … und (eine) Vierzimmerwohnung …"*

20 The Patzwahl family moved to the two-bedroomed flat ten years ago *„Also ich bin vor zehn Jahren … eingezogen …"*

21 They moved into their current flat two years ago. *„… und hier seit zwei Jahren wohnen wir …"*

2

Herr Winter wohnt in **einer** Eigentumswohnung. Die Wohnung hat vier Zimmer und **einen** Keller. Die vier Parteien haben **eine** Waschküche und **einen** Fahrradkeller zusammen. Seine Wohnung hat **keinen** Dachboden.

Herr Hartmann wohnt in **einem** Einfamilienhaus mit **einer** Wohnfläche von 140 m² und mit einem großen Garten.

Die Möhles wohnen in **einem** Zweifamilienhaus.

Frau Storr wohnt in **einem** Doppelhaus. Ihr Büro ist **in dem** Dachgeschoß. *(Note that* in dem *is usually contracted to* im.*)*

Frau Patzwahl hat jetzt **eine** Vierzimmerwohnung. Früher wohnte sie in **einer** Dreizimmerwohnung.

3

1 Ist Karl da? Nein, er ist in die Stadt gefahren/gegangen.

2 Wo ist Heti? Sie ist im Schlafzimmer.

3 Wohin ist Lutz gefahren? Er ist ins Dorf gefahren/gegangen.

4 Ich suche Herrn Hartmann. Er ist im Haus.

5 Wissen Sie, wo Margret ist? Sie ist in den Keller gegangen.

6 Haben Sie Axel hier gesehen? Er ist in den Garten gegangen.

7 Wo ist Benno? Er ist in die Küche gegangen.

8 Ist Christine da? Nein, sie ist auf dem Balkon.

4

The words that are spelt in *Hörabschnitt 8* are Belfast, Clwyd, Xavier, Quorn, Lougherne, Jarrow, Kempton.

5

1 a two-family house *Zweifamilienhaus*
2 b first floor *im ersten Stock*
3 b ground floor *im Erdgeschoß*
4 a surface area *Wohnfläche*
5 b rent *Miete*

6

1 Frau Rösner has lived in Lustnau for 13 years. „... *ich wohne seit dreizehn Jahren ... in Lustnau.*"
2 The landlord also lives in the house. „... *im Erdgeschoß wohnt der Hauseigentümer ...*"
3 The flat is 98 m². „... *die Wohnfläche beträgt 98 Quadratmeter.*"
4 The rent is DM 1,200 per month. „*An Miete zahlen wir 1 200 Mark im Monat.*"

7 Your answers should be something like these.

Advantages The flat was very nice. It was very big.
Disadvantages The rent was very high. There was too much traffic. They lived right on the high street. There was too much noise and pollution. There were too many cars. Her daughters had nowhere to play.

8 Model answers are provided in *Hörabschnitt 10*, and the written version is in the transcript booklet.

9 In your answer you might have covered some of the following points:

– Wo wohnen Sie?
– *Ich wohne in* (name) *(in einem Dorf, in einer Stadt, in der Stadtmitte, am Stadtrand, in einem Vorort in Südengland, Schottland, Nordirland). Das ist eine Stadt (ein Dorf, ein Stadtteil von ...).*
– Wohnen Sie in einem Hochhaus?
– *Ich wohne in einem Haus (in einer Doppelhaushälfte, in einem Bungalow, in einer Wohnung im dritten Stock).*
– Wie viele Zimmer haben Sie?
– *Ich habe/wir haben ...*
– Was für Zimmer gibt es in Ihrer Wohnung oder in Ihrem Haus?
– *Ich habe/wir haben eine Küche, Toilette, Eßecke, Diele, ein Wohnzimmer, Eßzimmer, Badezimmer, ein/zwei Schlafzimmer.*
– Wohnen Sie gerne dort? Warum oder warum nicht?
– *Ich wohne gern dort. Ich habe die Gegend gern, wohne gern auf dem Land.*
– Wo haben Sie früher gewohnt?
– *Ich wohnte in* (name) *(Ich habe früher in [name] gewohnt.)*
– Warum sind Sie umgezogen?
– *Ich habe eine neue Stelle bekommen ..., (mein Haus war zu klein, wir hatten keinen Garten).*

Lerneinheit 6

2 Here are the answers, together with extracts from the *Hörbericht*, which should have given you the clues you needed.

1 Sixty to seventy percent of people who work in Tübingen commute to work. „... *60 bis 70% der Leute, die in Tübingen arbeiten, pendeln.*"
2 They commute because they cannot afford the rents and the price of land in Tübingen. „... *sind nicht in der Lage, die Mietpreise oder Grundstückspreise in Tübingen zu bezahlen.*"
3 The average number of people travelling in each car is 1.1. „... *im Durchschnitt ein Auto mit 1,1 Personen besetzt ist ...*"
4 Cars are allowed only on the edge of the estate. „... *müssen die Autos am Rande der Siedlung bleiben.*"
5 Frau Patzwahl has lived in Schafbrühl for ten years; she is married; she has four children. „*Frau Patzwahl wohnt seit zehn Jahren mit ihrem Mann und ihren vier Kindern in Schafbrühl.*"
6 The recording of Frau Patzwahl was made on her balcony. „*Jetzt steht sie auf ihrem Balkon.*"
7 There are a stream and a pond in the courtyard by her house. „... *wo der Teich ist ... vom Teich aus fließt der Bach durch den Innenhof.*"

8 Cars are allowed only on the edge of the estate; the estate is child-friendly; the children can play in the stream; there is a good community feeling; there are good social contacts; you meet neighbours, friends; children meet each other. *„... müssen die Autos am Rande der Siedlung bleiben ... Schafbrühl ist kinderfreundlich: Es gibt sogar einen kleinen Bach ... Dort können die Kinder mit Wasser spielen ... ein starkes Gemeinschaftsgefühl; gute soziale Kontakte; ... trifft man immer Nachbarn, Freunde, die Kinder begegnen sich immer."*

3

1 Die **Verkehrsprobleme** in der Stadt sind besonders schlimm.

2 Die meisten Pendler sind **nicht in der Lage**, die Miet- und Grundstückspreise zu bezahlen.

3 Die Autos **sind im Durchschnitt** mit 1,1 Personen besetzt.

4 **Jeden Tag** ist Tübingen praktisch eine Großstadt durch die Einpendler.

5 Schafbrühl ist eine neue **Siedlung.** Die Autos **müssen am Rande** der Siedlung bleiben.

6 Zwischen **den Häusern** gibt es Innenhöfe, wo die Kinder **spielen** können.

4 **Sechzig bis siebzig** Prozent der Leute, die in Tübingen arbeiten, sind Pendler. Sie pendeln, weil sie **nicht in der Lage sind**, **die Mietpreise und die Grundstückspreise zu bezahlen**. Sie fahren meistens mit dem **Auto**. **Viele** Autos kommen in die Stadt. Die Pendler fahren in die Stadt, um **zu arbeiten oder um zu studieren**.
Seit den **80er** Jahren gibt es eine neue Art Siedlung. Sie heißt Schafbrühl und liegt **am Stadtrand** (**am Rande der Stadt**). Die Häuser sind um **Innenhöfe** gruppiert. Schafbrühl hat **ein** starkes Gemeinschaftsgefühl und die sozialen Kontakte sind **gut**.

5 Model answers are provided in *Hörabschnitt 11*, and the written version is in the transcript booklet.

6 Model answers are provided in *Hörabschnitt 12*, and the written version is in the transcript booklet.

7 Here are some possible questions – yours may be a bit different. Alternative versions are given in brackets.

Interviewer Wie fahren die meisten Leute (Pendler) in die Stadt?

Frau Hüber Die meisten Leute fahren mit dem Auto in die Stadt. (Einige fahren mit dem Bus und einige wenige fahren mit dem Rad.)

Interviewer Warum wohnen diese Leute nicht in der Stadt?

Frau Hüber Sie wohnen nicht in der Stadt, weil es zu teuer ist. Die Mietpreise sind zu hoch.

Interviewer Wie viele Personen sitzen im Durchschnitt in jedem Auto? (Sind die Autos voll?)

Frau Hüber Im Durchschnitt sitzen nur 1,1 Personen in jedem Auto. Es gibt viel zu viele Autos in der Stadt. Wir haben aber eine neue Siedlung, wo man praktisch ohne Auto leben kann.

Interviewer Seit wann gibt es (haben Sie) diese neue Siedlung?

Frau Hüber Die Siedlung gibt es seit 1980.

Interviewer Wo liegt sie?

Frau Hüber Sie liegt am Stadtrand.

Interviewer Gibt es Parkplätze? (Wo sind die Parkplätze?)

Frau Hüber Parkplätze? Ja, es gibt Parkplätze, aber sie sind am Rand der Siedlung.

Interviewer Was ist zwischen den Häusern?
(Note that here the preposition zwischen *takes the dative and that* Haus *is in the plural. In the dative plural you add an* -n *to the noun, so* Häuser *becomes* Häuser**n**.*)*

Frau Hüber Es gibt Innenhöfe dazwischen.

Interviewer Wie sind die Innenhöfe?

Frau Hüber Die Innenhöfe sind sehr schön. Es gibt Teiche und Bäche.

8 Here is one possible version.

Tübingen hat große Verkehrsprobleme. Viele Leute, die in Tübingen arbeiten, pendeln jeden Tag mit dem Auto. Sie wohnen außerhalb der Stadt, weil sie nicht in der Lage sind, die Mietpreise und die Grundstückspreise in der Stadt zu bezahlen. Es gibt zu viele Autos in der Stadt und sie bringen Lärm und Verschmutzung. Das ist nicht gut für die Lebensqualität.

Am Stadtrand gibt es eine neue Siedlung: Schafbrühl. In Schafbrühl müssen die Autos außerhalb der Siedlung bleiben. Es gibt Innenhöfe in der Siedlung und die Kinder können dort spielen (wo die Kinder spielen können). Die Siedlung ist sehr kinderfreundlich. Es gibt dort ein gutes Gemeinschaftsgefühl und gute soziale Kontakte.

Lerneinheit 7

1 Here are the answers to the questions, together with extracts from the video which should have given you the clues you needed.

1. Dr. Setzler lives in a one-family house. *„Ich wohne ... in einem Einfamilienhaus."*
2. The house has seven rooms. *„... das Haus besteht aus sieben Zimmern ..."*
3. He says they call the garden the biggest living room. *„... und das größte Wohnzimmer, sagen wir, ist unser Garten."*
4. Tanya Lindl lives in the centre of town. *„... direkt in der Innenstadt ..."*
5. Possible problems she mentions are the telephone and the bath. *„... da steht das Telefon wahrscheinlich nie still, und im Bad gibt's wahrscheinlich auch die ganze Zeit Probleme ..."*
6. Sibylle Metzger's flat has three rooms, a kitchen and a large balcony. *„... wir haben drei Zimmer für uns zwei, und eine Küche und einen großen Balkon ..."*
7. Günter Leypoldt lives about 20 minutes from the town centre. *„... ungefähr zwanzig Minuten von der Stadtmitte entfernt."*
8. Gesine Jüttner has shared a house with her parents for a year. *„Seit einem Jahr wohne ich ... gemeinsam mit meinen Eltern."*
9. Gesine Jüttner has about 70 m^2 of the house. *„Ich persönlich habe in dem Haus zirka siebzig Quadratmeter Wohnfläche."*
10. Frau Stabenow lives in a big rented block. It is a prefabricated building. *„Ich wohne in einem größeren Mietshaus ... Es ist natürlich Plattenbau ..."*
11. The flat is small. *„... in diesen kleinen Wohnungen ..."*
12. Daniela Krafak and her boyfriend decided to move in together. *„... und jetzt haben wir uns entschlossen, zusammenzuziehen ..."*
13. They moved into a flat together in September. *„... und sind im September zusammen in eine Wohnung hier in Leipzig gezogen."*
14. Frau Frenzel's flat is 106 m^2. *„... unsere Wohnung ist erstmal 106 Quadratmeter ..."*
15. The Frenzel's flat is in an old building. *„... daß wir in 'ner Altbauwohnung wohnen ..."*
16. Frau Baumeister lives in a three-family house. *„Wir wohnen in einem Dreifamilienhaus ...".*
17. A single parent with two children lives in the middle flat in Frau Baumeister's house. *„... in der Mitte wohnt eine alleinerziehende Mutter mit zwei Kindern ..."*

2
1 Wilfried Setzler 2 Günter Leypoldt
3 Ruth Stabenow 4 Sibylle Metzger
5 Daniela Krafak 6 Renate Baumeister
7 Tanja Lindl 8 Günter Leypoldt
9 Angelika Frenzel 10 Gesine Jüttner

3 These are the prepositions in the order in which they were used in the video sequence: *seit; in; mit; von; aus; mit; in; in; in*

4 Here are the descriptions of flats and houses, complete with direct or indirect articles. Some alternatives are given in brackets.

1. Ich wohne in **einer** kleinen Wohnung in **einem** Hochhaus. Meine Wohnung ist in **der** Stadtmitte und ich wohne dort seit **einem** Jahr.

2 Ich wohne mit **(m)einem** Freund zusammen. Unsere Wohnung ist sehr schön und besteht aus **einem** Wohnzimmer, **einer** Küche und drei weiteren Zimmern. Im Sommer essen wir auf **dem** Balkon.

3 Ich wohne in **einem** Haus mit **einem** Garten. Man kann direkt von **dem (vom)** Wohnzimmer in **den** Garten gehen. Das Haus liegt an **dem (am)** Stadtrand und ist zwei Kilometer von **der** Stadtmitte entfernt. Ich kann also zu Fuß in **die** Stadt gehen, was sehr praktisch ist.

5 Model answers are provided in *Hörabschnitt 13*, and the written version is in the transcript booklet.

6 Here is one possible version. When checking what you have written, look out for the word order, the articles and the endings of the adjectives and the form of the verbs.

Die Familie Schelling wohnt seit einem Monat in einem Einfamilienhaus. Sie haben 130 Quadratmeter Wohnfläche und einen großen Garten. Das Haus liegt im Osten der Stadt. Sie wohnen gern am Stadtrand. Es liegt 6 Kilometer von der Stadtmitte entfernt. Sie wohnen in der Nähe vom Sportzentrum entfernt. Es gibt eine Bushaltestelle vor der Tür.

Siegfried Braun und Gisela Klausewitz wohnen seit zwei Jahren in einer Wohnung in der Stadtmitte. Sie haben drei Zimmer, eine Küche, ein Bad und einen großen Balkon. Die Wohnung ist 120 Quadratmeter groß. Sie wohnen nur 500 Meter vom Bahnhof entfernt und es gibt Geschäfte in der Nähe.

Lerneinheit 8

1 Here are the answers, together with extracts from the accounts, which should have given you the clues you needed.

1 Frau Stabenow's flat is on the outskirts of Leipzig. *„... in einer kleinen Wohnung am Stadtrand ...“*

2 She likes it because it is quiet; the neighbours are friendly; she meets friends; she likes walking around in Leipzig. *„... weil die Lage ruhig ist und die Nachbarn freundlich sind ... treffe ich immer Freunde ... mache oft Stadtbummel in Leipzig, was mir sehr gefällt.“*

3 Frau Baumeister likes living there because she likes the southern way of living; she likes being in the open air. *„Das Lebensweise in Süddeutschland gefällt mir sehr ... wir sehr gern in der Natur sind.“*

4 Dr. Setzler likes living there because he has good social contacts and friends and it is very practical living in the town centre. *„Ich habe hier viele soziale Kontakte und Freunde. Mein Haus steht in der Stadtmitte, was ich sehr praktisch finde.“*

5 Herr Rübling lives in a new house in a part of the town that he finds beautiful and he has many relations and friends in the town. *„Ich wohne ... in einem neuen Haus am Stadtrand, eine Gegend, die ich sehr schön finde ... Ich habe hier viele Verwandte und Freunde.“*

2 Here are the personal pronouns you should have listed. They are all in the dative case.

Frau Stabenow: Es gefällt **ihr** dort sehr gut.
Herr Rübling (und seine Frau): Leipzig gefällt **ihnen** gut.

These are the possessive adjectives:

Frau Stabenow: **ihre** Freunde; **ihre** Kinder
Frau Baumeister: **ihr** Haus; mit **ihrem** Mann
Dr. Setzler: mit **seiner** Familie; in **sein** Büro; **seine** Kinder
Herr Rübling: mit **seiner** Frau

3

1 **Frau Stabenow** Leipzig gefällt **ihr**. Sie trifft **ihre** Freunde. Ihre Kinder wohnen in einer anderen Stadt.

2 **Frau Baumeister Ihr** Haus steht in einem Dorf. Süddeutschland gefällt **ihr** sehr. Sie geht mit **ihrem** Mann oft spazieren.

3 **Dr. Setzler** wohnt mit **seiner** Familie in der Stadtmitte. Er kann zu Fuß in **sein** Büro gehen. **Seine** Kinder können auch zu Fuß einkaufen gehen.

4 **Herr Rübling** Mit **seiner** Frau wohnt er in einem neuen Haus. Leipzig gefällt **ihnen** gut.

4

1 **Frau Stabenow** Die Lage **ist ruhig**. Die Nachbarn **sind freundlich**. Wenn sie das Haus verläßt, **trifft sie Freunde**. Spazieren gehen gefällt **ihr sehr**.

2 **Frau Baumeister** Die Lebensweise in Süddeutschland **gefällt ihr sehr**. Sie macht gern **Wanderungen im Wald**. Sie ist **gern in der Natur**.

3 **Dr. Setzler** Er fühlt **sich sehr wohl in Tübingen**. Wohnen in der Stadtmitte ist **sehr praktisch**. Er geht zu Fuß **in sein Büro**.

4 **Herr Rübling** Er fühlt **sich ganz zu Hause in dieser Stadt**. Er wohnt mit **seiner Frau in einem neuen Haus**.

5

1 Frau Schreiner geht gerne ins Konzert.
2 Herr Neuner geht abends in die Kneipe.
3 Nein, er ist um die Ecke.
4 Er fährt mit dem Rad.
5 Frau Schelling fährt mit dem Bus und der S-Bahn.
6 Ihre Fahrt dauert zwei Stunden.
7 Weil sie gern in der Natur sind .
8 Er hat ein Haus gebaut.

6

1 Sie mag Magdeburg, weil … **b** ihre Familie und Freunde dort wohnen. **c** es viel Unterhaltung und Kultur gibt.

2 Bremen gefällt ihm, weil … **a** seine Wohnung in der Innenstadt ist. **b** der Supermarkt gleich um die Ecke ist. **c** er zu Fuß in die Kneipe gehen kann.

3 Sie mag Frankfurt nicht, weil … **a** es zu viel Verkehr und Hektik gibt. **b** die Mietpreise zu hoch sind.

4 Rostock gefällt ihm, weil… **a** sein Arbeitsplatz dort ist. **b** er sein Haus dort gebaut hat. **c** seine Kinder und Enkelkinder ihn dort besuchen/in der Nähe wohnen.

7 Your statements should be something like this.

Frau Stabenow wohnt gern am Stadtrand, weil die Lage ruhig ist und weil sie dort viele Freunde hat. Sie findet die Nachbarn freundlich. Sie fährt gern in die Stadt.

Frau Baumeister wohnt gern in Tübingen, weil die süddeutsche Lebensweise ihr gefällt. Sie macht auch gern mit ihrer Familie Wanderungen in die Natur.

Dr. Setzler fühlt sich sehr wohl in Tübingen, weil er dort viele Kontakte und Freunde hat. Die Familie wohnt in der Stadtmitte, was er sehr praktisch findet. Die Kinder können zu Fuß einkaufen gehen und Dr. Setzler kann zu Fuß in sein Büro gehen. Die Geschäfte und einige Gaststätten sind in der Nähe.

Herr Rübling hat sich ein Haus am Stadtrand gebaut, und wohnt gern dort. Es gefällt ihm in Leipzig, weil er viele Freunde und Verwandte in der Stadt hat.

8 Here is a suggestion.

Ich bin in einem Dorf groß geworden, aber für mich ist die Stadt wichtig, weil ich gern ins Kino gehe.

Die Verkehrsverbindungen in der Stadt sind gut. Wir haben einen Bahnhof in der Nähe und die Autobahn ist auch nicht sehr weit entfernt. Das ist wichtig, weil mein Mann in der nächsten Stadt arbeitet.

Die Stadt hat einige schöne Parks, wo meine Kinder spielen können. Es gibt ein Freizeitzentrum. Ich gehe dort einmal die Woche hin. Meine Kinder gehen gern schwimmen. Leider ist das Schwimmbad ziemlich weit entfernt. Man muß mit dem Bus hinfahren. Wir können nicht mit dem Rad fahren, weil die Straße gefährlich ist. Es gibt auch Geschäfte und Supermärkte in der Nähe.

Lerneinheit 9

1 You should have taken notes along these lines.

Wo Herr Pietrowski früher wohnte
Karl-Marx-Stadt/Chemnitz; kleine Wohnung; zwei Zimmer; negativ: Ohne Komfort und Luxus, keine Heizung, Küche teilen, Bad und Toilette im Treppenhaus; positiv: Jeder kannte jeden, gutes Gemeinschaftsgefühl; Kinder konnten überall spielen, wenig Verkehr.
Wo Herr Pietrowski jetzt wohnt
Leipzig seit 1970; kleine Wohnung; Hochhaussiedlung; Plattenbau; Balkon; sechster Stock; zwei Zimmer (Wohnzimmer mit Kochecke, Badezimmer, Schlafzimmer); lebt gerne dort – hat alles, was er braucht; Supermarkt um die Ecke, Post und Sparkasse, in der Nähe, Bushaltestelle vor dem Haus.

2 Model answers are provided in *Hörabschnitt 16*, and the written version is in the transcript booklet.

3 Here are the answers, together with extracts from the article which should have given you the clues you needed.

1. The purpose of the project is to give the homeless the chance to lead a normal life. *„Die Funktion dieses Hauses ist es, Obdachlosen die Chance zu geben, ein normales Leben zu führen."*
2. The hostel was rebuilt and extended. „… *wurde das zerstörte Haus vollständig rekonstruiert und erweitert."*
3. The hostel can accommodate 59 homeless people. *„Jetzt können 59 Wohnungslose … dort eine Unterkunft finden."*
4. The hostel opened in 1991 and burned down in 1992. *„Das Haus wurde 1991 eröffnet und dann ein Jahr später durch einen Brand zerstört."*
5. The hostel has a reception area, kitchens on each floor, day rooms and rooms with 2 beds. *„Es hat Rezeption, Etagenküchen, Aufenthaltsräume und Zwei-Bettzimmer."*
6. Homeless people can stay all day. *„Hier in diesem Haus können Wohnungslose … rund um die Uhr bleiben."*

4 Here are the answers, with quotations from *Hörabschnitt 17.*

1. Forty-two men and women have already moved in. *„Es haben bereits 42 Männer und Frauen Quartier bezogen …"*
2. Yes, 85% have regular jobs. *„85 Prozent von ihnen haben Arbeit …"*
3. People have a beer, play cards or watch TV. *„… wo sie dann ein Bier trinken oder Karten spielen … Fernsehen … ist … eine beliebte Beschäftigung am Abend."*
4. Yes, this hostel is much better than others. *„… natürlich ist dieses neue Haus viel viel besser als die anderen."*
5. The negative aspect is that there is a need for more hostels. *„… immer mehr neue Obdachlosenheime gebraucht werden."*

5 Here is the completed transcript.

„Ja, Meine Funktion also – ich bin Leiter des Hauses. Leider **haben wir ein großes Problem** mit Obdachlosigkeit in Leipzig, und so war nach dem Brand dieser Wiederaufbau dringend notwendig. Es haben bereits **42 Männer und Frauen** Quartier bezogen, und das sind grundsätzlich Leute mit guten Integrationschancen. **85 Prozent von ihnen haben Arbeit,** gehen also einer geregelten Arbeit nach und **kommen abends wieder hierher,** wo sie dann **ein Bier trinken oder Karten spielen**. **In den Aufenthaltsräumen** sind auch Fernseher, und Fernsehen ist natürlich eine beliebte Beschäftigung am Abend."

6 The interview should run like this.

Interviewer	Guten Tag, liebe Zuhörer und Zuhörerinnen. Ich spreche jetzt mit dem Leiter des neuen Obdachlosenheims. Guten Tag. Sie leiten das neue Obdachlosenheim. Darf ich Ihnen einige Fragen stellen, bitte? Wie viele Obdachlose wohnen jetzt schon hier?
Sie	*Im Moment wohnen 42 Männer und Frauen hier.*
Interviewer	Ist die maximale Kapazität erreicht?
Sie	*Nein, 59 Bewohner haben hier Platz.*
Interviewer	Wie viele Menschen sind in Leipzig als obdachlos registriert?
Sie	*Es gibt über 1 200 Obdachlose.*
Interviewer	Wie ist das „Haus für Wohnungslose" eingerichtet?
Sie	*Wir haben eine Rezeption, Etagenküchen und Aufenthaltsräume.*
Interviewer	Wie viele Personen sind in einem Zimmer?
Sie	*Die Zimmer sind zumeist Zweibettzimmer.*
Interviewer	Wie lange ist das Heim offen?
Sie	*Das Heim ist rund um die Uhr offen, 24 Stunden pro Tag.*
Interviewer	Was hat der Neubau gekostet?

Sie	*1,1 Millionen Mark.*
Interviewer	Wir danken Ihnen für das Gespräch.

Lerneinheit 10

1 Here are the answers, with extracts from the newspaper article, which should have given you the clues you needed.

1 There are owner-occupied and rented flats. *„… mit modernen Eigentums- und Mietwohnungen …"*

2 The local people would like: a car-free environment; green areas; courtyards; shops nearby; to have bigger car parks on the edge of the estate; no environmental damage; environmental protection measures. *„… eine verkehrsfreie Umgebung … mit Grünanlagen und Innenhöfen, Geschäften in der Nähe, und größeren Parkplätzen nur am Rande der Siedlung – und ein klares Nein zur Umweltverschmutzung und Ja zum Umweltschutz."*

3 The big disadvantage is that the B 27, which carries a lot of traffic, cuts Südstadt off from Tübingen. *„Die vielbefahrene Umgehungsstraße B 27 schneidet die Südstadt von Tübingen ab."*

2

1 Heike und Peter Reus finden die Südstadt ideal für Kinder, weil es einen Kinderspielplatz gibt und weil ihre Straße verkehrsfrei ist.

2 Frau Heck gefällt es dort nicht, weil ihre Wohnung weit von der Bushaltestelle entfernt ist.

3 Frau Meier fühlt sich sehr zu Hause, weil es ein gutes Gemeinschaftsgefühl in ihrem Wohnblock gibt, und weil die Mieten günstig sind.

3 Here are the answers, with clues from the invitation.

1 The main points of concern are:

- how they are to cope with the extra traffic *„Wie sollen wir denn diesen zusätzlichen Verkehr verkraften?"*
- where multistorey car parks are to be built *„Wo werden Parkhäuser gebaut?"*
- which local streets will be traffic-free *„Welche Anwohnerstraßen werden verkehrsfrei?"*
- whether a community centre is needed *„Brauchen wir dann nicht auch ein Bürgerhaus?"*
- where the new playgrounds should be *„Wo sollen neue Kinderspielplätze entstehen?"*
- where young people will meet *„Wo treffen sich die Jugendlichen?"*
- whether there should be a meeting place for senior citizens *„Wie wär's mit einer Seniorenbegegnungstätte?"*
- whether planners have thought about leisure and sports facilities *„Haben die Planer auch an Freizeit- und Sporteinrichtungen gedacht?"*
- whether there will be an indoor swimming pool *„Bekommen wir ein Hallenbad?"*
- whether there will be a few quiet corners left on the new estates where people can take a breather. *„Bleiben bei der Verstädterung unseres Stadtviertels noch ein paar ruhige Ecken zum Verschnaufen?"*

2 The organisers of the *Bürgerinitiative* are keen for locals to express their ideas so that they don't get served up with something they don't like the taste of. *„… nicht etwas serviert bekommen, was uns nicht schmeckt."*

3 You are asked to bring your ideas. *„Bringen Sie ruhig alle ihre Ideen mit!"*

4 Es gibt viele Parkplätze in Waldfried – sie befinden sich am Rande der Siedlung. Die Straßen in der Mitte der Siedlung sind alle verkehrsfrei. Die Bewohner haben ein Bürgerhaus. Das gefällt ihnen sehr gut. Kinder können in den Innenhöfen zwischen den Häusern spielen und es gibt auch ein Jugendzentrum. Man hat eine Begegnungsstätte für Senioren/SeniorInnen gebaut. Es gibt ein Sportzentrum, aber kein Schwimmbad, und zwei kleine Parks/kleine Grünanlagen. Das Gemeinschaftsgefühl ist sehr gut. Die meisten Leute fühlen sich dort zu Hause. Es gibt aber auch Probleme. Die Verkehrsverbindungen sind nicht gut genug und es gibt zu wenige Vierzimmerwohnungen für große Familien und

Einzimmerwohnungen für jüngere Leute. Es gibt keine Geschäfte in der Nähe.

5 Here is the sort of dialogue you should have written.

Heidrun	*Hallo. Hier Bauer.*
Sie	Hallo Heidrun, hier ist (*Ihr Name*). Nächste Woche ist ein Treffen der Bürgerinitiative Südstadt. Ich werde vorher vielleicht nach Waldfried in Pfäffingen gehen, um einige Fragen zu stellen. Ich möchte wissen, wie es dort zugeht.
Heidrun	*Gute Idee.*
Sie	Möchtest du mitkommen?
Heidrun	*Ja, sicher. Wann möchtest du gehen?*
Sie	Wie wäre es mit Donnerstag?
Heidrun	*Um wieviel Uhr?*
Sie	Am Abend. Um 7 Uhr?
Heidrun	*Nein, das geht nicht. Leider bin ich verabredet.*
Sie	Wie wäre es mit Mittwoch abend?
Heidrun	*Ja, das geht. Sagen wir um 7 Uhr?*
Sie	Ja. Wo treffen wir uns? Bei mir oder bei dir?
Heidrun	*Das ist mir egal. Wir treffen uns bei dir. (Sagen wir, bei dir.)*
Sie	In Ordnung. Bis Mittwoch.
Heidrun	*Ja. Bis dann. Tschüs.*

6 Here is an example of the sort of dialogue you should have written.

Sie	Herr Rach. Guten Abend. Mein Name ist (*Ihr Name*) und ich bin Mitglied der Bürgerinitiative Südstadt. Es gibt in der nächsten Woche ein Treffen und ich habe gehört, daß Sie sich dafür interessieren.
Herr Rach	*Ja, das interessiert mich sehr.*
Sie	Möchten Sie mitkommen?
Herr Rach	*Ja, gerne. Wann ist es?*
Sie	Es ist am 9. Februar. Am Dienstag. Geht das?
Herr Rach	*Ja, das geht. Ich möchte gern kommen.*
Sie	Gut. Ich freue mich.
Herr Rach	*Um wieviel Uhr ist es?*
Sie	Es ist um 8 Uhr im Bürgerhaus.
Herr Rach	*Danke. Wo liegt das?*
Sie	Das ist hier in der Nähe, in der Weltingerstraße.
Herr Rach	*Wo treffen wir uns?*
Sie	Wie wäre es bei Ihnen?
Herr Rach	*Gute Idee. Um wieviel Uhr?*
Sie	Um Viertel vor acht?
Herr Rach	*Ja, In Ordnung. Am Dienstag um Viertel vor acht.*
Sie	Ja. Bis Dienstag abend. Auf Wiederhören, Herr Rach.
Herr Rach	*Auf Wiederhören.*

Lerneinheit 11

1

1 Nein, Frau Kiefer wohnt mit ihrem Kind und ihrer Freundin zusammen.

2 Frau Kiefer hat ein Kind.

3 Nein, sie wohnt in einer Wohnung.

4 Nein, Frau Kiefer ist nicht verheiratet. Sie ist alleinerziehende Mutter.

5 Sie war am Anfang skeptisch, weil Südstadt am Rande der Stadt liegt und weil es keine Kinos und keine großen Geschäfte gibt.

6 Sie fühlt sich sehr wohl.

7 Südstadt ist durch die B 27 von der Stadt abgeschnitten

8 Sie hat eine Wohnung gemietet, weil sie nicht in der Lage war, eine Wohnung zu kaufen.

		RICHTIG	FALSCH
9	*„Am liebsten wäre mir alles ohne Auto."*	☐	☒
10	*„... dreimal in der Stunde. Am Samstag vielleicht zweimal und am Sonntag kann man das fast vergessen."*	☒	☐
11	*„Die Linie 1 fährt nur einmal in der Stunde ..."*	☐	☒

2

1. Frau Kiefer wohnt mit einer Freundin zusammen, weil es billiger ist, eine Wohnung zu teilen … weil sie beide alleinerziehende Mütter sind.
2. Frau Kiefer war am Anfang skeptisch, weil Südstadt am Stadtrand liegt … weil es keine großen Geschäfte gibt.
3. Frau Aziz ist nichr sehr zufrieden, weil sie lieber keinen Wagen besitzen würde … weil die Busverbindungen schlecht sind.

3

Ich habe **einen** Sohn und ich wohne mit (**m**)**einer** Freundin zusammen. Sie hat auch **ein** Kind. Wir wohnen seit **einem** Jahr in **einer** 4-Zimmer-Wohnung in **der** Stuttgarterstraße. Ich fühle mich sehr wohl hier. **Im** Wohnblock habe ich jetzt viele Freunde, und für **die** Kinder gibt es **einen** guten Spielplatz ganz in **der** Nähe. Wir haben **keinen** Garten, aber es gibt schöne Innenhöfe, wo man draußen sitzen kann.

4

Here are the sort of answers you should have written.

Frau Schneider	Seit wann wohnen Sie hier, Frau Uhland?
Frau Uhland	*Ich wohne hier seit einem Jahr. Es gefällt mir gut. Die sozialen Kontakte sind gut.*
Frau Schneider	Sind die Wohnungen groß?
Frau Uhland	*In diesem Wohnblock haben die Wohnungen 100 m². Einige haben einen Balkon.*
Frau Schneider	Das ist sicher groß genug für Sie?
Frau Uhland	*Ja. Ich habe eine schöne Küche, zwei Schlafzimmer und ein Wohnzimmer mit einer Eßecke.*
Frau Schneider	Wie finden Sie die Mietpreise?
Frau Uhland	*Die Mieten hier sind sehr günstig. Ich bin nicht in der Lage, eine Wohnung zu kaufen. Es ist wirklich toll, eine Wohnung hier zu haben.*
Frau Schneider	Es gibt es also Platz genug für Sie und die Familie?
Frau Uhland	*Ja. Tisch und Stühle sind in der Ecke und ich habe ein großes Sofa und einen Fernsehapparat. Bei meiner Arbeit und mit zwei Kindern bin ich abends todmüde und ich sehe viel fern.*
Frau Schneider	Ja, das mache ich auch.
Frau Uhland	*Wie wäre es jetzt mit einem Kaffee bei mir?*
Frau Schneider	Gerne. Danke sehr … Und wie sind die Verbindungen?
Frau Uhland	*Die Busverbindungen in Südstadt sind nicht sehr gut. Ich fahre meistens mit dem Auto.*

5

Clues from the adverts are included, which should have helped you.

1 a *„Hobbyraum … im Keller …"*
2 a *„mit Balkon an der Sonnenseite"*
3 a *„WM/Trockner"*
4 a *„… zentraler … Lage …"*
5 b *„… einmalige Lage."*
6 b *„… inkl. Garage …"*
7 a By process of elimination! A lift is mentioned in **c**; **b** wouldn't need a lift as it is an *Einfamilienhaus*.
8 c *„… 3. OG. (Obergeschoß)"*
9 a *„… Hobbyraum mit WC/Dusche …"*
10 c *„… Bad, Sep. Dusche …"*

6

1h **2**d **3**g **4**a **5**b **6**e **7**c **8**i **9**f

Lösungen Thema 2

Lerneinheit 1

1 Here are the answers, with quotations from the text, which should have given you the clues you needed.

	RICHTIG	FALSCH
1 *„Dr. Setzler ist in **Pforzheim** großgeworden ...“*	❑	☒
2 *„Hans-Peter Baumeister ist ... in Norddeutschland geboren.“*	☒	❑
3 *„Walter Utz ... stammt aus Tübingen.“*	☒	❑
4 *„Renate Baumeister ... ist durch ihren Beruf als Erzieherin nach Tübingen gekommen und ist **nicht** dort geboren.“*	❑	☒
5 *„Peter Bosch ist gebürtiger Tübinger.“*	☒	❑
6 *„Alice Kurz kommt aus dem Nordschwarzwald.“*	☒	❑
7 *„Tanja Lindl ist in **Heilbronn** geboren.“*	❑	☒
8 *„Wolfgang Fritz ist im Dorf Drejesingen geboren.“*	❑	☒
9 *„Wolfgang Fritz ist Schwabe.“*	☒	❑
10 *„Sie ist in der **Türkei** geboren ...“*	❑	☒

2 Here are the answers, with quotations from the video, which should have given you the clues you needed.

1 Dr. Setzler said that there were very few 'original inhabitants'. *„ ... die Stadt Tübingen ... hat ... nur ganz wenige, Ureinwohner'.“*

2 The three words he uses to describe what Tübingen is like are modern, European and multicultural. *„... im Prinzip ist das eine moderne europäische Stadt, multikulturell ...“*

3 The three nationalities that you can meet in Tübingen are Italian, Greek and Turkish. *„... hier gibt's Italiener, hier gibt's Griechen, hier gibt's Türken ...“*

4 Herr Baumeister was born in Salzgitter. *„... ich bin in Salzgitter geboren ...“*

5 He says that Salzgitter was founded about 60 years ago. *„... die vor zirka 60 Jahren gegründet worden ist.“*

6 Herr Utz was born in Tübingen *„Hier in Tübingen geboren ...“*

7 Frau Baumeister grew up near Stuttgart. *„... in einem kleinen Dorf ... in der Nähe ... von Stuttgart.“*

8 She grew up in a small village.

9 The words Herr Bosch uses to describe where he comes from are *ein geborener Schwabe* – i.e. he was born a Swabian.

10 Calw is a small town. *„... aus einer kleinen Stadt, die heißt Calw.“*

11 The town Tanja Lindl comes from, Heilbronn, is 100 km from Tübingen. *„Ich komme aus Heilbronn ... hundert Kilometer weg.“*

12 Herr Fritz was born in Drejesingen and grew up in Hagelloch. *„Ich bin geboren ... in Drejesingen ... und aufgewachsen dann in Hagelloch ...“*

13 Frau Braun grew up partly in Turkey, partly in Germany. *„... ich bin teils in der Türkei, teils hier aufgewachsen.“*

14 She misses her family in Turkey, but when she is there on holiday, then she misses Germany „... *natürlich habe ich Sehnsüchte. Meine Familie lebt in der Türkei. Aber wenn ich im Urlaub dort bin, dann habe ich wieder Sehnsucht hierher.*"

3 Where there is more than one way of completing the sentence, alternatives are given.

1 Dr. Setzler fühlt sich als **Tübinger**, aber er **ist** nicht in Tübingen **geboren**. Er ist als Student nach Tübingen **gekommen**.

2 Hans-Peter Baumeister **ist** kein **Tübinger/Schwabe** wie seine Frau. Er **kommt aus** dem Norden.

3 Herr Utz **ist gebürtiger** Tübinger, und **hat** sein ganzes Leben dort **verbracht**.

4 Frau Baumeister **kommt/ist** nicht aus Norddeutschland, wie ihr Mann. Sie ist Schwäbin und **ist** in einem Dorf in der Nähe von Stuttgart **aufgewachsen/ großgeworden**.

5 Peter Bosch **ist Schwabe**.

6 Alice Kurz **stammt/ist** aus dem Schwarzwald.

7 Wolfgang Fritz **ist in** Hagelloch **großgeworden/aufgewachsen**.

8 Frau Braun ist nicht in Deutschland **geboren**. Sie **stammt/ist** aus der Türkei.

4

1 Her parents left Sri Lanka for political reasons. *„Ihre Eltern kamen als politische Flüchtlinge aus Sri Lanka."*

2 She is now a German citizen. „... *inzwischen deutsche Staatsbürgerin.*"

3 She has just finished her studies at a music college. „... *und hat gerade ihr Studium an der Musikhochschule beendet.*"

4 His parents came to Schwaben. *„Seine Eltern ... ins schwäbische Bad Urach kamen ...*"

5 They are now German citizens. „... *erhielten ihre Staatsbürgerschaft ...*"

6 He is a member of the German parliament. „... *ihr Sohn für die Bündnisgrünen in den Bundestag gewählt wurde.*"

7 She left the Lebanon with her parents because of the civil war. „... *bis der Bürgerkrieg begann.*"

8 She is studying journalism and history and working in a photographic agency. „... *studiert Publizistik und Geschichte. Nebenbei jobbt sie bei einer Fotoagentur.*"

9 She plans to go to the Lebanon with her father to obtain an impression of the country. *„In diesem Jahr will sie mit ihrem Vater in den Libanon reisen, um von diesem Land ... einen Eindruck zu bekommen."*

5

1 Cem Özdemir *„Seine Eltern, die vor 30 Jahren aus der Türkei ... ins schwäbische Bad Urach kamen, erhielten ihre Staatsbürgerschaft ...*"

2 Nadja Masri „... *lebte aber mit ihren Eltern im Libanon ...*"

3 Nadja Masri „... *bis der Bürgerkrieg begann.*" The article goes on to say that she can hardly remember the Lebanon „... *Land, an das sie sich kaum erinnert ...*"

4 Chaya Mettananda „... *hat gerade ihr Studium an der Musikhochschule beendet. Sie hat schon zahlreiche Engagements ... bekommen.*"

5 Cem Özdemir *„Seine Eltern, die ... ins schwäbische Bad Urach kamen, erhielten ihre Staatsbürgerschaft ... 1994.*"

6 Chaya Mettananda „... *wurde ... in Deutschland geboren. Ihre Eltern kamen ... aus Sri Lanka.*"

6

1 *Er ist gestern* ***gekommen****.* He came yesterday.

2 *Ich habe in Dresden* ***gewohnt****.* I lived/have lived in Dresden.

3 *Wir sind gestern nach Tübingen* ***gefahren****.* We travelled to Tübingen yesterday.

4 *Uschi ist hier in Hagelloch* ***geblieben****.* Uschi stayed/has stayed here in Hagelloch.

5 *Gestern bin ich sehr früh ins Bett* ***gegangen****.* Yesterday I went to bed very early.

6 *Das Buch hat mich sehr* ***interessiert****.* The book interested me a great deal.

7 *Klaus hat absolut nichts* ***gemacht****.* Klaus did/has done absolutely nothing.

8 *Ah! Da ist das Telefonbuch. Ich habe es überall* ***gesucht***. Ah! There's the telephone book. I've looked for it everywhere.

9 *Vorige Woche haben wir Spielbergs neuen Film* ***gesehen***. Last week we saw Spielberg's new film.

10 *Brigitte hat dieses Paket heute* ***gebracht***. Brigitte brought/has brought this parcel today.

7

1 Die Miete war mir zu hoch. Ich habe 800 DM im Monat **bezahlt**.

2 Wann beginnt der Film? Hat er schon **angefangen**?

3 Meine Kindheit habe ich in Schlesien verbracht. Ich bin dort im Hause meiner Großmutter **großgeworden**.

4 Die Wohnung war schon in Dezember fertig. Wir sind im Januar **eingezogen**.

5 Was ich gestern abend gemacht habe? Ich habe nur **ferngesehen**.

6 Am Wochende habe ich Freunde in Bremen **besucht.** Wir sind **spazierengegangen**.

8

1 Frank **ist** einkaufen **gegangen**.

2 Uschi **ist** gestern **umgezogen**.

3 Sie **haben** Tennis **gespielt**.

4 Sie **hat** in Berlin **studiert**.

5 Er **hat** den ganzen Tag im Bett **verbracht**.

6 Ich **habe** die Adresse **gefunden**.

7 Wir **haben** eine Wohnung **gemietet**.

8 Ich **bin** mit dem Auto/Wagen **gefahren**.

9 Sie **sind** um 11 Uhr **gekommen**.

10 Ich **bin** nicht lange **geblieben**.

9 Here are the answers, with quotations from *Hörabschnitt 1*.

1 In her childhood. *„... ich bin als Kind öfters in Schlesien gewesen."*

2 Her relatives were farmers. *„Meine Verwandten ... die hatten fast alle so Bauerngüter ..."*

3 She enjoyed nature, the countryside and the farming. *„Ich habe die Natur und die Landschaft und die Landwirtschaft auch geliebt."*

4 She helped with the farming. *„Ich hab' auch im Krieg dann dort mitgeholfen noch in der Landwirtschaft ..."*

5 She also liked being in Leipzig. *„Ich bin eigentlich auch gerne hier in Leipzig gewesen."*

6 Because her parents' house was in the country and on the edge of the forest. *„... bin ich auch so etwas mehr im Grünen und am Waldrand großgeworden."*

10 habe ... geliebt; habe ... mitgeholfen; habe ... empfunden; bin ... gewesen; bin ... großgeworden

11 Model answers are provided in *Hörabschnitt 2*, and the written version is in the transcript booklet.

12 Your answers may be different in some respects from this version. If so, check your version carefully against the texts in *Lerneinheit 1*, checking in particular that the word order is correct.

– Ihr Verwandter stammt aus Deutschland?

– *Nein. Er ist (im Jahre) 1924 in Frankreich geboren. (Er stammt aus Frankreich und ist dort 1924 geboren.)*

– Er hat aber in Deutschland gelebt, oder?

– *Ja. Er ist in Sachsen aufgewachsen/großgeworden. (Er hat seine Kindheit in Sachsen verbracht.)*

– Wo war er im Krieg?

– *Er hat den Krieg in Frankreich bei Verwandten verbracht. (Er war in Frankreich bei Verwandten.)*

– Er ist aber in Deutschland auf der Uni gewesen, nicht wahr?

– *Ja. Er hat 5 Jahre in Berlin studiert. (Er hat seine Studienzeit in Berlin verbracht. Er hat dort 5 Jahre studiert/verbracht.)*

– Und danach?

– *Danach ist er Geschichtslehrer geworden. (Er ist Geschichtslehrer in Paris geworden./Er war Geschichtslehrer in Paris.)*

Lerneinheit 2

1 Here are suggested answers.

1. Rudolf Kost betrachtet Tübingen als seine Heimat, weil er dort geboren ist und weil seine Familie seit Jahrhunderten dort ansässig ist.
2. Rudolf Dobler bezeichnet Tübingen als seine Heimat, weil sein Großvater und Vater aus Schwaben stammen und weil es ihm sehr gut in Tübingen gefällt.
3. Dr. Wilfried Setzler beschreibt Tübingen als seine Heimat, weil er dort seine Freunde hat, weil er sich dort auskennt, und weil er sich dort wohl fühlt.
4. Für Hans-Peter Baumeister ist Tübingen seine Heimat, weil seine Familie dort ist, weil sie ihre sozialen Kontakte dort haben und weil seine Arbeitsstelle dort ist.

2

1. Ihre Heimat ist da, wo sie gerade ist.
2. Nein. Sie stammt aus Glauchau/nicht aus Leipzig, sondern aus Glauchau.
3. Sie beschreibt sich als Leipzigerin.

(As you can see from the transcript booklet, Frau Stabenow says den Wunsch *and not* dem Wunsch. *This may be because when she began the sentence, she had not decided what verb to use at the end of the sentence. The verb she eventually used required the dative* dem Wunsch *rather than the accusative* den Wunsch.*)*

4. Er betrachtet sein Dorf als seine Heimat.
5. Weil seine Familie dort ist.
6. Seine Familie und sein Dorf bedeuten ihm besonders viel.
7. Nein. Ihre Mutter stammt aus Thüringen und ihr Vater aus dem Sudetenland.
8. Sie sind durch ihren Beruf in Rostock ansässig.
9. Dorothea Vogel ist in der DDR aufgewachsen.
10. Sie bezeichnet sich als Ostdeutsche.

3 Here are one person's reasons for regarding somewhere as her *Heimat.*

Ich betrachte Milton Keynes als meine Heimat, weil ich seit 22 Jahren hier wohne. Es gefällt mir hier, weil meine Familie und meine Arbeit hier sind und es gute soziale Kontakte gibt. Aufgewachsen bin ich aber nicht in Milton Keynes, sondern an der Südküste Englands.

4 Everyone's family tree will be different – but check back against the Baumeister-Neukamm *Stammbaum* to make sure you have included the words for all family members.

5

2. Die Tochter der Schwester meines Vaters. Das ist **meine Kusine**.
3. Die Mutter meines Vaters. Das ist **meine Großmutter**.
4. Der Sohn des Bruders meiner Mutter. Das ist **mein Vetter**.
5. Die Tochter meiner Eltern. Das ist **meine Schwester**.
6. Der Bruder meiner Mutter. Das ist **mein Onkel**.
7. Ich!

6

2. Die jüngere Schwester meines Mannes **ist im Jahre** 1944 **geboren**.
3. Die Tochter meines Bruders **heißt** Bianca.
4. Der Mann meiner Mutter **ist im Jahre** 1922 **geboren**.
5. Der älteste Vetter meiner Kinder **heißt** Michael.
6. Die Nichte meines Bruders **heißt** Lucy.

7

1. The *neue Länder* are in the east of Germany, the area covered by the former *Deutsche Demokratische Republik*.
2. The number of single-occupier households has increased considerably there.
3. The Statistical Office of the Federal Republic has published this information.
4. The statistics tell us that 1.9 million people live alone.
5. The consequence of the 2% growth is that more than one in every four is a single-occupier household.
6. In the *alte Länder* there was also an increase in the number of single-occupier households.

7 The overall position in Germany is that one third of households contain single people.

8 In Berlin over 50% of households are single-occupier households.

9 This trend has been constant since the early '80's.

10 The three sectors mentioned in the article are house- building, food and leisure.

11 In 2010 almost every second household will be single.

1993 haben in Deutschland rund **1,3 Millionen** Frauen und etwa **0,2 Millionen** Männer ihre Kinder allein erzogen. Die Zahl der Alleinerziehenden ist zwischen 1991 und 1993 um rund **100 000** Personen gestiegen. Etwa **40** Prozent der alleinerziehenden Männer und Frauen sind geschieden. Ungefähr ein **Drittel** der Männer und Frauen sind ledig.

Lerneinheit 3

1

1. They define *Heimat* and where it is for them.
2. He mentions Germany, Italy and Sweden.
3. Herr Naber and Herr Thassioulis come from Jordan and Greece.
4. Professor Bausinger says that clubs are the life of villages. Herr Winter confirms this by saying that the choir does not meet just to sing, but supports many festivals by taking part and also helps in the parish. („*Es ist nicht nur, daß wir ... unsere ... Singstunde haben, sondern wir feiern auch andere Feste, wir helfen auch in der Gemeinde.*") Note the use of *nicht ... sondern ...*

2

1. Frau Lotzmann liebt ihre Stadt, weil **sie dort einfach zu Hause ist**.
2. Auch wenn sie wegzieht, betrachtet die junge Frau im Gasthaus Tübingen als ihre Heimat, weil **ihre Eltern dort wohnen**, weil sie **dort Freunde hat**, weil **sie dort arbeitet** und weil **sie sich dort wohlfühlt**.
3. Herr Mayerhofer bezeichnet Leipzig als seine Heimat, weil er dort viele Schul-, Studien- und andere Freunde hat, weil er in Leipzig in die Schule gegangen ist, weil **er dort studiert hat**, weil **er dort seine Frau kennengelernt hat**, weil **er dort geheiratet hat** und weil **seine Kinder alle dort geboren sind**.

3 Riccardo Delfino ist Straßenmusikant von Beruf. Er ist in Krefeld geboren, aber sein Vater ist Italiener/ist in Italien geboren. Er hat in vielen Ländern gewohnt – in Schweden, Italien und Deutschland – und er ist ständig auf Reisen. Er weiß nicht mehr, wo seine Heimat ist.

4

1. Jettenburg liegt in der Nähe von Tübingen.
2. Dort gibt es einen Musikverein und einen Männergesangverein.
3. Herr Naber kommt aus Jordanien.
4. Er wohnt im Dorf seit fünf Jahren.
5. Deutschland ist seine zweite Heimat.
6. Er hat die Menschen gern, aber er mag das Wetter nicht.
7. Herr Thassioulis kommt aus Griechenland.
8. Er lebt seit 30 Jahren in Deutschland.

5

1. Man hat immer gesagt, Dorfkultur ist Vereinskultur.
2. Die Männer des Gesangvereins treffen sich jeden Freitag.
3. Sie singen an Weihnachten und an Ostern.
4. Der Gesangverein hat ihm geholfen, Leute kennenzulernen und eine neue Heimat aufzubauen.

(You may have noticed the *-n* ending on *Herr* in questions 3 and 4. In both questions, *Herr* is in the dative case (after *laut* in 3 and *helfen* in 4). In common with almost all masculine nouns which form their plural in *-n* or *-en*, *Herr* adds *-n* to the accusative, genitive and dative cases in the singular as well.)

6

1. Deutschland ist zur/zu ihrer zweiten Heimat geworden.
2. Die Mehrheit der Ausländer wohnt seit mehr als zehn Jahren in Deutschland.
3. Viele kennen das Land ihrer Eltern (*i.e. genitive – of their parents*) nur als Urlauber.
4. Sie tragen ein Zehntel zur Wirtschaftsleistung bei.

7

Ausländer in Deutschland 8,8 Millionen
Türkei 1 855 000
Ex-Jugoslawien über 900 000
Italien 558 000
Griechenland 346 000
Österreich 185 000
Rumänien 167 000
Spanien 134 000
Niederlande 114 000
USA 104 000

8

The words for nationality can be grouped by ending as follows.

Group 1 Italiener Österreicher Spanier Amerikaner
Group 2 Griechen Rumänen Türken Kurden

9

1. Ein Mann aus Polen ist ein **Pole**.
2. Eine Frau aus Großbritannien ist eine **Britin**.
3. Leute aus Amerika sind **Amerikaner**.
4. Eine Frau aus Frankreich ist eine **Französin** und ein Mann ist ein **Franzose**.
5. Ein Mann aus der Schweiz ist ein **Schweizer** und eine Frau ist eine **Schweizerin**.
6. Eine Frau aus Italien ist eine **Italienerin**.
7. Ein Mann aus Spanien ist ein **Spanier**.
8. Eine Frau aus der Türkei ist eine **Türkin** und ein Mann ist ein **Türke**.

10

1. They came from Cambodia.
2. Because their own family had been killed in the war.
3. His ambition is to become a self-employed carpenter.

12

1. Sie hatten ihre Eltern verloren.
2. Freunde in der ganzen Welt
3. Gäste aus drei Kontinenten
4. das Land ihrer Zukunft
5. es wurde ihre zweite Heimat
6. eng zusammen
7. alle vier sehen sich als Geschwister

13

Model answers are provided in *Hörabschnitt 5*, and the written version is in the transcript booklet.

Lerneinheit 4

1

1. Bettina says she does not know Leipzig very well. She has not seen much of it.
2. After the coffee comes, they talk about where Bettina lives and what kind of accommodation she is looking for.
3. Orhan tells Thomas that he is having a party and that Thomas will be getting an invitation.
4. Thomas tells Bettina that he is divorced and that he has a son.
5. Thomas wants to perform music in clubs.
6. Thomas invites Bettina to an evening at the Moritzbastei.
7. Sonja says she is not interested in what Bettina tells her.

2

Some alternative versions are given in these answers.

1. Bettina und Thomas sitzen am Fenster.
2. Bettina ist (erst) seit drei Wochen dort.

(*Note that Bettina says* „Erst seit drei Wochen hier“. Erst *means 'only' or 'just', here.*)

3. Thomas wohnt dort seit vier oder fünf Jahren.
4. Sie ist Lehrerin von Beruf.
5. Bettina findet die Schüler undiszipliniert.
6. Bettina wohnt bei einer Freundin in Connewitz.
7. Sie sucht eine etwas größere Wohnung, eine Wohnung mit einem Gästezimmer oder einem großen Wohnzimmer. (Sie möchte eine größere Wohnung haben.)
8. Bettina hat Tübingen verlassen, weil die Stadt zu kleinbürgerlich für sie war. (Weil sie lieber in einer Großstadt wohnt.)
9. Orhan kommt/stammt aus der Türkei.
10. Kai ist fast 7 Jahre alt.
11. Nein. Thomas ist nicht verheiratet. Er ist geschieden.

12 Nein. Sein Sohn wohnt bei der Mutter/bei Thomas Ex-Frau/bei der Ex-Frau von Thomas.

13 Thomas macht Straßenmusik, um Geld zu verdienen/weil er Geld verdienen muß/will.

14 Die Moritzbastei ist ein Café mit einem Bierkeller und Veranstaltungsräumen.

15 Thomas lädt Bettina für morgen abend ein.

3 Here is a suggested version with some variations. When checking your answer, pay attention to the perfect tenses – the form and position of the auxiliary verbs and the past participles.

Ich habe Thomas in der Grimmaischen Straße getroffen und wir sind in ein Café – das Café Corso – gegangen. Wir haben über die Arbeit gesprochen./Ich habe ihm von meiner Arbeit erzählt. Er ist Student/Er studiert auf der Hochschule für Musik und Theater und er ist außerdem Straßenmusikant, weil er Geld verdienen muß/will/möchte. Sein türkischer Freund ist vorbeigekommen. Er hat ihn zu einer Party eingeladen. Thomas hat von seiner Familie erzählt. Er ist geschieden und hat einen kleinen Sohn. Er hat mich (für) morgen abend in die Moritzbastei eingeladen.

4 Thomas would get invitation 2 if it is intended for Kai as well, as Orhan mentioned. He would get invitation 1 only if it were just for him. Invitation 1 uses the familiar singular *du bist* and *sag*, and invitation 2 uses the familiar plural *ihr seid* and *sagt*.

5

a This is addressed to more than one friend. The clues are *euch*, *sagt*, *ihr*, *euer*.

b This is a formal invitation.The clues are *Sie*, *Ihr*.

c This invitation is to one friend. The clues are *dich*, *sag*, *du*, *dein*.

7 Complete versions of the conversations are given in the transcript booklet.

9 This is how the conversation should run.

Frau Braun	**Guten Abend**, Herr Bürgermeister. **Wie geht es Ihnen**?
Bürgermeister	**Guten Abend**, Frau Braun. Sehr gut, danke. **Und Ihnen**?
Frau Braun	Auch gut, danke. Schön, daß **Sie gekommen sind**. **Kommen Sie** doch 'rein. Darf ich **Ihnen** Sybille Schneider, meine Nachbarin, vorstellen?
Bürgermeister	**Guten Abend**, Frau Schneider. Freut mich, **Sie** kennenzulernen.
Frau Schneider	Guten Abend, Herr Bürgermeister. Schön, daß Sie kommen konnten.

8

Greetings	Introductions and responses	Enquiring how someone is and responding
Hallo!	Darf ich dir meinen Freund Bernd vorstellen?	Wie geht's euch?
Guten Abend!	Freut mich, dich kennenzulernen.	Mir geht's gut.
	Freut mich auch.	Was ist mit deiner Mutter? Geht es ihr wieder besser?
	Bernd, das ist Ülkü, eine Freundin von Sultan.	Danke, gut.
	Darf ich Ihnen meine Nachbarin, Frau Schneider, vorstellen?	Wie geht es Ihnen?
	Darf ich euch Herrn Holzner vorstellen?	Sehr gut, vielen Dank.

Other such polite phrases you might have added.

Greetings	Introductions and responses	Enquiring how someone is and responding
Guten Morgen!	Freut mich.	Danke, sehr gut.
Guten Tag!		Danke, es geht.
Grüß Gott!		Wie geht's (dir)?
Servus!		
Grüezi!		

10 Model answers are provided in *Hörabschnitt 7*, and the written version is in the transcript booklet.

Lerneinheit 5

1 **Wilfried Setzler** ist zwischen fünfzig und fünfundfünfzig Jahre alt. Er hat einen graumelierten Bart und einen Schnurrbart. Er trägt **eine Brille** und er **lächelt**, während er **spricht**. Wie Herr Kost und Herr Dobler ist er **im Freien**.

Tanja Lindl hat lange, rötliche **Haare**, ein rundes **Gesicht** und sie trägt **eine Brille**.

Ruth Stabenow hat blonde, kurze wellige **Haare**. Sie trägt **eine Brille** und Ohrringe.

Thomas Walter hat einen kleinen Schnurrbart und braune Haare. Er hat ein schmales Gesicht. Er **lächelt** nicht, sondern sieht ernst aus.

Dorothea Vogel sieht auch **ernst** aus. Sie hat ein blasses **Gesicht** und eine hohe Stirn.

Hans-Peter Baumeister lächelt ein bißchen. Seine Haare sind fast weiß aber er hat schwarze Augenbrauen. Er hat einen **Schnurrbart** und einen **Bart**, und er trägt **eine Brille**. Er ist Mitte vierzig. Seine Frau, **Renate**, sitzt neben ihm. Sie hat dunkelbraune Augen und glatte, **rote** Haare. Sie trägt **Ohrringe**. Sie ist Anfang vierzig.

2

1. Er hat einen **graumelierten** Bart. Er trägt eine Brille.
2. Er hat weiße Haare und **schwarze** Augenbrauen. Sein Bart ist graumeliert. Er trägt eine runde Brille.
3. Herr Utz ist ein **alter** Mann. Er hat **graue** Haare und ist glattrasiert.
4. Sie hat **blaue** Ohrringe, **glatte**, **rote** Haare und trägt keine Brille.
5. Herr Bosch hat **kurze**, graue Haare.
6. Ihre Haare sind **braun** und kurz.
7. Sie ist eine junge Frau mit **langen**, roten Haaren.
8. Er ist ein junger Mann. Er hat **kurze**, **braune** Haare.
9. Sie ist eine **junge** Frau mit **schwarzen** Haaren.

3 Gesine Jüttner ist gebürtig**e** Leipzigerin. Sie ist Mitte 30. Sie hat schulterlang**e**, rot**e** Haare und dunkelbraun**e** Augen mit schmal**en** Augenbrauen. (*Note: it is* schmalen *because* mit *is followed by the dative.*)

Günter Leypoldt hat ein glattrasiert**es** Gesicht. Er wohnt in Tübingen im alt**en** Teil der Stadt.

Sibylle Metzger ist Studentin. Sie trägt groß**e**, silbern**e** Ohrringe. Wo wohnt sie? Sie wohnt mit zwei ander**en** Frauen in einer schön**en** Wohnung mit einem groß**en** Balkon in Tübingen.

Daniela Krafak wohnt in Leipzig. Sie teilt eine groß**e** und schön**e** Wohnung mit ihrem Freund.

Tanja Lindl wohnt in der sehr schön**en** Altstadt von Tübingen. Wie sieht sie aus? Sie hat ein rund**es** Gesicht, eine hoh**e** Stirn und sie trägt eine rund**e** Brille.

Ruth Stabenow hat eine klein**e** Wohnung in einer ruhig**en** Lage in Leipzig. Sie hat gut**e** Freunde in ihrem Wohnblock.

Hans-Peter Baumeister wohnt mit seiner Frau und seinen Kindern in einem modern**en** Haus in Tübingen. Er hat einen graumeliert**en** Bart, und er trägt eine rund**e** Brille.

4

1. He calls him tall and cheerful. (The usual word for tall is *groß*.)
2. He says he had a beard and round spectacles.
3. She says he is always happy and open-minded.
4. Sibylle has red hair. She is very nice and cheerful.
5. The man didn't speak to Anna because he cannot stand her.
6. He thinks she is stupid and unpleasant.
7. She has green hair and wears a lot of make-up.
8. She asks who he was talking to for such a long time.
9. He says she is very nice, rather quiet but interested in everything.
10. She can't stand him.
11. No.
12. She says that he is obstinate and arrogant. He gets on her nerves.

5 Your descriptions should be similar to these.

Sibylle hat rote Haare und die Frau findet sie immer lustig und freundlich.

Anna hat grüne Haare, sie ist geschminkt, und der Mann findet sie dumm und unsympathisch.

Der Mann findet **Angelika** nett. Sie ist ruhig, aber sie interessiert sich für alles.

Die Frau findet **Peter** nicht unfreundlich, aber stur und arrogant.

6 Here are the answers, with clues from the adverts.

1 e *„Tel. 44 87 26 täglich 19–21 Uhr."*

2 c *„gesch. (1 Kind); mit viels. kulturellen Interessen "*

3 f *„Nichtraucher"; „Unternehmer"; „interessiert sich für … gemütl. Zuhause."*

4 a *„spät. Ehe mögl.."; „mit viels. Interessen … Reisen"*

5 d *„mit Sinn für Humor"; „(wenn mögl. mit Bild)"*

6 b *„Witwe"*

7 c *„möchte zuverlässigen … Mann … kennenlernen"*

8 e *„möchte … dynamische Lebensgefährtin … kennenlernen"*

9 b *„dunkel u. schlank"*

10 a *„freut sich auf begeisterungsfähigen, aufgeschlossenen Partner"*

7 Model answers are provided in *Hörabschnitt 9*, and the written version is in the transcript booklet.

Lerneinheit 6

1

2 Rudolf Dobler trägt eine dunkelblaue **Jacke,** einen blauen Pullover und einen **karierten** Hut.

3 Wilfried Setzler hat einen **dunklen/schwarzen** Mantel und ein **weißes** Hemd an. Er trägt einen gelben **Schal,** aber keine **Krawatte**.

4 Tanja Lindl trägt einen dunkelgrünen **Pullover**.

5 Ruth Stabenow hat eine lila Bluse und einen lila **Pullover** an.

6 Thomas Walter hat einen weißen **Schutzhelm** auf. Er trägt ein **grünes Hemd** und eine **braune** Öljacke.

7 Dorothea Vogel hat zwei blaue Pullover an, einen hellblauen und einen **dunkelblauen**.

8 Hans-Peter Baumeister hat **einen schwarzen Pullover** und **ein weißes Hemd** an. Seine Frau, Renate, trägt ein buntes Halstuch und **einen schwarzen Pullover**.

(You might have wondered why the adjectives don't decline in *eine lila Bluse* and *einen lila Pullover.* Some adjectives of colour do not change their endings – *lila* and *rosa* (pink) are two.

Hell and *dunkel* can be added to a colour to indicate tone, e.g. *hellgrün, dunkelblau*. Note that *dunkel* loses its *-e-* when it has an ending, e.g. *eine dunkle Krawatte.*)

Lerntip

1 c **2** b **3** d **4** a

2 Did you spot all these items of clothing?

1 Zwei Frauen sprechen miteinander. Die Frau auf der linken Seite hat **eine blaue Regenjacke/einen blauen Anorak** an und die andere Frau trägt **eine weiße Regenjacke/einen weißen Anorak**.

2 Zwei Senioren stehen auf der Straße und unterhalten sich. Die Frau trägt **einen schwarzen Mantel** und **Handschuhe**, und der Mann trägt **einen (dunklen)/ dunkelblauen Regenmantel** und **einen schwarzen Hut**.

3 Fünf Kinder und eine junge Frau gehen spazieren. Die Kinder haben alle bunte **Kleidung/Anoraks** und **Hosen** an und die junge Frau trägt eine braune Jacke, **eine Jeans** und **braune Schuhe**.

4 Vier junge Leute unterhalten sich. Zwei stehen und zwei sitzen. Die zwei, die stehen, tragen **Lederjacken** und einer von ihnen trägt eine **Jeans**, und der andere trägt eine **weiße Hose**. Beide tragen **schwarze** Schuhe.

5 Ein Mann und eine Frau gehen am Marktplatz vorbei. Sie trägt **einen hellbraunen Regenmantel**, und er hat **eine weiße Regenjacke** an.

3

1. Uwe Kürten trägt meistens Jeans und Hemden.
2. Im Winter trägt sie Leggings.
3. Weil es zu ihren Augen und ihren roten Haaren paßt.
4. Weil Andreas Schnitter oft im Freien ist.
5. Weil sie ihm nicht stehen.
6. Nein, Tanja Polinski trägt dieselben Sachen in der Freizeit wie bei der Arbeit.
7. Albrecht Winter trägt einen Anzug, weil er oft mit Kunden zu tun hat.

4

1. Herr Kürten mag Pullis, Jeans und Hemden.
2. Anzüge mag er nicht.
3. Frau Unterberg trägt sehr gern Leggings.
4. Zum Ausgehen trägt sie einen Rock und einen Pullover.
5. Frau Reus trägt bei besonderen Anlässen ein schwarzes Kostüm.
6. Sie trägt Schuhe mit hohen Absätzen zu besonderen Anlässen.
7. Herr Schiffer trägt selten formelle Kleider.
8. Richtig.
9. Richtig.
10. Im Büro gibt es keine Vorschriften.
11. Graue Anzüge sind nicht Herrn Winters Geschmack.
12. Er trägt einen Anzug, wenn er mit Kunden zu tun hat.

5

1. She likes to wear loose shirts or blouses.
2. Tight clothes don't suit her.
3. She likes to wear comfortable clothes.
4. She likes to spend a lot of money on clothes.
5. He has no choice about what he wears because he's in a management position (literally: a leading position) in a bank.
6. At work he wears a dark suit, or jacket, a white shirt and a discreet (literally: decent) tie.
7. At the weekend he wears sporty clothes.
8. He also mentions cotton trousers.

6

1. Diese Lehrerin braucht keine **schicke** Kleidung zu tragen. Bei **der** Arbeit trägt sie meistens **bequeme** Kleidung. Zu besonderen **Anlässen** gibt sie gern viel Geld **aus** und kauft sich schöne **Kleider**.
2. Dieser Mann ist Manager **bei** einer Bank und **hat** viel mit wichtigen **Kunden** zu tun. Deshalb trägt er **einen** dunklen Anzug und ein **weißes** Hemd.

7&8

Model answers are provided in *Hörabschnitte 11* and *12* respectively, and the written versions are in the transcript booklet.

Lerneinheit 7

1

Here are the answers with extracts from the video, which should have given you the clues you needed.

1. Gesine Jüttner comes from Leipzig. „*... ich selber würde mich erstmal als Leipzigerin schlechthin bezeichnen.*"
2. The people of Leipzig are very open to anything new. „*... mit der typischen Eigenart, aufgeschlossen zu sein für alles Fremde.*"
3. She sums herself up as a real local patriot. „*Ich bin also 'n ausgesprochener Lokalpatriot!*"
4. Leipzig has the oldest trade fair in Germany. „*Wir haben ... die älteste Messe Deutschlands ...*"
5. The town is famous for books, sport and science. „*... berühmt in der ganzen Welt als die Stadt des Buches, des Sports, der Wissenschaft.*"
6. The town has the the second oldest university in Germany. „*Wir haben die zweitälteste Universität in Deutschland ...*"
7. It has fine museums. „*Wir haben schöne Museen.*"

2

1. Georg Rübling has lived in Leipzig for 25 years. „*Meine Heimat ist seit 25 Jahren Leipzig ...*"
2. He considers Leipzig his home town because his work has been there; his friends and some of his relatives also live there; he has

spent most of his life there and intends to spend the rest of his life there. *„... weil ich hier meine Arbeit hatte, weil ich meine Freunde hier habe, einige Verwandte, und weil ich ja auch fast den größten Teil meines Lebens schon hier verbracht habe und den Rest meines Lebens hier verbringen werde."*

3 He used to live in Grünau, 10 minutes away. *„... in Grünau ... ungefähr 10 Minuten von hier entfernt ..."*

4 They decided to build a house on their land because they used to spend the summers there anyway. *„... weil wir den ganzen Sommer über ohnehin auf diesem Grundstück gewohnt haben."*

5 They intend to move in by Christmas. *„... wir beabsichtigen, bis Weihnachten einzuziehen ..."*

3 Here is a suggested description of Herr Rübling and his building plans.

Herr Rübling betrachtet Leipzig als seine Heimat, weil er seine Freunde dort hat/weil seine Freunde dort wohnen/leben, weil er dort einige Verwandte hat/weil einige Verwandte dort wohnen und weil er den größten Teil seines Lebens dort verbracht hat/weil er schon 25 Jahre dort wohnt. Er wird den Rest seines Lebens dort verbringen.

Er hat früher in Grünau gewohnt. Er hat aber ein Grundstück, wo er und seine Frau den Sommer verbringen. Dort bauen sie ein Haus. Sie beabsichtigen, bis Weihnachten einzuziehen.

4

1 Professor Rotzsch is talking about the effects of the *Wende*. *„Wir haben jetzt nach der Wende 1989 ..."*

2 He is particularly happy about the opportunity to travel and get to know many west German cities. *„... die Möglichkeit wieder zu reisen ... Und ich freue mich sehr, daß ich nun jetzt erst viele westdeutsche Städte kennenlernen darf ..."*

3 He says that the east German cities suffered a lot after the war and were not looked after. *„... und sehe den Status dieser Städte im Verhältnis zum Verfall unserer Städte, die nach diesem Krieg enorm gelitten haben, und die nicht gepflegt wurden."*

4 In Germany. *„... ich fühle mich schon in Deutschland zu Hause ..."*

5 He was 15. *„... ich war fünfzehn Jahre, als dieser Krieg zu Ende ging ..."*

6 Because he can feel at home in Europe. *„Und deswegen freue ich mich so sehr, daß wir durch diese Verbindung mit Frankreich oder auch jetzt mit Großbritannien die Brücken schlagen können, um in Europa zu Hause zu sein."*

5

1 Deutschland liegt in der Mitte/im Herzen Europas.

2 Deutschland hat neun Nachbarstaaten.

3 Deutschland wird als Durchgangsland bezeichnet, weil es Nordeuropa und den Mittelmeerraum verbindet und weil es West- und Osteuropa verbindet.

4 Deutschland ist Mitglied der Europäischen Union und der NATO.

5 Es ist eine Brücke zu den osteuropäischen Staaten.

6 Read through the transcript of *Hörabschnitt 13* and check your answers. The data in Activity 6 is set out in the same order as in the transcript.

7 Model answers are given in *Hörabschnitt 14*, and the written version in the transcript booklet.

Lerneinheit 8

2

1 c *„... geboren bin ich in Breslau ..."*

2 e *„... wir wurden 1946 mit dem Rest der deutschen Bevölkerung evakuiert ..."*

3 b *„... in Ostfriesland ... und dort verbrachten ... die ersten drei Schuljahre ..."*

4 f *„... in Gelsenkirchen, ging dort aufs Gymnasium, machte dort Abitur ..."*

5 a *„... ich ging nach dem Abitur für zwei Jahre zur Bundeswehr nach Oberbayern ..."*

6 d *„... begann ich meine Studien in Tübingen."*

3 This is a suggested answer.

Harald Winck ist in Polen geboren. 1946 ist seine Familie nach Ostfriesland gekommen. Dort ist er drei Jahre in die Schule gegangen. 1951 ist seine Familie ins Ruhrgebiet gezogen. Dort ist er aufs Gymnasium gegangen und hat Abitur gemacht. Dann ist er für zwei Jahre zur Bundeswehr nach Oberbayern gegangen. Danach hat er in Tübingen studiert. Jetzt wohnt er in Tübingen.

4

	RICHTIG	FALSCH
1 *„Ich war Student noch …“*	☒	☐
2 *„… mit etwa damals 70- bis 75jährigen älteren Herren …“*	☐	☒
3 *„… einer erzählte, daß er in Mannheim beim Militär gewesen sei.“*	☐	☒
4 *„… da waren Bayern, da waren Schwaben, da waren Hessen …“*	☒	☐
5 *„Da waren wir ganz international …“*	☒	☐

6 Harald Winck says *„Man ist Deutscher in zweiter Hinsicht erst, oder in Konkurrenz mit einer anderen Nationalität.“* In his view, being German takes second place to being a Swabian or a Bavarian, unless you are comparing yourself with someone from another country entirely.

5 1c 2b 3a 4c

Lerneinheit 9

1 The twelve prepositions used are: *an; aus; bei; bis; durch; entlang; für; in; nach; über; von; zu.*

Here are the prepositions as they appear in the text.

durch die Schweiz *accusative*

entlang den Grenzen *dative*

von Österreich *dative*

im (**in** dem) Schweizer Kanton *dative*

durch den Bodensee *accusative*

über den Rheinfall bei Schaffhausen *accusative*

nach Basel *dative*

von dort fließt er **über** Straßburg *accusative*

bis er **bei** Rotterdam *accusative, dative*

in die Nordsee *accusative*

bis Ende *accusative*

Note that *bis* is never used with an article. It is used alone with a time (*bis 5 Uhr,* until 5 o'clock), or with another preposition (*bis zum nächsten Mal,* until next time, *bis zum Mittelmeer,* as far as the Mediterranean).

für große Transportschiffe *accusative*

bis Ludwigshafen *accusative*

von der Nordsee *dative*

bis **zum** (zu dem) Mittelmeer *dative*

über den Rhein-Main-Donau-Kanal *accusative*

bis **zum** Schwarzen Meer *dative*

in den letzten Jahren *accusative*

am (**an** dem) Niederrhein *dative*

von großer Bedeutung *dative*

im Rheintal *dative*

aus der Römerzeit *dative*

am Rhein *dative*

von der wichtigen politischen Bedeutung *dative*

im Mittelpunkt *dative*

in Worms *dative*

zum Beispiel *dative*

im 5. Jahrhundert *dative*

nach der Nibelungensage *dative*

in den Rhein *accusative*

2

1 **Von** der Schweiz **bis** in die Nordsee fließt der Rhein **durch** sechs Länder.
2 Von Schaffhausen fließt der Rhein **entlang** der Grenze zwischen Deutschland und der Schweiz.
3 Nördlich von Basel fließt der Rhein ungefähr 170 km **entlang** der Grenze zu Frankreich.
4 Danach fließt er **durch** das Bundesland Rheinland-Pfalz.
5 **Über** den Rhein-Main-Donau-Kanal ist die Schiffahrt bis zum Schwarzen Meer möglich.
6 Der Mittelrhein ist **seit** 1900 schiffbar.
7 Heute fahren Frachtschiffe bis **zum** Mittelmeer.

8 Wie die Elbe mündet der Rhein **in** die Nordsee.

9 **Für** den Handel ist der Rhein sehr wichtig.

10 Der Rhein fließt **bei** Rotterdam in die Nordsee.

3

1 Von **der** Rheinquelle in der Schweiz bis zur **der** (**zur**) Mündung sind es mehr als 1 000 km.

2 Der Rhein fließt zwischen Bregenz und St. Gallen durch **den** Bodensee.

3 Seit 1900 ist der Fluß zwischen **der** Stadt Basel in der Schweiz und **der** deutschen Stadt Mannheim schiffbar.

4 Der Rhein fließt entlang **der** französischen Grenze.

5 Nach **dem** Ruhrgebiet fließt der Rhein langsamer.

6 Für **die** Industrie ist der Rhein eine wichtige Verkehrsader.

7 Die Sage der Nibelungen stammt aus **dem** 13. Jahrhundert.

8 Hagen hat das Rheingold bei Worms in **den** Fluß geworfen.

9 Auf dem Niederrhein herrscht reger Schiffsverkehr.

10 Vor Rotterdam fließt der Rhein durch **eine** Landschaft, die sehr flach ist.

4

der Rhein; der Wasserweg; fließen; entspringen; der Rheinfall; münden; schiffbar; die Binnenwasserstraße; die Flutkatastrophe; die Überschwemmung; der Niederrhein

5

Die Elbe ist der wichtigste **Wasserweg** in Norddeutschland. Sie **mündet** nördlich von Hamburg in die Nordsee, aber ihre Quelle liegt weit im Süden. Dieser Fluß **entspringt** in den Bergen der Tschechischen Republik und von dort **fließt** er in einer nordwestlichen Richtung durch Deutschland. Die Elbe ist auf ihrer ganzen Länge in Deutschland **schiffbar**. Dann und wann, im Frühling oder im Winter, gibt es in der Nähe von Hamburg **Überschwemmungen**.

6

Here are the answers, together with extracts from the article, which should have given you the clues you needed.

1 The people in the affected areas cannot assume the worst is over yet. *„Die Menschen in den … betroffenen Regionen … können noch nicht aufatmen."*

2 Recent heavy rain and snow have caused the floods. *„Nach neuen heftigen Regenfällen und Schneetreiben …"*

3 Six *Länder* are affected by the flooding. *„… Hessen, Rheinland-Pfalz, Baden-Württemberg und Niedersachsen … Nordrhein-Westfalen und Bayern."*

4 In Göttingen the floods are the worst for almost 50 years. *„Die Region Göttingen erlebt derzeit das schlimmste Hochwasser seit fast 50 Jahren."*

5 The Weser is flooding near Göttingen. *„Die Weser erreichte … 6,21 Metern."*

6 In Köln a few suburbs are flooded. The old town has survived so far. *„… einige Vororte … unter Wasser stehen, blieb die Altstadt … verschont."*

7 The Mainz authorities forecast a disastrous Rhein flood. *„… das Hochwasserzentrum in Mainz warnt bereits vor einer verheerenden Rhein-Flut."*

8 At the weekend the levels of December 1993 could be reached or exceeded. *„Zum Wochenende könnten die Pegelstände vom Dezember 1993 erreicht oder überschritten werden."*

9 The problem on the Mosel has been caused by heavy rain. *„Starke Regenfälle haben eine neue Flutwelle ausgelöst."*

7

1 Göttingen hat das schlimmste Hochwasser seit Jahren **erlebt**.

2 Am Donnerstagabend hat das Wasser einen Stand von 6,21 Metern **erreicht**.

3 Auch der Rhein ist wieder **gestiegen**.

4 Die Altstadt von Köln ist verschont **geblieben**.

5 Das Hochwasserzentrum von Mainz hat vor einer Rhein-Flut **gewarnt**.

Lerneinheit 10

1 Here is a suggested summary.

Frau Schmidt ist in Leipzig geboren. Ihr Vater stammt aus Leipzig, aber ihre Mutter ist in Berlin geboren und in Österreich aufgewachsen (.:. hat ihre Kindheit in Österreich verbracht). Nach dem ersten Weltkrieg haben ihre Eltern in Leipzig geheiratet. Sie ist in Leipzig zur Schule gegangen und hat dort ihren Mann kennengelernt. Sie waren 44 Jahre verheiratet.

2 Ich bin 31 Jahre alt und komme aus Rumänien. In meiner Heimat **habe** ich Abitur **gemacht,** dann **bin** ich zum Militär **gegangen**. Danach **bin** ich ins Ausland **gegangen**, zunächst nach Griechenland. Da **habe** ich eine Hotelfachschule **besucht** und jetzt bin ich Hotelfachmann.

Nach zwei Jahren **bin** ich nach Deutschland **gekommen**, und hier arbeite ich jetzt als Hotelkaufmann.

Ja, mit den Menschen habe ich eigentlich keine Probleme, so gut wie keine Schwierigkeiten. Ich **habe** viele Deutsche **kennengelernt**. Die meisten sind sehr kontaktfreudig und versuchten immer wieder zu helfen, wo etwas zu helfen war.

3

1. Er ist in Rumänien **geboren**.
2. In Rumänien ist er zur Schule **gegangen**.
3. Er hat dort den Militärdienst **gemacht**.
4. Danach hat er Rumänien **verlassen**.
5. Er ist nach Griechenland **gegangen**.
6. Dort hat er eine Ausbildung in einer Hotelfachschule **gemacht**.
7. Er ist nach Deutschland **gereist/gefahren/gegangen/gekommen**.
8. Mit den Menschen hat er keine Probleme **gehabt**.
9. Er hat die Deutschen sehr kontaktfreudig **gefunden**.
10. Deutschland hat ihn an seine Heimat **erinnert**.

4 Here is a suggested summary.

He grew up in Romania, where he did his military service. He trained at a college of hotel management in Greece. After two years he moved to Germany, where he now works as a hotel manager. Most of the Germans he has got to know are very sociable and helpful.

He feels at home in Germany. Many things remind him of Romania, such as buildings, streets, the climate, the vegetation and the people.

5 Here are the answers, with quotations from the text, which should have given you clues.

1. Weil er zu jung ist. *„Er ist sieben Jahre alt …"*
2. Weil er Disneyland besuchen möchte. *„Und er fährt ins Disneyland nach Paris."*
3. Er hat drei Geschwister. *„… eines von vier Geschwistern."*
4. Sie lebt seit Toms Geburt von staatlicher Hilfe. *„… lebt seit Toms Geburt von staatlicher Hilfe."*
5. Nein. Sie hat nur die älteren Kinder alleine aufgezogen. *„Ihre älteren Kinder … hat sie alleine aufgezogen."*
6. Er durfte nicht in Deutschland arbeiten, weil er Ausländer/Ägypter ist. *„Der Vater … ist Ägypter und durfte bis vor kurzem nicht in Deutschland arbeiten."*

6

1. Er hat die ersten Jahre **seines/des** Lebens in Rumänien verbracht.
2. Die Dauer **seines/des** Aufenthalts in Griechenland war zwei Jahre.
3. Die meisten **seiner/der** Kollegen waren sehr kontaktfreudig.
4. Der Mann **seiner** Mutter stammt aus Ägypten.
5. Der Preis **eines/des** Kostüms war sehr hoch für die Familie.
6. Der Traum **des** Jungen, ist einen Computer zu kaufen.

7

2. Der Parthenon ist ein griechisches Gebäude.
3. Edamer ist ein holländischer Käse.
4. Der Neckar ist ein deutscher Fluß.
5. Paella ist eine spanische Spezialität.
6. Verdi ist ein italienischer Komponist.
7. Baseball ist ein amerikanischer Sport.
8. Ein Ferrari ist ein italienischer Wagen.

9 Der Dudelsack ist ein schottisches Instrument.

10 Cricket ist ein englischer Sport.

11 Döner Kebab ist eine türkische Spezialität.

8 The correct order is as follows.

b Am Wochenende feiert das pfälzische Dorf Iggelbach seine Weinkerwe. Die Kerwe beginnt am Freitagabend.

h Der Bürgermeister eröffnet das Fest und lädt alle zur Weinprobe ein.

d Zur Eröffnung singen die Gesangsvereine von Elmstein und Iggelbach Weinlieder.

c Am Samstag feiern die Leute ab 14 Uhr im Festzelt, und ab 20 Uhr spielen die „Pfälzer Musikanten".

a Der Kerwe-Umzug beginnt am Sonntag um 14 Uhr auf dem Zimmerplatz und zieht die Dorfstraße hinunter bis zum Kerweplatz. Dort hören alle die Kerwerede.

e Höhepunkt ist die Verlosung eines Schweins am Sonntagnachmittag.

g Der traditionelle Montagsfrühschoppen fängt dieses Jahr um 10 Uhr an.

f Am Dienstag endet die Iggelbacher Kerwe mit einem Heringsessen.

9 Here is a possible version, using eleven examples of the perfect tense.

Am Wochenende hat das pfälzische Dorf Iggelbach seine Weinkerwe gefeiert.

Die Kerwe **hat** am Freitagabend **begonnen**. Der Bürgermeister **hat** das Fest **eröffnet** und alle zur Weinprobe **eingeladen**. Zur Eröffnung **haben** die Gesangsvereine von Elmstein und Iggelbach Weinlieder **gesungen**. Am Samstag **haben** die Leute ab 14 Uhr im Festzelt **gefeiert**, und ab 20 Uhr **haben** die „Pfälzer Musikanten" **gespielt**. Der Kerwe-Umzug **hat** am Sonntag um 14 Uhr auf dem Zimmerplatz **begonnen** und ist die Dorfstraße **hinuntergezogen** bis zum Kerweplatz. Dort **haben** alle die Kerwerede **gehört**. Höhepunkt ist die Verlosung eines Schweins am Sonntagnachmittag **gewesen**. Der traditionelle Montagsfrühschoppen **hat** dieses Jahr um 10 Uhr **angefangen**. Am Dienstag **hat** die Iggelbacher Kerwe mit einem Heringsessen **geendet**.

Lerneinheit 11

1 So einer wie ich, ich meine: In meinem Alter, ist heute verunsichert. Ein Beispiel: Nachbarn geben eine große Party. Als meine Frau und ich geklingelt haben, öffnet uns die Hausfrau. „Schön, daß **ihr** kommt," sagt sie. Und ich denke: „Duzen wir uns denn?" Ich weiß es nicht genau, aber eins weiß ich: Wenn ich jetzt sage: „Wir haben **Ihnen** diese Blumen mitgebracht," dann klingt das fast frostig. Man sagt heute besser: „Wir haben **euch** diese Blumen mitgebracht." Und nach ein paar Gläsern Wein sagen dann sowieso alle **„du"**. Das ist heute so.

Nur der ältere Herr mit Krawatte sagt den ganzen Abend ganz klar **„Sie"** zu allen Gästen und fühlt sich dabei auch wohl.

Die dritte Möglichkeit ist, immer eine ganze Gruppe gleichzeitig anzusprechen, und das universale **„ihr"** zu verwenden. Damit macht man bestimmt nichts falsch!

2

1 He feels uncertain about how he should reply to the hostess's welcome.

2 He decides to use *euch* (the informal mode of address) instead of *Ihnen* (the formal mode of address).

3 People will all use the informal *du*.

4 The older gentleman uses the formal *Sie*.

5 The third option is to address people *en masse*, using *ihr*.

3

1
- Guten Tag Frau Bauer. Darf ich **Ihnen** meinen Mann vorstellen?
- Guten Tag Herr Bowes. Freut mich, **Sie** kennenzulernen. Seit wann sind **Sie** in Marburg?
- Ich bin schon eine Woche hier.
- Und gefällt **Ihnen** unsere Stadt?
- Ja, sehr.
- Also, mein Mann und ich, wir möchten **Sie** zu uns einladen. Könnten **Sie** morgen abend zu uns kommen?
- Ja. Danke sehr. Um wieviel Uhr?

2 Mutter Da seid **ihr** endlich!

Axel Hast **du** lange warten müssen?

Mutter Ja. Warum seid **ihr** so spät?

Axel	Naja. Das Auto, **du** weißt wie es ist.
Mutter	Ach. Axel, wie oft habe ich **dir** gesagt, daß **du** diese alte Klapperkiste verkaufen sollst!
Axel	Ja. Ich weiß schon. Also, wie geht's **dir**?
Mutter	Gut danke. Und **euch** beiden?
Britta	Einigermaßen. Sag mal, ist deine Enkelin bei **dir**?
Mutter	Ja. Seit gestern. Sie freut sich sehr auf euren Besuch. Auf **dich** besonders, Britta. Aber komm mal 'rein.

4 Here are two more examples.

1 Lehrerin, Anfang 40, freut sich auf toleranten und begeisterungsfähigen Partner. Kulturelle Interessen: Reisen, Theater und Lesen.

2 Unternehmer, Mitte 50, aufgeschlossener und sportlicher Typ, möchte zuverlässige, und humorvolle Lebensgefährtin bis 50 für gemeinsame Zukunft kennenlernen.

5 Here are some possible answers. Note the adjectival endings.

1 Der Gentleman-Boxer liebt toll**e** Klamotten. Er mag auch sportlich-elegant**e** Kleidung. Er trägt gern Hosenträger und Mützen.

2 Der Fußballspieler hat am liebsten bequem**e** Jeans und bunt**e** T-Shirts. Aber manchmal trägt er auch ein klassisch**es** Outfit.

3 Der Formel-1-Weltmeister liebt sein**en** Renn-Overall. Er trägt gern leger**e** Kleidung, aber er mag auch fein**e**, weiß**e** Hemden.

6 Here are two descriptions.

1 **Angela Winter** Sie ist Mitte 30. Sie ist groß. Sie hat lange, schwarze Haare und trägt eine Brille. Sie trägt ein blaues Kostüm/einen blauen Anzug, ein buntes Halstuch und einen Regenmantel.

2 **Gerhard Reuter** Er hat kurze, graue Haare und einen Vollbart. Er ist Anfang 50. Er trägt keine Brille. Er trägt einen weißen Anzug.

7 The correct order is c, h, i, a, e, f, b, d.

8 Here is a suggestion for the life history.
Er ist in Berlin-Charlottenburg geboren und in der Nähe vom Alexanderplatz aufgewachsen. Er und seine Freunde haben in den Ruinen gespielt. Er ist in Berlin zur Schule gegangen und hat dort Abitur gemacht. Später ist seine Familie in den Westen gegangen. Er hat studiert und dann im Ausland gearbeitet. Nach 40 Jahren hat er Berlin wieder besucht. Er wollte die Welt seiner Kindheit wiedersehen, aber alles war fremd. Das war das letzte Mal, daß er dorthin gefahren ist. Berlin ist nicht seine Heimat.

9 In **seinem** Reisepaß steht, daß er in Berlin geboren wurde. Zwar hat er **seine/die** Kindheit dort verbracht und hat dort auch **das** Gymnasium besucht, aber er betrachtet Berlin nicht als **seine** Heimat. In **der** großen Ruine die Berlin damals war, waren ihm sogar **die** neuen Häuser fremd. Mit **seinen/den** Eltern hat er **die** Stadt verlassen und hat ein neues Leben **im** Westen angefangen.

10

S	X	T	S	O	P	G	T	A	C
E	T	Q	F	R	J	R	K	F	Z
P	R	A	T	H	A	U	S	O	T
T	I	S	D	U	X	B	L	H	A
K	K	H	P	T	A	D	V	N	L
I	G	R	L	U	P	G	M	H	P
R	Y	F	A	R	O	L	D	A	K
C	W	M	T	M	M	E	A	B	R
H	B	O	Z	H	Z	B	T	N	A
E	W	D	C	N	E	D	A	L	P

der Bahnhof station
die Burg castle
der Dom cathedral
die Kirche church
der Laden shop
der Markt market
der Parkplatz car park
der Platz square
die Post post office
das Rathaus town hall
der Stadtplan town map
der Turm tower, steeple

11

S	V	A	E	I	F	P	O	N	K
T	H	P	J	Q	L	P	C	S	H
R	H	U	T	U	A	L	R	U	G
U	Z	L	H	V	H	O	H	K	D
M	K	L	R	C	C	C	O	A	M
P	L	I	O	W	S	B	S	R	E
F	F	Y	C	X	T	D	E	O	H
J	A	C	K	E	Z	P	N	N	H
M	N	D	V	L	E	T	N	A	M
B	A	D	E	A	N	Z	U	G	H

der Anorak anorak
der Badeanzug bathing costume
der Handschuh glove
das Hemd shirt
die Hose trousers
der Hut hat
die Jacke jacket
der Knopf button
der Mantel coat
der Pulli pullover, jumper
der Rock skirt
der Schal scarf
der Schuh shoe
der Strumpf stocking, (long) sock